India-Pakistan
Themes Beyond Borders

Nikhil Chakravartty

India-Pakistan
Themes Beyond Borders

Selections from
Nikhil Chakravartty's Writings

Selected and Edited by
Anil Nauriya
Ravi M. Bakaya
Razia Ismail Abbasi
Sumit Chakravartty

AAKAR

India-Pakistan: Themes Beyond Borders

First Published 2004
First Aakar Edition 2019

ISBN 978-93-5002-615-1

Published by
AAKAR BOOKS
28 E Pocket IV, Mayur Vihar Phase I
Delhi 110 091, India
www.aakarbooks.com

Printed at
D.K. Fine Art Press, Delhi

Contents

Prefatory Note

This is a selection from Nikhil Chakravartty's writings covering a period of thirty-three years (1964-97) relating to India-Pakistan ties, including also developments in Jammu and Kashmir. These were published in the weekly *Mainstream*, New Delhi, the journal which he had founded, and also in the daily newspapers *The Hindu*, *The Times of India*, *Hindustan Times*, *The Pioneer* and *The Tribune*.

Nikhil Chakravartty passed away in New Delhi on June 27, 1998.

These writings were collected together in his memory on the occasion of his ninetieth birth anniversary on November 3, 2003. The date of publication of each piece is carried at the end of the piece.

—A.N., R.M.B., R.I.A., S.C.

Foreword

Selections from the writings of Shri Nikhil Chakravarty's (Nikhilda as we used to call him) were published in 2004 under the title: *India-Pakistan: Themes Beyond Borders*. I am glad to know that the Aakar Book has decided to bring out a reprint of the book. This is a very wise and timely decision. In the political climate prevailing in India today, issues relating to India-Pakistan relations have been pushed to the backburner. The very mention of the need to revive these relations is regarded as anti-national. In this context, it is extremely important for readers in India to know about the importance of these relations for peace and security in the two countries and in the region as a whole, and the factors which hold out promises for injecting a new life into these relations. These issues were of abiding interest to Nikhilda and have been dealt with in this book in his typically lucid and directly communicable style and within the framework of a broad vision. I hope this reprint would enable the readers to see Indo-Pak relations not as a taboo but as a challenge. I regard it as a great honour to have been afforded this opportunity of writing a brief Foreword to this volume.

Even if we did not have the total blanket of mistrust and animosity spread over India-Pakistan relations by the present BJP Government and there would have been a genuine desire on the part of India to take these relations to new heights, the conditions currently prevailing in Pakistan make the realisation of this objective a more unenviable task than what it was during the time of Nikhilda. The groundswell of public opinion in favour of peace with India that Nikhilda had witnessed during his various trips to Pakistan, has dissipated itself in the dreary desert of religious fanaticism on both sides of the border. We have spoken about the conditions in India. In Pakistan, the extremist religious elements, which successive governments spawned, trained and armed, to be used against its neighbours, India and Afghanistan, is set about to devour the state. The Pakistani Taliban have spread their net all over the country and have penetrated the major political parties, legislatures, armed forces and educational and cultural establishments in the country.

After Partition, Pakistanis belonging to various sections of society were assailed by the apprehension that India would seize the first opportunity available to it, to undo Partition. India had to declare from time to time that such an objective was the farthest from its intention. Even when India found itself in a favourable bargaining position vis-à-vis Pakistan, it did not display any such ambition. In spite of this, the feeling that India would seek to force reunification on Pakistan continued to persist in that country for a very long time. This apprehension of Pakistan was ultimately laid to rest during the late Prime Minister Atal Behari Vajpayee's sojourn in Lahore when he paid a visit to Minar-e-Pakistan and, from that symbol of Pakistan, pronounced India's full respect for the sovereignty of Pakistan. Pakistan's fear of India undoing Partition was an issue still debated spiritedly during Nikhilda's time. That is why he has dealt with this theme in a number of essays included in the book.

Nikhilda was categorical that the thought of undoing Partition "is not only unrealistic but also dangerous". But he believed that the two countries should come together at least emotionally and, if possible, also institutionally. He wrote : "But surely we can think of something short of reunification." As the last resort, he was a strong believer in and for several years, actively worked for "bringing the peoples of the two countries together, without hurting the sovereignty of the other country". In this connection, he also referred to the idea of a India-Pakistan Confederation mooted by Dr Rammanohar Lohia but also attributed to Pandit Deen Dayal Upadhyay. Nikhilda himself did not specifically endorse this idea. The maximum distance that he travelled in this direction was India and Pakistan taking "a lead together to establish a South Asian Common Market". Whatever the source of its emanation, the idea of a Confederation between India and Pakistan is not well thought out and is even dangerous. Whatever the intention behind it, Pakistanis are bound to regard it as another device conjured up by India to bring about reunification. Besides, before reaching the stage of Confederation, one has to go through manifold stages each of which is beset with numerous pitfalls. It will be a diplomatic folly of colossal dimension for any Government of India to formally put forward the Confederation idea for Pakistan's consideration.

In the present circumstances, the only route for the two countries to march together is normalisation of trade and investment, preferential trading arrangement, selective harmonisation of economic policies–all leading to a free trade arrangement and possibly a comprehensive economic partnership agreement. Before the present government came to power, the two countries had already started marching in that direction, of course, with its usual ups and downs and Pakistanis at long last had come to realise that a more intense economic relation-ship with India was a very important means of serving its national economic interest, particularly for overcoming the stagnancy in its economy which has prevailed over several years.

Nikhilda was a strong votary of improvement in India-Pakistan relations. His approach to the subject has been very well summed up by Shri K.R. Narayanan, a former President of India, in his introduction to this book: "The pre-dominant and recurring theme (of the book) is to harness the common humanity of both the countries for durable peace and friendship." Nikhilda's faith in improved India-Pakistan relations rested mainly on what he perceived to be the tremendous goodwill for each other prevailing in both the countries and the common culture and heritage of the two countries. He personally experienced this in his several extended visits to Pakistan. Giving an impression of the visits, he wrote: "The overpowering impression which will abide with me is the abundance of friendly feelings towards India in all sections of the people of Pakistan."

Peace between the two countries is essential in order, among other things, to prevent future wars between the two countries. Such a war will be beyond anyone's control and inflict such horrendous damages as to reduce India and Pakistan to the category of forgotten episodes of modern history.

In the chapter in the book entitled 'Walls must come down', he refers to the reunification of Germany and the optimism prevailing at that time regarding the reunification of Korea and states: "All the post-war partitions are dis-appearing and walls coming down, then why should not India and Pakistan come together?" He was still expecting a breakthrough in the relations between India and Pakistan in the penultimate article in the volume, written in May 1997, about a year before his death.

In contrast to this positive and futuristic approach of Nikhilda, today a good deal of our diplomatic skills and resources are devoted to isolating Pakistan from the comity of nations, and in the process further isolating India from Pakistan. How frustrated our present-day diplomats must be feeling in being obliged to follow an essentially negative policy towards Pakistan which has no bearing on our national interest or ideals. Going by the dictates of history, geo-political considerations and vision for the future, this policy does not make any sense. All the alternatives of dealing with our neighbours and other countries in the region which we have tried through the creation of forums which exclude Pakistan, are destined to fail and have in fact failed.

As a pivotal issue in Indo-Pak relations, the Kashmir problem is accorded the prime of place in the collection of Nikhilda's essays in this volume. As early as in 1992, Nikhilda discerned "total alienation" of the Kashmiri people from India. He wrote: "...the measure of the alienation of the sections of the people from the authority of New Delhi had reached almost a point of no return." He noticed that "militants practically run the valley; whereas the troops control the border". After one of his visits to Pakistan, he wrote: "Practically nobody in Pakistan believes that India would ever recover even a semblance of authority in the Valley".

The above perception of the Pakistanis brought about a radical change in the Pakistan Government's stand on Kashmir. Once they realised that the Kashmiris were totally alienated from India and that it was unlikely that India would be able to win back their confidence, Pakistan started harping the tune that the solution of the Kashmir dispute should be according to the will of the Kashmiri people and that they should be involved in any negotiation for finding such a solution. Earlier, Pakistan's official stand was that Kashmir was an issue between India and Pakistan and the question of the acceptance of a solution bilaterally arrived at was not terribly relevant.

In this context, a question that frequently crops up is whether an improvement in India-Pakistan relations is a pre-condition for solving the Kashmir issue. This author has always believed that for India the priority should be to solve the Kashmir problem with our own Kashmiris. Till the late 1980s, when the alienation of the Kashmiri people had not reached the level depicted by Nikhilda, there were several windows of opportunity of solving the Kashmir problem with our Kashmiri citizens. The last one that I recall was at the time of the release of Shabbir Shah from prison after which he made a strong plea in several of the meetings addressed by him for solving the issue between the Kashmiri people and the Government of India. After his release, he enjoyed tremendous popularity in the Valley where each of his meetings was attended by tens of thousands of people. But the Government of India, while making the usual helpful noises, did not come out with any concrete suggestion and did not engage Shabbir Shah in any worthwhile dialogue. Today the same Shabbir Shah is regarded as India's enemy No. 1 and is frequently incarcerated in prison.

If we would have taken advantage of any of these windows of opportunity, apart from avoiding the bloodshed and suffering that has taken place in Kashmir and is still rampant there, we would have been in a much stronger bargaining position to solve this problem with Pakistan, which we are committed to do under the Simla Agreement. Building good relations with Pakistan is by itself an important objective to be pursued, but in the then prevailing situation it was not necessarily a pre-condition for solving the problem with our own Kashmiris. But today the alienation of the Kashmiri people has gone to such an extreme extent that an improvement in India-Pakistan relations has indeed become a pre-condition for solving the problem with our own Kashmiris.

In one of his essays, Nikhilda has written that "a thaw can come only if the Government can indicate the extent of autonomy it is prepared to grant". Such an indication can indeed provide a way out of the current difficult situation. In the ultimate analysis, what the Kashmiris have been asking for is Azadi which can be interpreted as the maximum amount of autonomy short of sovereignty, though for compelling political reasons, they have not said it in so many words. If autonomy short of sovereignty is the only way out short of secession of Kashmir or its opting for Pakistan, then why not face the issue headlong, and as Nikhilda suggested, start the talks with our Kashmiris with a unilateral offer of the maximum possible measure of autonomy?

With these words, I commend this reprinted volume to readers in India. I hope this would serve as a timely reminder of the significance of our relationship with Pakistan and persuade the government to reverse the present counter-productive policy towards this country.

New Delhi **Muchkund Dubey**
May 10, 2019

Introduction

Over quarter of a century, the general reading public, particularly the more intellectually inclined in the subcontinent, had looked forward avidly to the editorials and other writings of Nikhil Chakravartty in *Mainstream* for illumination and understanding of the bewildering developments within the region since 1947. It is, therefore, with nostalgia and great expectations that we turn to the present volume, focusing on Indo-Pak relations, containing Nikhilda's precious writings on the complexities of developments in the subcontinent since 1947, and look for his analysis of the issues involved with flashes of prophetic ideas the relevance of which now strike us with added poignancy.

The predominant and recurring theme of this publication is to harness the common humanity of both the countries for durable peace and friendship. This is an urge and aspiration, which has been articulated since 1945, almost anticipating the tragic division of India. When Partition of India became inevitable, Jawaharlal Nehru, sitting in a cell in a British jail, wrote in his book *Discovery of India:* "It is obvious that whatever be the future of India, even if there is regular partition, the different parts of India will have to cooperate with each other, in a hundred different ways." And after the Partition took place, he declared his belief that "it is to India's advantage that Pakistan should be a secure and prosperous state with which we can develop close and friendly relations". Qaid-e-Azam Mohammed Ali Jinnah, expressing the same sentiment to the press, had said that "now that the division of India has been brought about by a solemn agreement between the two Dominions, we should bury the past and resolve that despite all that has happened we shall remain friends. There are many things which we need from each other as neighbours, morally, materially and politically, and thereby raise the prestige and status of both the Dominions." Almost a year after the Indo-Pak war of 1965 President Ayub Khan, addressing the Royal Institute of International Affairs, London, had said: "The geopolitical imperatives of our location on the map of the world make it necessary that for our survival we should have good neighbourly dealings with our three big neighbours, China, Soviet Union and India." I had said at the banquet hosted in honour of President Musharraf in Delhi that "it is this vision of the future articulated by the leaders of our countries that we have to pursue as the unfinished agenda of partition for resolving all the differences between us and for ensuring peace and prosperity for our peoples".

In 1967, on the second anniversary of the tragic armed conflict of 1965 between India and Pakistan, Nikhilda wrote in *Mainstream*: ". . .the struggle beyond the conflict for achieving enduring peace becomes a more difficult but a more compelling struggle." He then observed: "It is no platitude but solid hard truth that neither history nor geography, neither culture nor self-interest can justify the continuation of a state of armed peace in the relations between India and Pakistan."

Describing that the economies of both India and Pakistan are more dependant than those of Israel and the Arab states he appealed for paying heed to the wholesome urges for friendly ties that could be found in abundant measure among common peoples of both the countries. Through his brilliant pieces in "Passage through Pakistan", written in 1982, he recounted his first ever journey to that country and recollected fascinating experiences and interactions with a variety of people who unequivocally expressed their innermost desire for peace and good neighbourliness. "The overpowering impression," he wrote, "which will abide with me is the abundance of friendly feeling towards India in all sections of the people of Pakistan. I emphasise, all sections, because this goodwill transcends all barriers." "From the embittered Opposition leaders, gagged and immobilised," he further added, "to different layers of the establishment, high and low, young and old, from academics to professionals, the youth and the cultural elite—among them all there is an irrepressible desire to remain in friendship with India." An old man selling sun-dried apricot to Nikhilda along the Karakoram Highway and telling him that "you are not a mehman, you are a brother" and the warmth and friendship shown to him by the ex-serviceman, selling entry tickets at the museum at Mohenjodaro, and telling him that the ancient ruins there "belonged to you and me both" represented what he called the "effusion of friendly feelings in the populace towards India". "It is not a question," he wrote, "of anybody wanting to undo the Partition of 1947: it is a question of forging bonds of friendship between two neighbours with common heritage and organic cultural links." When a decade-and-a-half after his visit to Pakistan the Gujral doctrine was formulated to commence a new era of friendship and understanding with our neighbours, Nikhilda described it as "the biggest testimony of India's persistent anxiety for good neighbourliness". Only recently, we saw the spontaneous outpourings of love, affection and understanding from Indians across the country for baby Noor who was brought from Pakistan to Bangalore for heart surgery. To put our efforts for peace and friendship in historical context one may refer to Nikhilda's article written only four days before Prime Minister Nehru's death. He wrote: ". . .the Prime Minister, as an epilogue to his eventful life, seems to feel that if by friendly overtures suspicion could be dispelled even to a small measure inside Pakistan, the game would be worth the candle." At a time when India has extended the hand of friendship to Pakistan in spite of the unabated cross-border terrorism, the writings and ideas of Nikhil Chakravartty outlining the fascinating aspects of foreign policy vis-à-vis neighbours assume deep significance.

While appreciating the positive and heart-warming trends for friendship and peace from Pakistan we must understand the hard-headed approach of the military leaders of that country to see and comprehend their stand towards India based on compulsive hostility. In fact, the trend for irreversible democratisation in Pakistan would constitute a sure step for establishing peace between the two countries. Nikhilda wrote in the concluding piece in "Passage through Pakistan" that "in the struggle for democracy in Pakistan lies the future of friendship between the two countries of the same subcontinent".

One is struck by the breadth of vision of Nikhil Chakravartty and his ability to see through the complex social developments which affected the subcontinent. Many of his thoughts and ideas formulated and expressed in the early 1960s have come true. On May 23, 1964, four days before Jawaharlal Nehru passed away, he wrote that "the recent spate of communal violence has given rise to a serious apprehension that an ultra-communal leadership might dominate this country after Nehru, jeopardising democracy".

One fact which is of great historical significance and which is vital to understand our long march towards self-sufficiency in Defence production is the contribution made in this regard by the policies adopted by Krishna Menon to start Defence projects and undertakings on a long-term basis so that India would stand entirely on her own legs in building up the military strength. In 1965 Nikhilda put facts in perspective and acknowledged the role played by Krishna Menon in taking important steps for achieving self-sufficiency in Defence matters. He wrote: "Menon's tenacious emphasis on self-reliance in Defence during his tenure in the Cabinet has paid rich dividends in the present military campaign. Many among those who were critical of Menon as the Defence Minister can no longer belittle the long-range importance of his Defence Economics."

Two years before Bangladesh emerged as a sovereign and independent country Nikhilda had warned the Pakistani authorities through his writings in *Mainstream* that "General Yahya Khan's battalions in Dacca will face a situation ten times worse than the US in Vietnam if it really comes to a show-down with the Bengal peasantry spread all over the riverine districts". The consequences faced by the Pakistani military in 1971 are too well known to be recounted.

Today we are fighting against terrorists supported from across the border in the State of Jammu and Kashmir. The analysis given by Nikhilda to understand the emergence of communal forces in Kashmir is very instructive. He outlined that inter-communal marriages in Kashmir had become more frequent than in any other part of India and robust secularism of the Muslim peasants had prevented communal riots practically in the whole of the State. In early 1967 he had detected communal forces from within the country and beyond our frontiers beginning to poison the age-old amity and harmony among the Kashmiri people professing different faiths and warned that "a climate of mutual alienation had set in for the first time since independence".

The heroic fight put up by the people of Jammu and

Kashmir belonging to different creeds to drive away the Pakistani tribal infiltrators in 1947 brought to light the assertion of people's strength for remaining an integral part of India. Commenting on the accession of Jammu and Kashmir to India and the role played by ordinary people to fight against the Pakistan sponsored invasion Nikhilda wrote: "What is to be borne in mind is that even with a declaration of loyalty to India by the Maharaja—which in fact was not very vocal in those days—there could have been no chance of holding the advance of armed bands into the farthest corner of the Valley, had there been no Sheikh Abdullah and his band of patriotic workers who roused the entire people to put up the resistance. Perhaps in no other part of the country there was such an armed mass upheaval under a political leadership for accession to India as it happened in the Valley of Kashmir in 1947."

The present volume is valuable from the point of view of correctly understanding the evolution of our relationship with Pakistan and educating public opinion about certain historical facts so that those are appreciated in the proper perspective. It is appropriate that on the 90th birth anniversary of Nikhilda this publication is being brought out.

Congratulations are due to Sumit Chakravartty and others for bringing out this important book which will be of immense value for scholars, policy-makers, students and readers.

Narayanan K.R.

(K.R. NARAYANAN)

A Biographical Note

Born on November 3, 1913 in Silchar (Assam), Nikhil Chakravartty had his school education at Hindu School, Calcutta (1925–29), and college education in Presidency College, Calcutta (1929–35). He graduated with History Honours in 1933 and stood First Class First in MA (History) in 1935. Thereafter he went to Oxford where he studied in Merton College (1936–39) and in Oxford University's Honours School in Modern History (1939). On his return to India he taught Modern History in Calcutta University's Postgraduate Department (1940–44) before plunging into activist journalism as a special correspondent with the Communist Party organ *People's War* (1944–46) and *People's Age* (1946–48). Before that he married in India Renu Roy (who had also been in England when he was studying there) in 1942 and their only son Sumit was born in 1945. After serving a stint in the underground as an important communist functionary from 1948, he worked in *Crossroads* (1952–55) and *New Age* (1955–57). He then set up a feature news service, *India Press Agency* or *IPA,* and in 1959 shot into prominence with a report in the *IPA* on the activities of the then Prime Minister's PA, M.O. Mathai, that rocked Parliament forcing Mathai to resign. In 1962 he founded the current affairs weekly *Mainstream* and served as its editor from 1967 to 1992. Subsequently he became its Editorial Adviser. In 1975–77 he played a vital role in defence of press freedom during the Emergency; later in the eighties he alongwith other senior journalists fought doggedly against the Anti-Defamation Bill sought to be introduced in Parliament by the then Union Government and compelled the government to withdraw the legislation. He was a Member, Press Commission (1978–80), the Chairman, NAMEDIA Conference (December 1983), and the Chairman, NAMEDIA Foundation (media foundation of the non-aligned) since 1984 till his death. He was the President of the Editors Guild of India (1990–92) and a member of the National Integration Council for some time. He was also a member of the Indo-US Subcommission on Education, Culture and Media (1985–89). In 1990 he declined the Padma Bhushan Award conferred on him by the National Front Government with a letter to the then President pointing out that a journalist carrying out his professional obligations should not be "identified, in the public eye, with any particular establishment". A member of the Communist Party for forty years (1938–78), he was not associated with any political organisation thereafter. In November 1997 he was appointed the Chairman of the Prasar Bharati Board that was entrusted with the task to oversee and ensure genuine autonomy for the official media.

In the forties, he wrote incisive reports and reportages on the Bengal famine, the Tebhaga movement, resistance to communalism in Calcutta, anti-imperalist upsurge in Bengal, the remarkable mass awakening at the dawn of independence on August 15, 1947. In 1946 he was briefly arrested, charged with having leaked out valuable information to the public on the British authorities' secret plan to crush the national movement just before independence (known as 'Operation Asylum'). The case against him continued till independence when it automatically lapsed.

During the Emergency period (1975–77) he wrote fearlessly in *Mainstream* against the Emergency Raj braving censorship and this distinguished him from many of his colleagues who had succumbed to the pressures of the time. Finally, however, he had to close down *Mainstream* for a brief period at the fag end of 1976 when the censorship laws did not permit him to express himself in as bold a manner as the situation warranted. Besides his editorials in *Mainstream,* a small booklet, *Maruti to Mafia,* written by him (not in his own name) at that time caused consternation in the official circles. His depositions before the Shah Commission, set up in 1977 to probe the Emergency excesses, evoked wide public interest.

He visited several countries on journalistic assignments. His article on the events in Hungary in 1956, following a visit to that country soon after the Soviet intervention there, appeared in *New Age* and caused a stir as he had categorically refused to describe the developments there as reflective of any attempted "counter-revolution". He sharply criticised the CPSU organ, *Pravda,*in *Mainstream* once the Soviet leaders faltered in roundly condemning the Chinese aggression on India in 1962. He visited China, the former Soviet Union, the US, Iran, Poland, Germany, Romania, Pakistan, Afghanistan, Bangladesh, Sri Lanka, South Africa and met the leaders of these countries, including Mao Zedong, Ziaul Haq, Sheikh Mujibur Rahman. His pieces on China after the Tiananmen massacre in 1989 and Eastern Europe after the collapse of statist socialist structures there generated considerable discussion. His dispassionate analysis of the events in

Kashmir and fervent plea for Indo-Pak amity evoked a positive response in Pakistan.

In December 1996 he resigned from the National Committee for the Commemoration of the Fiftieth Anniversary of India's Independence on the ground that while several persons charged with corruption were included in it, quite a few individuals and institutions associated with the freedom struggle were kept out.

As the Chairman of the Prasar Bharati Board he visited almost all the North-Eastern States in 1997-98.

His active, creative life was brought to an end by a rapidly growing brain tumour. He was operated upon on May 20,1998 but did not regain consciousness thereafter. He passed away peacefully at New Delhi's G.B. Pant Hospital on June 27, 1998 at the age of 85. His wife had predeceased him in April 1994.

1

Sheikh Abdullah in New Delhi

Sheikh Abdullah's visit has churned up exciting speculations in all New Delhi circles about the future of Kashmir, of Indo-Pak relations and of him too as a political personality.

The unusually large number of talks that he has held in the Capital—together with his air dash to the South—has been objected to by none but the Jan Sangh and the loyal scribes of the fast-diminishing Bakshi lobby. Generally there is support in practically all sections of responsible opinion in New Delhi for the Government's decision that Sheikh Sahib after eleven years of detention should be afforded the fullest opportunity to exchange notes with whomsoever he desires, so that he may get the most exhaustive appraisal of different aspects of the Kashmir situation and thus form his own views with the fullest awareness of their impact on different sections of opinion in the country.

At the same time there has come up, not unexpectedly, a certain amount of uneasy impatience at the protracted nature of the talks, which has been made worse by some rather confusing, if not conflicting, statements by leading personalities both inside and outside the Government. The understanding, tacitly agreed to at the beginning, that airing of opinions should be withheld until at least some tentative decisions are reached, seems to have been forgotten.

The result is that just as Sheikh Sahib's concrete views could not be clearly made out of the jumble of statements he made in Kashmir in the three weeks following his release, it is also difficult to decipher New Delhi's own viewpoint with regard to the Kashmir problem. In fact, T.T. Krishnamachari's strong assertion in Parliament—made on the very day of Sheikh Sahib's arrival in New Delhi—against any re-examination of the question of accession of Kashmir into the Indian Union was made mainly with a view to dispel the confusion let loose by reports of the Government's drastic re-thinking on the issue, reports which did not spare TTK himself as being one of those prominently associated with free-thinking on Kashmir.

Confusion is perhaps worse confounded by some of those who kept close to the Sheikh during his stay in New Delhi. Among them, Jayaprakash Narayan's performance—particularly when he chose to address some of the MPs at Nath Pai's initiative—is regarded by observers here as unfortunate. While his anxiety to bring about friendly relations between India and Pakistan is shared by a very large body of opinion, his public pronouncements on Kashmir, especially on the touchy question of accession, considerably spoiled his effectiveness in contributing towards the settlement of the question itself. Many have felt here that if JP had strictly adhered to the tenets of quiet diplomacy, he would perhaps have been more successful without being handicapped by public misgivings about his open mind on the right of self-determination for any region of the country.

There were others who were conspicuous in their anxiety to keep Sheikh Abdullah's company but were actually a liability rather than a political asset for him. Minoo Masani's discomfiture both in Rajkot and Calcutta has dispelled the complacent Swatantra view that the far-flung corners of the country care very little whether Kashmir is kept inside the Indian Union or not.

J.J. Singh attending on Sheikh Abdullah has also come as a strange incongruity since he commands neither the standing nor the influence in New Delhi's public life which may stand the Kashmir leader in good stead. Rather, it has been taken as a gesture to the American lobby to which Singh professionally belongs.

Although the Sheikh's visit to Rajaji may have been prompted by his search for a formula on the Kashmir question—CR being known for his famous formula on partition—its impact has not been particularly wholesome since the Swantantra leader has made no bones about his readiness to let Kashmir go out of the Indian Union.

However, Sheikh Abdullah's own stand during his New Delhi talks has been far better than that of the self-appointed promoters of his cause. For one thing, it is now clear to New Delhi that Sheikh Sahib has no intention of letting Pakistan grab Kashmir. Despite the fact that a sizeable section of those who have been making noise on behalf of the Sheikh in the Valley are pro-Pakistan, neither he nor Afzal Beg is regarded here as having any soft corner for Pakistan.

In fact, his public pronouncements since his release have come as a disappointment for Rawalpindi since he has neither deviated from his abhorrence of the two-nation theory nor demanded implementation of the past UN resolutions on Kashmir which has become the stock-in-trade of the Pakistani case at the Security Council.

The impression that has gained ground in New Delhi is that Sheikh Abdullah is not making the right to secede the key point in his case for Kashmir. He has made it plain that he does not recognise the changes, constitutional and political, that have been effected in Kashmir's status and its relations with the Centre since his removal in 1953. In other words, he wants to go back to the point where the Delhi Agreement had left matters in 1952. While it is evident he is anxious that Kashmir should have a wide measure of autonomy—which he may interpret to his people as the substance of independence—he appears to have realised after his round of talks in New Delhi that there could possibly be no reversal of the accession of the State into the Indian Union.

As for Sheikh Abdullah's plea that the will of the people of Kashmir should be ascertained, responsible quarters in New Delhi seem to be agreeable to the holding of a general election in the State after Sheikh Sahib had come to an agreed decision on Kashmir. Such a general election will naturally take time.

Besides, New Delhi has made it clear to Sheikh Abdullah that there could possibly be no unilateral settlement with him, since the opinion of the present Kashmir Government carries weight here.

A point on which a number of leaders have laid stress in their talks with the Sheikh here as well as at Wardha is that the Kashmir leader must not forget or underplay his responsibility to the entire Muslim community in this country. Whether he wants it or not, circumstances have compelled him to look upon the Kashmir question from the angle of its bearing on the communal problem on an all-India scale. This is a role which he could perhaps have ignored ten years ago, but with the passing away of the revered old guard in the Muslim community, any realistic approach to the Hindu-Muslim relations demands that Sheikh Sahib should place before him an all-India perspective.

In this context, there is satisfaction in New Delhi that Sheikh Abdullah in his speeches has constantly harped on the need for Hindu-Muslim amity. Most of those who have met him have also laid stress on the present wave of communalism that has swept over both Pakistan and India and have urged him to play an all-India role and not confine himself to the narrow grooves of only one part of the country.

The balance-sheet of Sheikh Abdullah's visit to New Delhi is yet to be drawn up, but observers are on the whole agreed on the fact that the Prime Minister's warm hospitality for the Kashmir leader and providing him with the opportunity of meeting as many leaders and trends as he liked, proved a wise act of statesmanship, undoing much of the damage done in the past to the Kashmir question by Bakshi Ghulam Mohammad's provocative handling of it which, together with his reckless corruption, had raised a wall of antipathy between New Delhi and Srinagar.

The final outcome of this long-drawn process of delicate handling is not expected to be clear for quite sometime to come; but the initial round is certainly not without hope.

(May 9, 1964)

2

Indo-Pakistan Relations: New Perspective

Military aid has suddenly become the main topic of political discussion in New Delhi, almost downgrading Sheikh Abdullah's olive-branch mission to Pakistan and Nehru's repeat offer to Peking to open negotiations.

This is somewhat natural in view of Chavan's mission to Washington. But even a few weeks back, the Defence Minister's US trip was regarded in the Capital as of secondary importance to T.T. Krishnamachari's multipurpose approaches to America. It was also made clear from Washington recently when the Rao mission had just reached there, that no supersonic F-104 planes would be available for India. We were even offered the wise advice gratis that we should cut our arms coat according to our dollar cloth. A feeling of helpless frustration was about to creep in.

But this demoralisation was short-lived. Hard on the heels of the announcement of the Soviet offer of aid for Bokaro and the thousand-kilowatt transmitter, has come the disclosure of large-scale defence aid from Moscow. Alongwith the early delivery of 60 supersonic MIG-21s, the project for their manufacture in this country itself will be speeded up. What is perhaps more important is the offer of ground-to-air missiles and two ordnance factories, apart from helicopters and transport planes.

Although the Soviet supply of such top-priority defence aid had been known to informed quarters for quite sometime, it was purposely withheld even during the Defence debate in Parliament for important considerations: New Delhi was interested in seeing how far Washington would go on her own in helping India with large-scale arms aid, overruling Pakistani protests, while Moscow too was not prepared to announce such a defence aid programme to India so long as there was the least chance of a thaw in its cold war with Peking.

On either count a firm appraisal seems to have been reached. Alongwith Washington's polite refusal to supply India with F-104s, the experience of the latest round of back-stair Western lobbying in the Security Council has almost made it clear to New Delhi that there is no immediate prospect of the West withdrawing its generous patronage from Pakistan in her bellicose posture on Kashmir. The fact that the Western powers ignored Indian objection to Secretary General U Thant's good office being dragged into the picture has hardly pleased New Delhi. Matters were made worse in the closed-door informal sessions, in which the Western powers together with their underlings like the Ivory Coast and Morocco took a more threatening pose insisting on U Thant's mediation, to placate Pakistan.

The significance of the publicising of Soviet arms aid, according to observers in the Capital, is that Moscow's antipathy to Peking's adventurist preoccupations has reached the point of no return. The Chinese charge-sheet against Khrushchev that he is backing India against China—in diplomacy, propaganda, and in military aid—is no longer going to deter the Soviet Union from coming out strongly in support of India. Together with the Soviet Premier's current demonstration of solidarity with the UAR this new Moscow accent ensures a powerful prop for the non-aligned diplomacy as its bargaining capacity with the West goes up and to that measure helps to strengthen the independent status of these countries.

While Chavan's hands are thus strengthened, it is suspected in some circles in the Capital that the "leak" about the Soviet arms aid—significantly made in reputed American journals close to the present Administration—was so timed as to overpower the extreme anti-India lobby in the US Congress which could be expected to react if it could be made to realise that its veto on military aid to India would only facilitate Moscow getting the upper hand in India. The Congress scuttle of the Bokaro project has not been forgotten in New Delhi.

The immediate political impact of this development is being watched in the Capital. This will no doubt enhance Chavan's standing. So far his style was cramped by TTK's overlordship, who was also trying to pave the way for private US capital intruding into Indian defence: the way he has pulled quite a few strings in recent months to bring the Lockheeds in—and sometimes even prophesying the collapse of the MIG project—was hardly to Chavan's liking.

Together with Bokaro, this coming in of Soviet aid for defence in a big way is likely to deflate the image of TTK—which, incidentally, is largely the handiwork of himself and his ICS entourage—as the saviour who alone can bring from abroad the much-needed foreign aid, economic and defence. It has been noticed here that already the news has been given out that Chavan will soon be heading a Defence mission to Moscow. In the delicate balance of forces that exists in New Delhi today, this unexpected build-up of Chavan may have significant repercussions on the Centre's political alignments.

With this prospect of large-scale Defence aid, New Delhi will have to inevitably go in for proper planning of our entire Defence network. The question which is being posed now is: against whom have we to defend ourselves? In the context of the closer rapprochement between Rawalpindi and Peking, the answer is not difficult to find. The Defence planning has to be for the entire border that faces both China and Pakistan.

If this is the perspective that New Delhi holds before itself today, what is the meaning of the Prime Minister's friendly approach to Pakistan?

Observers have taken note of a number of significant developments towards the evolution of what might seem to be a new approach to Pakistan. First came the Prime Minister's declaration in Parliament that for the purpose of a settlement with Pakistan, even constitutional changes should not be ruled out. Then came his conspicuously friendly handling of Sheikh Abdullah and finally his pronouncement at the Bombay AICC, coming out in open support of the Sheikh's mission to bring about Indo-Pak amity. At the same time, Chagla in the Security Council laid special emphasis on mutual talks to the exclusion of third party intervention.

In circles critical of Pakistan, both from the Right and the Left, these constitute an ominous pointer towards a policy of appeasement. A closer examination of these important moves do not bear out any likelihood of a capitulation on the basic issues involved. Rather they point to a very important reappraisal of Indo-Pak relations.

It appears that the recent spate of communal violence has given rise to a serious apprehension that an ultra-communal leadership might dominate this country after Nehru, jeopardising democracy.

With this disturbing background, the Prime Minister seems to be in a mood to support any initiative which can help to restore sanity and goodwill between the two neighbouring countries. It was in this context that he has practically under-written Sheikh Abdullah's visit to Pakistan in search of a solution to this vexed question rather than for a constitutional formula with regard to Kashmir.

On the approach to Pakistan there seem to be two distinct schools in the Capital. According to one, if Pakistan could be mollified by settling the Kashmir issue, there should be no objection to making major concessions in the interest of long-term amity between the two countries. Rajagopalachari and the Swatantra Right belong to this school.

The other school firmly believes that the entire basis of Pakistan rests on stirring up hatred against India, and it is this negative foundation of Jinnah's two-nation edifice which will be a perpetual source of irritation and acrimony for India. While agreeing with the second school insofar as the origin of Pakistan is concerned, the Prime Minister as an epilogue to his eventful life, seems to feel that if by friendly overtures, suspicion could be dispelled even to a small measure inside Pakistan, the game would be worth the candle.

Behind this move, there is also a groping for what may be called strong support for Indo-Pak goodwill inside

Pakistan itself. With the developments in East Pakistan, a section of opinion in this country, particularly among the more enlightened section in West Bengal, has started rethinking on how to undo the bane of the Partition. Some are even urging for a positive policy in anticipation of the likelihood of East Pakistan seceding as an independent state.

While responsible opinion in New Delhi considers these as slightly premature, there is a definite exploring here for working up a solid body of friendly opinion inside Pakistan. It is this point which Sheikh Abdullah also hinted at his New Delhi utterances when he expressed his anxiety to create a 'base' inside Pakistan.

So far as the Sheikh is concerned, he is reported to be naturally toying with a number of suggestions for the solution of the Kashmir tangle. One of these is rather interesting: the creation of a de-militarised Kashmir to be guaranteed by both India and Pakistan. Some of his friends say that such a de-militarised Kashmir may be retained formally inside the Indian Union but with large-scale facilities for Pakistanis in the matter of trade and free access of the Valley.

But it is not yet clear whether Sheikh Sahib will raise all these suggestions during his first round of talks in Pakistan. More likely, he will go in for probing the attitude of the present ruling junta in Pakistan. While observers in New Delhi are very cautious about anticipating the reception that the Sheikh is likely to get from President Ayub, the general feeling here is that Pakistani rulers will not entertain any basic change from their stand which is annexation of Kashmir through the facade of a plebscite. In such a situation, Sheikh Abdullah's olive branch may wither away in the scorching summer of West Pakistan;

and at that stage he will take a more realistic view about the future of Kashmir as part of the Indian Union.

There is also the possibility that his visit in the Pak-occupied "Azad" Kashmir area, if it is permitted by Rawalpindi, will show him the contrast in its conditions with those prevailing on this side.

There are also indications that inside Sheikh Abdullah's camp three different trends are pulling in different directions. One is the frankly pro-Pakistani wing; the second one wants an independent Kashmir; and the third which seems to be of a considerable size, is for Kashmir remaining inside the Indian Union but with the restoration of the internal status quo as it was in 1953. If Sheikh Abdullah comes back empty-handed from Pakistan, it is more than likely that the pro-independence trend will merge into the pro-India group, while the ranks of the pro-Pakistanis will be heavily depleted.

Meanwhile, the Sadiq Ministry seems to be confidently on the saddle, and Bakshi Ghulam Mohammad's fulminations about bringing it down are totally baseless. The latest position, according to reliable authority, is that Bakshi does not command the support of more than a dozen MLAs inside the Legislative Party, while the National Conference itself has totally cracked up in the Kashmir Valley.

The prospect of stability returning in the beautiful but storm-tossed Valley seems to be not gloomy at all.

(May 23, 1964)

3

Whitehall Underwrites Rawalpindi

The political seismograph in New Delhi fluctuated violently in the week preceding the Independence Day, and the balance was partially restored only after the news of the recapture of the three Pakistani posts in Kargil boosted the drooping morale. In fact, the Kargil success neutralised to a large measure the impact of the Jan Sangh's mammoth demonstration in the Capital on the opening day of Parliament.

Yet the shock this time seemed to be much less severe than what was felt in October-November 1962 in the wake of the Chinese invasion. This is because in terms of military operation this is of a much smaller dimension, and, secondly, the authorities in New Delhi had forewarnings about the elaborate preparation for mass infiltration into the Valley from Pakistan. Although there were, no doubt, some lapses in intelligence alertness at the initial stage, the realisation of the gravity of the new Pakistani attack has not been underestimated in the Capital. In fact, the Prime Minister's frank warning before the Opposition leaders that the Kashmir crisis should not be expected to be short-lived had a sobering effect.

This was noticeable in another significant aspect of New Delhi's reaction. The fact that the armed infiltrators could come as far as the inner line of Srinagar itself was never concealed, and its logical corollary that they could secure support from a section of the people was not denied, though at the same time the magnificent role played by the Kashmir Chief Minister has to a large measure scotched the canard that Sadiq had no mass base.

The advantage of a well-armed force masquerading in civilian attire, exploiting to the full the fact that many of them could hide among their own relations and acquaintances on this side of the Cease Fire Line has never been denied by New Delhi—in fact, some of the responsible authorities could be heard to draw thoughtless parallels between the infiltrators in Kashmir with the Vietcong guerillas. At the same time significance is equally attached to the fact that in many cases the security forces got at the infiltrators only with the active cooperation of the local villagers.

The Kashmir Government was not completely taken aback by this new style of Pakistani offensive. In fact, a similar development was vaguely apprehended soon after Sheikh Abdullah began his long trip abroad. And this was nipped in the bud with the large-scale arrest of the Plebiscite Fronters. Besides, the link between the Plebiscite Front and the Pakistan-occupied Kashmir has always been detected by the Jammu and Kashmir authorities. It is also becoming clearer now in New Delhi why the Union Home Ministry took no chances with Sheikh Abdullah on his return, and for this the Ministry preferred to be misunderstood by many rather than give up its own appraisal of the danger of letting the Sheikh have his freedom.

The signing of the Kutch Cease-Fire Agreement did create a feeling—as the Prime Minister himself has honestly confessed—that the Ayub regime might perhaps prefer to switch on to a new phase of peaceful relations between the two countries. The impression was reinforced by the report that President Ayub went out of his way to assure the new Indian High Commissioner about Pakistan's earnest desire for friendship with India: he even wanted to dispel the suspicion that Pakistan was ganging up with Peking against India.

This perspective was however scotched not only by the recent intelligence reports which warned about the preparations on the other side of the Cease Fire Line, but by the news from Karachi that the Pakistan Government would in the next fiscal year go in for a 12 per cent increase in military budget, slashing down the allocations for the development programme.

Many theories are current in non-official circles in New Delhi about Ayub's real objective in the present Kashmir operation. It is generally held here that after making tenacious efforts to include Kashmir within the purview of the projected arbitration over the Kutch Cease Fire, Rawalpindi had to seriously think of other means of forcing the Kashmir issue to the forefront.

Simultaneously, the expectations that Sheikh Abdullah with his demand for self-determination would provide the necessary lever from inside Kashmir also came to naught with the Sheikh's return back to detention. In fact, the training of the so-called Mujahid commandos had long been in hand, originally meant to be thrown into the Valley when Sheikh Abdullah's men would stage a big round of disturbances over some issue or the other. The failure of the Plebiscite Front to stir up the necessary degree of trouble as per the original plan deprived the Operation Infiltration of a convincing alibi and thereby exposed it to the full brunt of the counter-offensive of the regular security forces.

The persistence of the operation even after the detection of this initial miscalculation has been impelled by Rawalpindi's hope that the continuation for long of the clashes inside the Valley, would help to "internationalise" the Kashmir dispute. For instance, at the coming Afro-Asian Conference, scheduled to be held at Algiers in November, disputes between two member-states would not be taken up. But this ban might not work if the Kashmir issue could be presented as a case of active struggle for self-determination or endangering peace in the area.

Pakistani calculations, as far as could be made out from diplomatic circles in New Delhi, are that once the Algiers Conference includes the Vietnam crisis on its agenda—with obviously strong bias against the USA—it would press for the discussion on Kashmir quoting what it regards as the similarity in the features of the two situations.

It is therefore clear that Rawalpindi would do its best to prolong the present disturbances by hit-and-run tactics—presenting these under the respectable label of a guerilla war—instead of going in for a major show-down which is doomed to be defeated. As far as could be judged from New Delhi at the moment, Rawalpindi is not going to risk any escalation of the conflict into a full-scale Indo-Pak war.

How have the great Powers been reacting to the latest Kashmir developments and what is the degree of their involvement?

Peking's open commendation of the infiltrators—complete with the "Revolutionary Council" and the

"Voice of Kashmir" radio—has not come as a surprise to the official quarters here. Reports have been current here for a long time about Chinese experts helping in the training of Pakistani guerillas, and these were never denied by the Peking Radio, so alert in refuting even minor items in the Indian press.

More than these reports, the very pattern of the present round of Pakistani operation in Kashmir—with armed subversion as its key feature—has led even the more cautious of New Delhi observers to believe that Rawalpindi has got its inspiration and encouragement from Peking in opening up the new offensive in Kashmir. Chou En-lai's granting of interview to Sheikh Abdullah in Algiers last April—arranged through Pakistani authorities—was no doubt meant to demonstrate Chinese official encouragement to political elements in Kashmir opposed to New Delhi.

More significant was the conference of Chinese and Pakistani officials in Cairo on June 21 and 22. According to reports received from non-Western quarters (and by no means hostile to Peking), one of the items discussed at this conference was how to take definite action to checkmate India's position in the Afro-Asian world and to explore possibilities of taking up issues through which India could be put into difficulty. It has not gone unnoticed here that the diplomat who has held the largest number of consultations with Pakistan Foreign Office during the present Kashmir crisis has been the Chinese Ambassador.

In this connection, the timing of the present operation has a significance of its own. For armed subversion in the Kashmir Valley, winter affords better chances of success since the mobility of the regular security forces is greatly hampered by the snows, particularly on the

Banihal. But the Pakistan authorities preferred the present season presumably counting on the advantage that till mid-November, the Indian defence forces locked in confrontation with the Chinese Army in the High Himalayas would not be able to divert any extra contingent to the Kashmir Valley.

Rawalpandi's close understanding with Peking however does not preclude its exploiting to the maximum its relations with the Western powers. And here lies the essence of the free-style diplomacy that President Ayub has developed, trying, with total lack of inhibition, to make the best of both worlds. In fact, taking advantage of the complicated international situation, Ayub has been manoeuvring, throughout, to keep the initiative for any action in his own hands.

Obviously, the huge accumulation of US arms in Pakistan itself acts as a spur for adventurist action. Washington opinion seems to be divided on how to tackle Rawalpindi. One school, the die-hard pro-Pakistan lobby with its base in CIA, disapproves of any move that might annoy Pakistani authorities. Their single, unwavering objective is to see that the U-2 base at Peshawar is not placed in jeopardy at all: for this, it would rather have the gamble of permitting Ayub to go in for any adventure—including hobnobbing with Peking—so long as he did not give in to Moscow and scrap the Peshawar U-2 base.

Against this, the other school, mostly entrenched in the State Department, would be worried about Ayub's growing understanding with Peking, and to a minor extent, about the outcome of any anti-India intransigence with the use of US arms, which, it fears, would spoil the US position in India. It is the interaction of these conflicting pulls which accounts for the extraordinary phenomenon that while President Johnson holds up the Aid-Pak Consortium meeting, there comes no veto on Rawalpindi wangling more supplies of US supersonic fighter planes in this very period.

Official quarters in New Delhi have noticed a change in Washington's attitude this time in contrast to its reaction at the time of the Kutch crisis. While B.K. Nehru had found Talbot very stiff towards India during the Kutch conflict—threatening to come out in open support of Pakistan in case of any counter-attack by India—this time he found Rusk in a different frame of mind, expressing concern, and not refuting the Indian charge of Pak complicity in the Kashmir clashes. It is also understood that Chester Bowles has reported to Washington pointing to the participation of outside elements in the clashes in the Kashmir Valley, thereby practically confirming the Indian case of Pak infiltration. It is also not without significance that the pro-US lobby in the Capital has now been openly criticising Ayub and even Swatantra Party has deviated from its traditionally pro-Pak stand—presumably reflecting the changed US attitude towards the Pakistan Government's present action in Kashmir.

In the UN Secretariat also, there is a noticeable change after U Thant's initial piece of advice to India to exercise restraint. It is learnt that General Nimmo, Chief UN Observer, in his latest report, has mentioned the coming in of armed personnel from across the Cease Fire Line. New Delhi observers tend to believe that the marked absence of any follow-up pronouncement after Indira Gandhi's public reaction on return from Srinagar complaining against the UN circles silence at Pak violation of the Cease Fire Line, was due to this change in the stand of U Thant.

In marked contrast to the cautious US stand, New Delhi authorities have almost had a sense of shock at the British attitude. The Government has felt offended at the way Cyril Pickard, Assistant Under-Secretary in the British Commonwealth Relations Office, totally subscribed to the Pakistani version of the Kashmir events when our High Commissioner called on him to discuss the crisis. Claiming to know more than other Governments, the British view, as conveyed by Pickard, has been that the disturbances in Kashmir are part of a "national uprising", touched off by the imprisonment of Sheikh Abdullah: he would not concede that the Pakistan Government had a hand in it.

What was more surprising was Pickard's assertion that he would try to convince Washington about the unwisdom of holding back aid to Pakistan and that both India and Pakistan should be treated on par in the matter of US aid. New Delhi circles are disturbed at this stiff stand of the Whitehall, and our High Commissioner is believed to have been instructed to convey to the British Government New Delhi's resentment at the British stand.

There is speculation in the Capital as to the reason behind this marked change in the British attitude from Wilson's affability during the Kutch crisis. One possible explanation is that after the split away of Singapore from Malaysia, the British strategy in the East faces a major fiasco, and in this context, the Whitehall is desperately anxious to find a niche for itself in Pakistan. This is no doubt facilitated by the strained relations between Washington and Rawalpindi, so that the British Government could muscle in and plead for Ayub's case in Washington. Pakistan's growing understanding with Peking creates no difficulty on this score, since in Mao

Tse- tung's power-politics map, Britain falls within the so-called "intermediate zone".

An interesting by-product of this far-from-friendly attitude of Britain is that New Delhi would rule out choosing any British personality as its nominee on the Kutch tribunal. A very distinguished VIP, for instance, had strongly suggested Lord Denning's name as India's nominee on the tribunal. But this seems to be out of question now in view of the worsening of New Delhi's relations with London over the Kashmir developments.

At the beginning of the Kashmir crisis, there was a feeling even in the highest quarters in New Delhi that it would be difficult to mobilise world opinion on a large scale because Pakistan would present it as the active struggle of the Kashmiri people for self-determination and as such many in the Afro-Asian world, particularly in Africa, might be confused over it. It is understood that New Delhi has been a little disappointed over Cairo's marked aloofness to the Indian position in Kashmir; there is hardly any recognition by the UAR of the fact that the present clashes were inspired by Pakistan. This is no doubt a matter of much deeper concern for New Delhi than Indonesia's rather flamboyant publicity in favour of the infiltrators claiming to be freedom fighters in Kashmir.

This pessimistic appraisal has been largely dispelled by the time these lines are being written. The fact that the UN Secretary General has not been able to dismiss the Indian allegation of Pakistani infiltration has helped to gain the hearing of other countries. Besides, the recapture of the Kargil posts has largely dispelled the growing impression that militarily Pakistan can score over India—a calculation which no doubt has its impact on the formulation of many Governments' stand in any dispute.

The way New Delhi has cancelled the invitation to Bhutto shows the same sense of self-confidence on the part of the authorities here.

With regard to the Soviet Union and the rest of the communist world minus China, New Delhi feels more assured today than it felt at the beginning. There was admittedly some amount of uncertainty here about Moscow's stand when the Soviet press published the version of both sides on the happenings in Kashmir. Later consultations with the Soviet leaders has made it clear to New Delhi that Moscow has not changed its stand on Kashmir either with regard to its position in the Security Council or it being part of India as Khrushchev had said ten years ago during his visit to Srinagar.

While the Soviet policy today takes a definitely positive attitude towards Pakistan, it is made abundantly clear that it would not be at the cost of Indo-Soviet amity. The Defence Minister has made the categoric assertion that he is convinced of getting arms aid unreservedly from Moscow.

The more hard-headed among New Delhi's political pundits also bank on the calculation that Moscow would not permit India being lost to Washington through any miserliness in Soviet support when it did not allow it to happen in the wake of the Chinese aggression in 1962.

At the same time there is an intelligent awareness in New Delhi that this advantage could be retained only if the disturbances in Kashmir could be put down effectively and soon. A festering sore in the beautiful Vale could only be to the advantage of Peking via Rawalpindi and of the West via London. Time is an important factor in the politics of the present crisis.

(August 21, 1965)

4

Statesmanship on Trial

Can it be said in all fairness that New Delhi—both its official and non-official sets—have been able to grasp the full implications of the Kashmir crisis today?

There is excitement, there is avid curiosity to know how things are in the trouble-tossed Valley, there are highly-strung, almost shrieking, clamours for action and more action. But there is yet to appear a determined body of opinion that can enforce sober appraisal of a very complicated situation—with many more knots to untie than any that this country has faced since independence.

What amazes any dispassionate observer is that while tub-thumping oratory and high-pitched heroics about replying to the challenge of Pakistan can be heard in many quarters, there is very little evidence of a sense of national emergency prevailing in the Capital. The fact that Sant Fateh Singh's suicide threat has now come up as an urgent issue shows that the Government has not yet been able to convey to responsible elements outside its own ranks the gravity of the Kashmir crisis. And the sordid character assassination that has become a favourite pastime of hoary-headed politicians from Uttar Pradesh in these very weeks cannot be passed off as the antics of an irresponsible Opposition: for they amount to an amazing display of ugly skeletons from the cupboard of the ruling party itself.

It is this inability of the powers that be to turn the nation's focus to the momentous happenings in Kashmir strikes one as one of the most ominous features of the present situation. One has only to recall the electrifying effect that the call of national emergency had on the country as a whole in the wake of the Chinese attack in October-November 1962.

While there is a reasonable amount of restraint in airing views about defence in these difficult times, one cannot completely ignore the questioning mood of a large-section of New Delhi opinion on vital issues which only the leaders of the Government could and should convincingly answer. There is an overwhelming body of support at the Government decision to recapture the strategic heights in Kargil across the Cease Fire Line. But with it has inevitably come back the question: was it at all justified that we should have vacated those very posts only a few weeks ago after their capture by the intrepid heroism of our jawans and young officers? We are rightly blaming the UN Observers for having failed, to say the least, to check the Pakistani intruders coming in large numbers across the Cease Fire Line. But why then was such faith on the effectiveness of the same UN Observers when we agreed to vacate the Kargil posts?

Although there is a healthy abstinence in apportioning blame for any shortcomings when the danger across the border continues to be real—such refreshing from the howling November storm three years ago—there is no denying the fact that even responsible Congress leaders who have visited Kashmir since the outbreak of the crisis have come back unconvinced about the reason why the

Army could not check the infiltration of the armed Pakistani bands earlier. Was it not a fact that weeks before the actual clashes those in authority in Srinagar had sensed the danger and did not hesitate to inform the appropriate authorities? Was the coordination between the State administration and the Army authorities as smooth and complete as one would want it to be, particularly in the crucial days at the beginning of the crisis? While the Prime Minister in his Red Fort speech on August 15 paid a tribute to Sadiq and his team, has there been the expression of the same degree of appreciation of the Kashmir Government's role on the part of all the Ministers of the Government? And why is it that neither the Prime Minister nor the Defence Minister has once visited Srinagar since the onset of the present crisis?

Looking around New Delhi, one is sometimes struck by the amazing intermixture of levity and ignorance in many of the open expressions of opinion on the Kashmir crisis. It is not a question of letting one solitary J. J. Singh to prescribe in public the partition of Kashmir and to proclaim his thesis that the Kashmiri Muslim does not regard himself as an Indian—a speech that has not only been distributed clandestinely in the Kashmir Valley itself, but picked up prominently by *Dawn;* there are other cases of serious let down of the Indian case in Kashmir indulged in without much inhibition right in the Capital itself. A particularly vocal MP, for instance, has not hesitated to repeat J. J. Singh's slander about the Kashmiri Muslim from a public platform within a hundred yards of the Parliament House, that is, outside the orbit of his parliamentary immunity. It is not that such cases have not attracted the attention of the Intelligence, but decision at the political level has yet been lacking. In contrast, the Government's swift and liberal use of extraordinary powers in the case of others engaged in protest demonstrations over food handling makes a mockery of DIR.

There are other specimens of extraordinarily misplaced thinking to be seen in the Capital. For instance, people placed in positions of responsibility are reported to have been talking loosely about the necessity of martial law in the troubled Valley. What such pundits—obviously not overburdened with political wisdom—do not seem to realise is that the active use of the Army in any place or occasion does not *ipso facto* warrant the use of the martial law. The fact that a properly constituted Government under the distinguished captaincy of a leader of the calibre of G. M. Sadiq has been in effective authority is a matter of tremendous political importance, particularly in the context of Pakistan's propaganda about a "national uprising" in Kashmir. But minds, conditioned by the depoliticalised quarantine of an alien rule, do not understand such political digits; and their intrusion into the decision-making sphere may very well harm national interest. And to most brass hats are reportedly talking in such terms, whose political repercussions they can hardly comprehend.

Fairly widely commented in the Capital is the Swatantra thesis of equating the Pakistani intrusion into the Kashmir Valley with the Vietcong's war against US occupation in South Vietnam. There is nothing unexpected in such political gymnastics on the part of the pro-US lobby in the Capital since they are in a sorry state at the fiasco of their Embrace-Ayub campaign: they also seem to be nervous that the public memory might not be so short as to forget their own earnest advocacy for a deal with Ayub at the expense of Kashmir. And so New Delhi observers have not been surprised at the diversionary tactic of the pro-US lobby, trying to confuse the true implications of the Kashmir crisis by comparing it with Vietnam.

But more surprising is the Government's inability in effectively refuting this piece of Swatantra propaganda, in Parliament and outside. That the logic of the Swatantra line implies the equation of the presence of the Indian Army in a portion of *Indian* territory with the US Armed Forces clamping down on the *foreign* soil of Vietnam has hardly been stressed in the Government's propaganda. In fact, the Swatantra line questions the very integration of Kashmir into India and provides fresh encouragement to Pakistan. Even this has so far received little notice in the polemics from the Treasury Benches.

There is another school in the Capital which faithfully campaigns, though with a certain amount of circumspection, for Bakshi Ghulam Mohammad's return to prominence. Their pleading for national unity boils down to the demand for the re-induction of Bakshi into the leadership in Kashmir. This has so far received little support, and rightly too. For, Bakshi's contribution in poisoning the Kashmiri people's opinion about Central patronage can hardly be overlooked; no political leader has through indiscriminate corruption tarnished India's image in Kashmir more than Bakshi Ghulam Mohammad. To think of bringing him back to leadership when charges of large-scale corruption against him are being investigated into amounts to undermining Kashmiri morale at this critical juncture.

As the compulsions of the military campaign against Pakistani raiders in Kashmir have led to the crossing of the Cease Fire Line, the awareness about the larger implications of a long-drawn-out Indo-Pak conflict is yet to be fully grasped in New Delhi. In an all-out Indo-Pak war, it is true that Rawalpindi has to reckon with India's undoubted superiority in counter-attack in the eastern region, since East Pakistan is no doubt Ayub's Achilles heel, both politically and logistically.

At the same time, such a perspective before India too is the least wholesome for her all-round economic development and political stability. There is also the danger of militarism undermining democracy in a protracted war. The danger of the non-aligned foreign policy being subverted by heavy dependence on arms giving Powers, is not also minimised. Fortunately, there is a sense of anxiety in the highest quarters in New Delhi—despite some conspicuous exceptions—at such a prospect. The desire not to let the Indo-Pak conflict in Kashmir escalate into a full-scale war is thus clearly discernible. And yet one cannot strongly vouch for a firm stand against any bellicose approach, because a political leadership, itself lacking in the towering stature of a Nehru and harassed by powerful pressure groups, might find itself at the crucial hour unable to go against the tide.

In a small scale this could be noticed over the Bhutto episode. Pakistan's Foreign Minister's New Delhi visit would have been the briefest possible—the actual talks might not have lasted even an hour—without any Munich-like capitulation in the offing. Although the External Affairs Minister himself was not reluctant to meet him, one could imagine Lal Bahadur Shastri's predicament as he had to face an angry Parliament questioning his entire policy towards Pakistan. In the bargain, we may have lost a point to Pakistani diplomacy making the maximum capital out of it in the Afro-Asian world.

Resilience in politics is never to be translated into waverings in foreign policy. For, a nation gains in stature abroad as its leadership combines firmness with tact, and does not mistake passion or frenzy with wisdom and statesmanship.

New Delhi today can hardly afford to miss this precept.

(August 28, 1965)

5

Stock Taking after the Ordeal

An ordeal by fire is not necessarily the best moment to expect a chastened mood in a nation. The upheaval through which New Delhi has just passed could hardly be expected to restore immediately the balance needed for a sternly objective appraisal of the six stormy weeks that preceded the Cease Fire in the early hours of September 23.

For New Delhi as for the entire country, it was an overwhelming experience, the trials and tribulations as also the emotional stresses of a modern war, the first that has come its way since independence. The tragic content of the spectacle of two neighbours, born out of the same parentage, being locked in bloody combat was almost lost in the sweep of a nation-wide fervour that identified what the President had characterised as "this wasteful bloodshed", with the crusade in defence of the motherland. What was perhaps missed by many was that on the other side of the front too the common humanity could look upon this very war with the same patriotic tenacity in defence of the soil of Pakistan.

One of the main reasons for this demonstration of pride

in the performance of the armed forces was the underlying feeling that they could this time redeem the honour that was lost three years ago with the cowardly retreat of the Commanding General in the NEFA against the Chinese Army. The national shame suffered at Sela and Bomdila in November 1962 was wiped off by the valour displayed at Haji Pir and Sialkot in September 1965.

Besides, as many of the friendly foreign observers could testify, this brief spell of war almost served, may be unreasonably, as a safety-valve for pent-up frustration in many spheres; while the event is as yet too near for the nation to fully add up the heavy toll that a developing country has to meet on account of a present-day war. Besides, some of the ugly facets of any war can hardly be escaped in our case and those who have visited the front lines have come back with a realistic understanding of what war means in terms of not only human misery but of its de-humanising compulsions as well.

In the emotional upsurge that has swept the country in these few weeks, a sense of oneness has scored over parochialism, and narrow communal fanaticism was, for the time being at least, kept at bay. No small contribution on this score was made by Sadiq and his intrepid band in Kashmir.

Perhaps the fact that our armed forces, whether on land or in the sky, united as one unwavering fraternity, could give a good account of themselves staved off the bitter anger out of which communal fury is often begot. How much of this striking secularism of today could stand the strain of any military setback at the front against the Pakistani troops is yet to be tested.

From New Delhi one could hardly notice any panic among the common people placed right in the battle zones. Though by the grim standards of twentieth-century war it was brief in duration and limited in extent, the fact that near-normalcy could prevail even in the sensitive areas throughout the time when the battles were on, particularly in the Punjab, is itself ascribed to the complete absence of sagging morale. Rather at one stage, early in the conflict, an amateurish tendency was noticeable, a tendency which, elated by the initial military successes, seemed to take an almost *Carthago-delenda-est* stand against Pakistan.

This cocksure outlook was very correctly scotched by the Defence Minister in Parliament at the height of the operations on September 10—a date which roughly marked the point of checkmate in the overall progress of our army in combat. And in this respect, the Army Chief himself displayed unusual common sense; meeting the press on the morrow of the Cease Fire, he refused to claim that the back of the Pakistan Army had been broken. The Field Commanders have also been remarkably circumspect in listing their own achievements. One is tempted to conclude that the political leadership itself was anxious not to delude the public with all exaggerated picture of military gains, for they have the sagacity to understand that it was the element of surprise in the Indian strategy at the initial stage that mainly ensured in a spectacular way the major operations being conducted mostly on Pakistani soil.

Two things, however, are conceded even by the severest of critical observers as solid Indian achievements: firstly the Kashmir Valley could be saved from Pakistan's military offensive; secondly, the superiority in arms, provided by the Pentagon, could not give Pakistan the runaway victory that the responsible leaders in Rawalpindi were reported to have had braggingly forecast to the Western diplomats just about a week before the full-scale operations started on September 1.

The political implications of these two achievements in the field are expected to be far-reaching, according to New Delhi authorities. In their calculation, the fact that India did not hesitate to face all the hazards of a full-scale war extending from Dwarka in the west to Bagdogra in the east, and actually succeeded in staving off the armed attack on the Kashmir Valley, should open the eyes of Pakistan's leaders, and their friends abroad, that no Government in India would or could let the Jammu and Kashmir State, as it is constituted today, to go out of the Indian Union. Any move for a political settlement of the Kashmir question will thus find it difficult to escape this reality. From New Delhi's point of view, the settlement of the Kashmir question has, thanks to this war, been reduced to fringe adjustments to the status quo in Kashmir.

Secondly, the psychological complex in favour of having indiscriminate arms aid, noticeable in certain well-known sections of the Right, has been largely removed; and in this way, the Shastri Government finds itself today in a better position to vindicate the Nehru policy of non-alignment in foreign affairs and reasonable self-reliance in defence production. It is not without significance that Indira Gandhi's exhortation that we have "to stand on our own feet and to bear the entire burden ourselves" has received wide acclaim even from circles which can hardly be identified with the Left.

It is in this context that one cannot escape noticing in New Delhi considerable slump in American prestige particularly with regard to its politics of military alliances. The discredit of the Patton tank in the eyes of the man in the street in India today may have been magnified due to ignorance of technical knowledge; but the discredit of the foreign policy based on the lavish gift of Patton tanks can hardly be concealed despite Chester Bowles' frantic lobbying and explanatory campaign in the Capital.

The setback for the Patton has helped to lift Krishna Menon's standing, for it is Menon's tenacious emphasis on self-reliance in Defence during his tenure in the Cabinet which has paid rich dividends in the present military campaign. Many among those who were critical of Menon as the Defence Minister can no longer belittle the long-range importance of his Defence Economics. It is therefore quite on the cards that Menon may be playing a more and more prominent role in the affairs of the Establishment. His trip to Cairo may be the opening of a purposeful phase.

Along with Menon, the prestige of the Congress Left, as also of the Left outside the Congress, has to some extent been enhanced. The case for building an independent economy has inevitably been strengthened by the positive experience of having indigenously-built defence equipment. The national oil policy of K. D. Malaviya has also got a boost, as much as the Swatantra crusade against the public sector in basic industries is expected to suffer a reverse.

But the battle for the Fourth Plan is going to be more difficult. Asoka Mehta will have to cross many more bridges, and even then the top priority for Defence is bound to shrink the Plan budget on other heads. Although public sector defence production has got the praise due to it, it would however be incorrect to conclude that planning in the new context will automatically set its face against powerful private interests in industry and finance.

Rather the present indications in New Delhi suggest that while the Government will stress on Defence as top priority, the argument is being sharpened that in order to relieve the burden of development on the taxpayer, the Government should allow greater scope for the private sector. The production of basic goods might be stepped up inside the country, but there is no guarantee that it would not pass on, to a large measure, to the Big Business. The battle for the public sector does not seem to be assured of automatic victory: the battle is yet to be fought and won by the Left.

The Congress Right is no doubt in disarray but nobody in New Delhi is naive enough to suggest that it has suffered a defeat. Morarji Desai is in difficulty of finding an issue with which to discredit the Shastri leadership, more firmly entrenched as it is as a result of the present crisis. S. K. Patil is under a cloud as it has come to be known that he could not fall in line with some of the crucial decisions on the present confrontation against Pakistan. His split Swantantraite personality seems to be suffering from the same agonising indecision as Masani himself.

At the same time, one has to recognise that the Jan Sangh in this crisis has been most prominently active. The Congress circles, however, point out that the Jan Sangh's anti-Muslim frenzy has been curbed because the fight against Pakistan has become an issue of national defence and not just a communal crusade. However, careful observers tend to agree that the Jan Sangh's election prospects have been enhanced since it can claim that its uncompromising antipathy to Pakistan has been vindicated.

Almost resembling the Swantantra, the Left Communist quandary has been most accentuated by the present developments. Namboodiripad's discomfiture is no longer a secret, since he has the unenviable task of reconciling his personal annoyance at the Pakistani and Chinese actions against India with the unalloyed pro-Peking leanings of some of the ultra-revolutionaries in his newly-found Party. The point of polarisation inside the Left Communist ranks seems to nave been reached.

What would be the political significance of the nation-wide tribute spontaneously showered on the Armed Forces? There is no doubt that the leadership of the Defence forces has not only come to be widely known all over the country but today commands the admiration of all sections of public opinion.

This is no doubt in keeping with the present national mood. How far the Armed Forces will play a significant part in the political life of the country time alone can show; and that too can be known only in times of crisis. At the moment, the attitude of the bulk of the officer class is echoed by a Field Commander receiving a team of Parliament Members with the words: "We are your servants." In the present temper in the Capital this expression of robust loyalty to the sovereign Parliament has not received the publicity it deserves.

In the sphere of foreign affairs, the Indo-Pak armed conflict has brought to the fore the question of this country's future links with the Commonwealth. An outstanding feature of New Delhi's political life today is that the Quit-Commonwealth slogan has become widely popular in the Congress circles. Although the Prime Minister disfavoured the presentation of a formal memorandum of protest to the UK High Commissioner by a group of MPs, it is an open secret that Shastri has not in the least discouraged the Congress members coming out sharply against India's continued association with the Commonwealth on the floor of the House. Bhagwat Jha Azad's resolution in the Lok Sabha practically got the green signal when the Prime Minister himself condemned the Whitehall stand at a public meeting in the Capital three days later.

While John Freeman has conveyed to Wilson the magnitude of Indian indignation at the British role in the Kashmir dispute, the British circles here seem to be confident that India would have second thoughts on the question of quitting the Commonwealth. Their calculations seem to be based on the assumption that secession from the Commonwealth would hit this country's foreign trade, and it will take time for India to work out an alternate trade pattern on a global scale. They also pin their hope on the pull of their lobby inside the Secretariat ranging from the External Affairs to the Finance Ministry.

The US embarrassment has been most acute over the stark realisation by all sections in India that Pakistan could fight the war against this country almost entirely with the American gifted arms. This is a point which the Government spokesmen have been directed to underline in their public pronouncements.

The general impression here about Washington's attitude is that it is opposed to the continuation of the Indo-Pak war as such; at the same time, there is a very strong suspicion that while anxious for a cease fire, the US authorities would exert the maximum pressure in the coming weeks for a political decision on Kashmir which will tend to favour Pakistan; although the demand for plebiscite seems to have lost weight in Washington, other proposals—including the J P plan for a variant of condominium—seem to be under the State Department's consideration. In other words, the US diplomatic pressure is likely to be stepped tip to force New Delhi to modify its present stand of complete integration of Jammu and Kashmir into the Indian Union. Not only Rajagopalachari's views but even Namboodiripad's declaration that the political status of Kashmir can by no means be regarded as settled has aroused interest in official US circles in the Capital.

The report that the Pentagon seems to favour the resumption of US arms aid to Pakistan has not come as a surprise here. Informed quarters in New Delhi have long held the view that the Pentagon and the CIA have never been alienated from President Ayub so long as he permitted the continuation of the U-2 base at Peshawar: on the other hand, the State Department has been annoyed by Pakistan's hobnobbing with Peking. Hence the strange spectacle of the Pentagon canvassing for arms for Ayub, while the World Bank repeatedly postponing the Aid-Pak Consortium meeting.

The argument trotted out by Bowles' men in New Delhi in apologia for the Pentagon move is interesting: So long as the Pakistan Government remained in loyal subservience to the US there was no danger of any attack on India: bellicosity in Rawalpindi came as a consequence of its moorings with Washington getting weakened. If Pakistan could once again be brought within the orbit of total US control, India would not have to fear any fresh armed attack from Pakistan.

This is no doubt an extraordinary piece of dollar dialectics by which the US arms gift were supposed to ensure peaceful proclivities in Pakistan, an argument which directly runs counter to New Delhi's bitter experience, gained over more than a decade, that it is the large-scale induction of US arms through military alliance that has heightened the danger of the Indo-Pak war. It appears that New Delhi opinion will considerably harden against Washington if the Pentagon proposal to resume arms aid to Pakistan is put through.

In contrast to Britain's sorry plight and the US discomfiture, Moscow at the moment is enjoying the sunshine of Shastri's confidence. Apart from the Soviet Union's traditional stand on Kashmir, which has always been favourable towards India, the Soviet leaders seem to have taken pains to explain to New Delhi that any accretion of the Soviet influence in Rawalpindi through patience and goodwill would in the long run be to this country's advantage, since it will to that extent neutralise Pakistan's leanings towards both Peking and Washington.

This rather daring experiment at international diplomacy on the part of Moscow has not created misunderstanding in New Delhi, though some pro-US commentators have started talking about Moscow's letdown. The Shastri Government was known to have decided to accept the Soviet offer of mediation in the very weekend that U Thant was here, that is, long before Kosygin's letter was formally replied to by Shastri. There is, however, a feeling of pessimism in certain circles here about the prospects of the proposed Tashkent summit, though there is not the least misgivings about the Soviet leadership's objective in promoting Indo-Pak peace.

With the regular war brought to an end by an uneasy peace that has accompanied the Security Council's mandate for a Cease Fire, there is speculation in New Delhi about the political crisis that is supposed to be brewing inside the Pakistani leadership. While President Ayub's responsibility for going in for the war is not denied, there is a general understanding here that the reported Ayub-Bhutto tension is a major upshot of the war which may turn out to be the decisive pointer to the future of Indo-Pak relations. Bhutto with his pro-Peking bellicosity is believed to have the support of a good section of the Army leadership: though Bhutto's political prestige may not have been enhanced by the fiasco of the much-proclaimed Chinese support in the war against India, the more truculent among the Generals have felt humiliated that the Cease Fire has come as an obstacle to their throwing Indian troops out of Pakistani soil.

On the other hand, President Ayub, according to this theory, has gone in for the Cease Fire precisely to prevent the Generals getting too powerful through the continuation of war while the public morale might have been embittered by his own failure to win Kashmir. The defiance of the Security Council Resolution appears to be the impact of the pro-Bhutto Generals' veto; both the factions at the same time are still hesitating to take the responsibility of going in full steam for a regular war with India. The fact of the Indian Army's presence on the Pakistani soil is for them a humiliating irritant, while the failure to trounce the Indian Army—which they might have complacently hoped to achieve—is acting as a deterrent against the resumption of full-scale war.

By this appraisal there seems to be a tug of war going on inside Pakistan between the Washington lobby and the Peking lobby, a tussle which has been accentuated as a result of the war. President Ayub, who has permitted himself the luxury of Chou En-lai's friendship as a lever for pressurising the US, never abandoned his links with Washington, he himself being the architect of the US-Pak military alliance in the Dulles days. In contrast to this, Bhutto has staked his whole political career on a determined entente with China in common belligerence against India. Whether this theory stems from wishful thinking or is a true indicator of events only the developments unfolding in the next few weeks will prove.

The Sino-Pak axis plans against India were believed to have been given the finishing touch when Chen Yi met Bhutto in Karachi after the Pak offensive had been mounted in the Chhamb sector. According to this blueprint, the Indian Army was expected to march into East Pakistan, finding it an easy target. Synchronising with this, Peking hoped to engineer a coup in Bhutan with the help of the disgruntled Dorji clique whose leader, the ousted Premier Lhendup Dorji, now in London, is believed to be in close touch with both Peking and the Whitehall. This projected coup was scheduled to give birth to a "Revolutionary Council" which would send out an appeal for help to "friendly powers" in their struggle against the Indian Army which by treaty is to come to the support of the King. Thereupon the Pak troops would try to push towards Bhutan through the narrow 60-mile gap of Indian territory that keeps Bhutan and East Pakistan apart, while the Chinese troops could march down from Bhutan. This way Assam and NEFA could have been sliced off from the rest of India, a geopolitical dream which Peking has long nurtured.

Unfortunately for Bhutto and his comrades in Peking, little Lal Bahadur Shastri did not oblige them by walking into their trap and Peking in the hurry had to cook up the complaint about the unused installations beyond Nathu La and of the missing yaks and the sheep. This was indeed poor substitute for the Grand design that banked on involving the Indian Army in a war with China via Bhutan and East Pakistan using the Pakistan Army as a baffle wall against any possible Seventh Fleet bombing.

It was but natural that the fiasco of this meticulously worked-out plan led Peking into a state of frustrated rage whose spit-over could be seen in the famous double-ultimatum and the note of condemnation at the bleating of the eight hundred sheep that turned up at the Chinese Embassy in New Delhi. Perhaps a sense of humour is a 'revisionist' sin.

(October 2, 1965)

6

How Far is Pindi from Washington?

New Delhi's sixty four-million-dollar question at the moment is: What precisely is the nature and extent of Washington's influence on Rawalpindi today?

In a sense, this is the key question around which Indian diplomacy in the Indo-Pak dispute has been revolving in the uncertain period ushered in by the Cease Fire. So far the only tangible thing that India has been able to extract from the US is the assurance that the original Pakistani clamour for a plebiscite in Kashmir on the plea that it is a case for the exercise of the right of self-determination, is not going to be underwritten by Washington.

At the same time, top-level US officials are believed to have made it clear to the Government of India that Washington would agree with Pakistan that discussion on the future of Kashmir, with a view to work out a formula agreeable to both the countries, must be taken up without delay. The Indian plea that the Cease Fire should be stabilised before any other question could be taken up seems to be hardly getting a hearing with the Americans.

The US diplomatic mission in the Capital in their high-powered off-the-record lobbying has let it be known that without India getting ready to let the question of Kashmir's political future be re-opened, it would be practically impossible for the US Administration to permit the inflow of PL-480 bounty into this country or keep to the commitments ranging from the private US participation in the fifth steel plant project to the allocation of foodgrains or the Aid-India Club assistance for the Fourth Plan. In other words, Kashmir is being brought forward as the centrepiece of US diplomacy, whether over the Plan-aid or food.

Even in the sphere of pure military supplies to Pakistan the latest round of developments throws interesting light. Our mission in Washington has been left in no doubt that a powerful section of the Pentagon is strongly in favour of continuance of arms aid to Pakistan: for this lobby, Pakistan is vitally important for the CIA's global network, and the important U-2 base near Peshawar cannot be left in jeopardy.

It is being given out by the US circles here that the State Department may not be in a position to hold out for very long in the face of this Pentagon pressure, and that the military aid to Pakistan can be withheld for sometime only if India complied with the US demand for the resumption of Indo-Pak negotiations on Kashmir. It is not without reason that wide publicity is being given about this subject by pro-Western quarters in the Capital.

Apart from the Pentagon lobby, it is known in New Delhi that Pakistan's two CENTO allies, Iran and Turkey, have given a squadron and a half of jet fighter aircraft to Rawalpindi. More important is the fact that Pakistan has been able to secure spares for her defence equipment from these two allies, since they all have the advantage of having standardised NATO specifications for arms.

This disproves the theory current in New Delhi for sometime that the Pakistan Army having supply of ammunition which would last only for a month would have been immobilsed if the war had continued a couple of weeks longer. With the help from her CENTO allies, there is no doubt that Pakistan could to a large measure replenish her losses in arms in the field of battle, which are assessed by informed observers as somewhere near thirty to thirtyfive per cent of her original strength; and the Western sources, even those which are not prejudiced against India, would prefer to place Indian losses at roughly the same proportion.

Another country from which Pakistan is reported to have received a response to her SOS is Saudi Arabia which is believed to have given a substantial quota of her dollar reserves (earned mainly as the royalty from the American oil concerns operating in that country) with which Pakistani agents have been trying to buy jet aircraft from private parties in northern Europe. Besides, there are reports of West German resumption of arms sales to Pakistan, temporarily stopped during the hostilities.

These Pakistani moves to replenish armed losses in the recent conflict have brought home to New Delhi the inescapable fact that although formally Washington has so far abstained from directly giving arms to Pakistan, the US Government has not put a stop to third parties providing US arms to her despite the fact that the US political influence over all these parties is definitely dominant. Incidentally, this is in marked contrast to the reported Moscow warning to Peking against escalating the war, delivered in the wake of the bellicose Chinese ultimatum in the last phase of the Indo-Pak war.

These developments have confirmed New Delhi in its

suspicion that the widely publicised Ayub-Bhutto rift is an American diplomatic concoction, devised with a view to pressurise India to negotiate with President Ayub over his claims on Kashmir. From the very beginning of the crisis, this story about a crisis in the Pak leadership has been discounted by the topmost circles in New Delhi. As an important VIP put it, the difference between President Ayub and his Foreign Minister, Bhutto, does not seem to be wider than the one between Shastri and Patil.

It is held here that Pakistan did not suffer so badly in the war as to let this difference between President Ayub and Bhutto widen into a full-scale rift. Only out of a decisive defeat at the front or as a result of an internal explosion can a political crisis come up in a set-up like the one prevailing in Pakistan; and on both these counts, the recent developments did not mark a decisive turning point.

The theory that Bhutto represents the anti-American and pro-Peking trend in the Pak hierarchy has been further weakened by a report received from an important source about very high level confidential confabulations that Bhutto held in New York with Goldberg, the US Ambassador to the UN, and with Dean Rusk as well. These confabulations are believed to have taken place on September 27, that is, less than a week after the Cease Fire.

It appears that Goldberg remonstrated with Bhutto for Pakistan's clumsy handling of the Kashmir situation and added that U Thant had informed him about India having irrefutable proof about the trouble-makers in the Kashmir Valley being Pakistani infiltrators trained by the Pak Army. This would be embarrassing for the US whose hands were already full with Vietnam.

Bhutto's reply was most revealing. He felt that the Goldberg assessment lacked a clear understanding of the developments that had come in the wake of the Rann of Kutch crisis: he reminded Goldberg that the whole question of Kashmir had been taken up by Pakistan with the State Department even before she had informed her CENTO allies; and it would not be possible for Pakistan to make a volte face on Kashmir, giving up the entire claim in this dispute.

Goldberg however advised Bhutto to go slow since the US delegation in the Security Council had to manoeuvre carefully in this crisis in view of the existence of the US-Pak military alliance. The Pak Foreign Minister agreed with this but stressed that unless the Kashmir question had been taken up soon, developments might take place which might be beyond the control of Pakistan, since the crisis was no longer the concern of Pakistan alone but of her more powerful allies as well. So, there should be mutual understanding between the US and Pakistan as to the next step to be taken.

Apart from this highly interesting report, it has come to be known here that certain important CIA officials had opined in Rawalpindi recently that U Thant's initiative had brought about premature results, for the US authorities, while finding it difficult to disagree with U Thant's positive stand, would not make too much of a fuss about the immediate and absolute cessation of hostilities.

With the developments in Indonesia there is a general impression here that the US is not placed in a state of isolation in Asia as she was at the beginning of the Indo-Pak crisis. Today she has secured a little more initiative to intervene in Asian affairs, thanks to the costly adventurism of the Indonesian Left.

With the awareness of this understanding of the US-Pak relations, New Delhi however does not envisage a fullscale war in the immediate future. The danger of Pakistani subversion or even armed clashes of sizable magnitude is not ruled out at least for the next six weeks. After that, with the snows blocking the path of the Chinese Army on the High Himalayas, it is possible for the Indian Army to throw practically its entire strength in any encounter with Pakistan, and this advantage continues definitely till the end of February.

It is therefore by this calendar of Himalayan snows that New Delhi has to weigh not only the import of Pakistani attitudes but also evaluate the importance of US-Pak understanding.

Meanwhile, speculation has started in the Capital about the significance of President Radhakrishnan's talks at Bucharest. Even before the President set out on his tour, it was known to informed circles in New Delhi that the Sino-Indian dispute would figure in the talks with the Romanian leaders. The reason why New Delhi has been interested in the subject is mainly due to the anxiety to assess the present trends in Peking. As part of the same essay, our Charge d'Affaires in Peking has been recalled here for consultation. The worldwide interest in Lin Piao's celebrated thesis delivered at the beginning of September as also reports about a tussle between the hardliners and the moderates in Peking have no doubt necessitated such an appraisal.

New Delhi's careful assessment of the Chinese mood at present does not seem to warrant any early rapprochement with Peking. At the same time, the Prime Minister seems to be anxious that all those powers which are likely to fall in for Peking's propaganda line, should be specially told about India's stand on the dispute and her readiness to settle it peacefully but with honour.

In this category falls not only Romania but France and the UAR as well, and India's accredited spokesmen and visiting dignitaries to both these countries are believed to have taken extra pains to emphasise the Indian stand on the dispute with China. If Peking chose to create trouble once again, such explanatory campaign at this stage would help to counter the Chinese propaganda poison against India; indeed this might help even to minimise any Chinese thrust since Peking would then think twice before attacking India. The raising of the Sino-Indian dispute in the Bucharest talks was thus not without the initiative from New Delhi's side.

Diplomatically, it is felt here, this is the opportune moment to neutralise Peking. And nowhere can it be done with greater effect than in Romania, since in the communist world, the distance to Peking is shorter from Bucharest than from Moscow.

(October 16, 1965)

7

Pakistan: Time for Initiative

This week two years ago, there took place one of the most tragic episodes in the annals of independent India—a regular armed conflict between India and her most initimate neighbour, Pakistan.

In the excitement of that conflict, particularly when it assumed the character of an onslaught by armed forces across the frontiers, it was but natural that the grim implications of a fullscale war between two neighbouring countries so closely interlinked as Pakistan and India are, could not be clearly realised. For, when frontiers are violated, particularly for nations which have newly won their independence, patriotic fervour cannot possibly be expected to take into account all the facets of a complicated reality; in other words, an armed conflict by itself hardly solves the problems that give rise to it. Rather, the struggle beyond the conflict for achieving enduring peace becomes a more difficult but a more compelling struggle.

It is the realisation of this aspect of the Indo-Pak conflict that led Lal Bahadur Shastri to say on the morrow of the successful Tashkent Conference: "We fought in the war with all our strength. Now we have to fight for peace with all our strength." The material loss sustained by this three-week war was severe indeed for both the countries: if it has cost India a thousand crores of rupees, it must have cost Pakistan as much, and neither the one nor the other in their economic stringency can afford the luxury of such an utter waste. And the bitter animosity left behind by such an armed confrontation in which the jawans gave their lives on both sides, in which civilians of both countries had to bear the brunt of a regular war, only helped to raise further the wall of estrangement between two closely-knit peoples. It is no platitude but solid hard truth that neither history nor geography, neither culture nor self-interest can justify the continuation of a state of armed peace in the relations between India and Pakistan.

The antipathy towards Pakistan in a considerable section of opinion in this country is born of a strange mixture. Many were embittered because a common homeland was partitioned: many others have not yet been able to overcome the passions roused by the bloody massacres that came in the wake of Partition; and still others have projected their hatred against Western imperialism towards Pakistan after the conclusion of the US-Pak military pact in 1954—a pact which the overwhelming body of people in this country regarded with good reason as a dangerous encroachment of the US Government into the Asian scene, one more link in its chain of military alliances all round the world.

But no objective appraisal of the political reality of today can be based on the understanding of the conditions of yesterday. Whether we liked it or not, Pakistan is as much a historical reality as Israel: in fact, the economies of both India and Pakistan are more inter-dependent than those of Israel and the Arab States. As for the justified abhorrence of membership of military alliances, it must not blind us to the new and significant developments in Pakistan's foreign policy in recent years: without underplaying the extent of influence that the US may still be wielding in Pakistan, particularly over its bureaucracy and a section of political opinion, one cannot ignore the fact that in recent years, Pakistan has shown a degree of resilience and unorthodox approach to both China and the Soviet Union, which run counter to the dictates of US-led military alliances; and to the extent that this exists and grows, the US hold over her is undermined. And we in this country will show a greater sense of realism if we too try to take note of these significant developments.

One point is often forgotten in our black-and-white attitude towards Pakistan. One of the main propaganda arguments by which reactionary forces in Pakistan have often whipped up frenzy in the common people is the menace of the Big neighbour, that is, India. If there is an effusion of misgivings, demonstrably shown, in this country at every piece of news of Pakistan getting military hardware from her own circle of friends and allies, there is no reason why intelligent people in this country should be unable to comprehend the extent of the fear that could be generated by interested circles in Pakistan at every piece of news about strengthening of India's military capacity. The tragedy of the situation is that every accretion of her arms and equipments is regarded by many in this country as adding to her military preparations against India, while every addition to our defence build-up is interpreted by many in Pakistan as posing a new threat to her security. It is in this context that one has to understand that if during the conflict of 1965, the halting of Pakistan's armed advance from Akhnoor to Barmer was hailed in our country as an expression of patriotic heroism, the resistance to Indian advance along the Ichogil canal and in the vicinity of Sialkot was acclaimed by the Pakistani masses as a demonstration of patriotic valour on the part of their jawans.

Many in this country are obsessed by the thought that Pakistan's preoccupation in foreign affairs is to be seen in a state of total hostility towards this country. What is missing in this appraisal is that the illusion of American invincibility prevalent in many parts of the world a decade ago has now been dispelled, and one can find today responsible sections in Pakistani hierarchy having a better grasp of what constitutes their national self-interest. Very little notice is taken in this country nowadays to many of the policy pronouncements of those in authority in Pakistan. It is worth noting, for instance, that in an address before the Royal Institute of International Affairs, London, on November 18, 1966, President Ayub said: "The geo-political imperatives of our location on the map of the world make it necessary that for our survival we should have good neighbourly dealings with our three big neighbours, China, the Soviet Union and India."

Apart from this sober realisation on the part of those in Pakistan who look at the world from the angle of power politics, one has to take into account the wholesome urges for friendly ties that could be seen in the common people over there. It would be short-sighted on our part to ignore, for instance, the powerful anti-imperialist stand of the overwhelming section of opinion in East Pakistan. There has often been an upsurge of anti-imperialist enthusiasm in the youth of East Pakistan, which on the eve of Tashkent had in a rousing manifesto declared: "We do not believe in the imperialist policy of trying to solve problems through war and hence we greet the coming

Tashkent Conference and wish it success." And even on the thorny issue of Kashmir, they appealed for settlement "through peaceful talks and negotiations outside the pale of imperialism".

Both these trends in Pakistan today—the hard-headed realism at the top and the democratic urge of the masses—need to be encouraged for the evolution of a positive approach towards India. And in this task, the role and responsibility of the leaders of public opinion in the country can hardly be underestimated.

This is a task which cannot be discharged by merely remaining correct on the diplomatic plane, confining oneself to only protocol proprieties. What is needed today is a bold *initiative* to break the ice that has once again accumulated after the thaw that was witnessed at Tashkent. Through sheer drift and inaction, a peculiar state of uncertainty has been reached in our relations with Pakistan, with the result that a chain-reaction of tensions can be worked up on both sides by those who have almost developed a vested interest in keeping the two peoples apart. It is thus not enough to keep ourselves only diplomatically correct: we have to ask ourselves, have we done our maximum best to overcome all the resistance that block the path to Indo-Pak reconciliation?

The Tashkent Declaration itself indicated a number of steps towards such reconciliation. On the level of propaganda, it laid down not only that "both sides will discourage any propaganda" against each other, but would also *"encourage* propaganda which promotes the development of friendly relations between the two countries". Can we honestly say that we have done everything on our part to compel the implementation of this?

It was also agreed at Tashkent that both the countries would work for "the restoration of economic and trade relations, communications as well as cultural exchanges" between the two countries. The record in this sphere is far from adequate. Two years have gone by since the 1965 hostilities, and yet even the lines of communication have not been restored: both sides are taking positions which are difficult to justify before the eyes of the world. One of the traits of Indian diplomacy in its heydays in mid-fifties was to tackle a deadlock by trying agreement on lesser issues until the hard core of the problem could be attacked: from Korea to Indo-China, this became the pattern of Indian intervention. And yet in Indo-Pak relations today, this common-sense approach seems to be lacking: if Rawalpindi is insisting on a package negotiation including Kashmir, New Delhi is insisting that all means of communications must open at the same time or none at all. Indira Gandhi has more than once expressed her eagerness to restore cultural exchanges between the two countries, but what concrete steps have been proposed or taken for the purpose?

It was agreed at Tashkent that India and Pakistan would "continue meetings both at the highest and other levels on matters of direct concern to both countries". After Sardar Swaran Singh's visit to Pakistan, no further step was taken in the matter. At one stage last year, the impression prevailed in New Delhi that not until the General Elections, would the Prime Minister be in a position to take any initiative in the matter. Six months have elapsed since the General Elections and there is no sign of a new initiative. Meanwhile, matters are allowed to drift—alarums come up occasionally, mutual expulsions of diplomatic personnel take place and the pandits in Kashmir take their own turn in helping to work up new tensions.

For, any drift in the situation does not ensure even the status quo. Other forces are bound to step in. The recent wave of Jan Sangh depredations from Kashmir to Ranchi are ugly pointers: and this will only encourage the Jan Sangh's opposite numbers in Pakistan to play their part with renewed gusto. But Jan Sangh politics cannot be held in the leash by mere exhortations against communalism, we have to realise that the question of combating communalism today is closely linked with the taking of a bold and positive move for a rapprochement with Pakistan.

Nobody in New Delhi is unaware of the present Government's difficulties in taking such an initiative. Its weak political standing inhibits it to a large measure. But the Prime Minister has to assert, as she did assert recently on the question of Dearness Allowances for the Central Government employees which the Deputy Prime Minister was resisting till the very end; for she has to realise that immediate stakes for a better understanding with Pakistan are high not only for the country but for her Government as well. As for Chavan, he was a co-architect of the Tashkent understanding; and today it is he as the Home Minister who has to bear the brunt of the offensive of the communal forces: and so long as the armed-truce relations with Pakistan prevail, such forces can never be quelled. For Chavan himself personally a bold stand for better relations with Pakistan will lift his national standing and silence those who whisper that he has a soft corner for the Jan Sangh. Political leaders have to realise that Shastri's moment of glory was reached really at Tashkent when he showed more courage in signing for peace than when he had to send the jawans to battle four months before.

The Left has a big responsibility in the matter. Gone are the days when a simplified understanding of world events could help, for Pakistan can no longer be branded as the mere spring-board of Washington's Asian adventures. The Socialists have to choose between the temptation for clap-trap popularity in the company of Jan Sangh and a more realistic, though more difficult, decision to campaign for a settlement with Pakistan. Some Communists have shown realism on this count, others also have to re-think: for it is no longer a badge of wisdom to dismiss the question of Indo-Pak settlement as a Jayaprakash fad or an American design.

The time for positive intervention by the democratic forces has come: and if the Left stands aloof, it will do so at its own cost.

(September 2, 1967)

8

Kashmir in Focus

Autumn has set in the beautiful Valley of Kashmir—the autumn of mellow fruitfulness. And in the breath-taking beauty of this rich land, one comes across today the spectacle of simmering tensions between brother and brother, tensions which were never in the past allowed to vitiate relations among Kashmiris of different communities.

The people of this picturesque Valley have passed through many an ordeal—two invasions in two decades and the convulsions following the deposition of one of their leaders. But none of these—not even the shock of the temporary loss of the Muslim Holy Relic three years ago—could weaken the bonds of communal harmony in Kashmir Valley that has been a precious asset for the whole of India. But today when one hears talks of communalism crossing the Banihal, it may be worth recording some of the impressions gathered during a brief visit to this enchanting Valley in distress.

What really is the crux of the Pandit agitation in Kashmir? The elopement of an allegedly minor Pandit girl with her Muslim office boss would by normal standards have been an issue of local excitement: there is no doubt of bungling by the police in handling the case, which was all the more thoughtless since there was the danger of the episode getting communal overtones—a danger which was least expected to be missed by the Kashmir administration with its record of vigilant anti-communalism for two long decades.

In fact, inter-communal marriages have throughout been more frequent in Kashmir than in any other part of India: cases of Pandit girls marrying Muslims, or Muslim girls marrying Hindus and Sikhs have been numerous, quite a few having taken place in recent months.

The reason why there was so much stir over this particular case of Parameshwari Handoo was that it was linked up with the dwindling economic status of the Pandit community. In their very first press conference, the Hindu Action Committee made it clear that their programme of struggle had been taken up "for restoring the rights that are being denied to them as citizens of free India" as "they have been undergoing continuous and unabated process of denial in all walks of life". In their representation to Chavan also they complained about their "disabilities and difficulties" as a community.

From the mere statement of this position one would possibly get the impression that the Kashmiri Pandit is being treated today as a second-class citizen in his own homeland. But a dispassionate study of the reality would show that this is far from the truth. Numbering roughly about sixty thousand, they constitute less than two per cent of the total population of the State. As against this, they still hold as many as 638 out of 2252 Gazetted posts in the State, thereby cornering more than 27 per cent of the higher-income Government jobs. The total number of non-Gazetted posts in the State is 44,529. Out of this, as many as 7136, or 18.25 per cent, are held by the

Kashmiri Hindus. (Incidentally, this shows that the Kashmiri Pandit as a relatively affluent community tends more towards the higher-income jobs.)

Perhaps no community in India is so favoured—not even the majority community in most of the States—with a population strength of less than two per cent it has been permitted to retain as many as 27 per cent of higher-income jobs and 18 per cent of the lower-income jobs under the Government.

This weightage in favour of the Pandit is more sharply brought out when one looks at the corresponding figures for the Muslim community. The Muslims constitute 68 per cent of the population of the State, but they hold only 42 per cent of the Gazetted posts and a little over 47 per cent of the non-Gazetted posts.

The charge of discrimination, if levelled against the Sadiq Government, becomes patently untenable when one looks at the figures of recent Government appointments. Of the 136 Gazetted appointments made since March 1966, the Muslims number only 45, while the non-Muslims (including Sikhs) were selected for as many as 91 posts, of which the Pandits bagged 47. Obviously, the badge of the community has not been the major consideration in the making of these appointments.

In the matter of educational facilities, one hears of the difficulty of the Pandit students getting admission into the Medical and Engineering Colleges. As for medical education, 104 went to Muslims in 1966, and 131 to non-Muslims. In the Regional Engineering College in Srinagar, the figures of admission in 1966 are interesting: Muslims 77, non-Muslims 127 (out of whom 60 are Kashmiri Pandit boys).

In the higher echelons of the bureaucracy, the non-

Muslims in Kashmir have an honoured place: the Chief Secretary, the Financial Commissioner, the DIG of Police, the Trade Agents are non-Muslims. Of the three High Court Judges, only one is a Muslim.

In terms of Government employment, therefore, if any community in Kashmir can have a grievance, one should think it is certainly not the Pandits. But the background to the undoubted sense of frustration which prevails among Pandits has a history behind it. Under the Maharaja rule before Independence, the Pandits monopolised all the Government jobs and the Muslims definitely were the have-nots, despite their being the majority community. As early as 1928, the then Prime Minister of the State, Sir Albion Bannerji, had compared the state of Muslims in Kashmir to a flock of sheep. One of the major causes of the uprising against the Maharaja rule in 1931 was the grinding economic impoverishment of the Muslim masses; this led to the appointment of the Glancy Commission which suggested measures for adequate representation of Muslims in Government services as also the spread of educational facilities. But the feudal autocracy of the Maharaja hardly made any efforts to improve conditions. In 1939 Sir Gopalaswamy Ayyangar, who was then the Maharaja's Prime Minister, added to the civil service recruitment rules of the State that in making appointments the Government would take into account the comparative representation of different communities in the State. This also did not improve matters and the last of the efforts in the direction were indicated by the Jha Commission which highlighted the inadequacy of Muslims in the matter of Government appointments and facilities for education.

After Independence, the successive Governments in the State have paid more attention to spreading education among all sections of the community rather than forcing an artificial percentage ratio in the matter of Government appointment; this in fact is the contrast between the Kashmir Government and the Muslim League Ministries of pre-independence days, particularly in Bengal and Punjab. With the spread of education, naturally the majority community has also thrown up a number of educated men eligible on grounds of merit for services; and so the monopoly held by the Pandit community has been undermined in a natural process. As a senior Kashmir leader put it to me with a total sense of unbias, the cake has remained constant while the clamour for shares have gone up, with the result that one who was having almost the whole cake for a long time has been finding that he has to share it with others equally entitled to it. It is in this way that the problem of educated unemployment, which has been growing all over the country, has got into a distorted focus in the mind of the Pandit community which looks at it with alarm as a serious inroad into their past privileged preserve.

In this connection it may be worthwhile noting the peculiar characteristics of the Pandit community. It is a closed tribe of highly cultured and widely educated men and women, who more than the Bengali *bhadralok* have kept themselves confined mainly to jobs instead of branching out to commerce and industry; nor one finds them engaged in agriculture, or the poorest section going in for factory work. Obviously the fate of such a community in the new economic set-up would be very trying: out of their closed-wall frustration any small incident could spark off an angry outburst.

One cannot say that the Kashmir Government is completely oblivious to this state of affairs. This is clear from the fact that right from the beginning Sadiq has refused to turn a deaf ear to the problem. Even before Chavan went to Srinagar, the Kashmir Chief Minister in a statement before the Assembly on August 31 said: "We live in a democratic age and have the proud privilege of being the citizens of the great Republic of India, and any differences or grievances which any section of the people may feel, can be discussed and thrashed out in a proper manner... I, on my part, assure them of all the consideration in examining their grievances." In the official statement at the end of his visit, Chavan mentioned: "The Chief Minister had already announced a decision to constitute a Committee which should examine all these and related matters (referring to the disabilities and difficulties of the Pandit community). Soon after a memorandum on this subject is made available to the Chief Minister by the Action Committee, the State Government would set up such a committee as would command universal confidence." Uptil this day, the memorandum from the Action Committee has not reached the Kashmir Government.

It is not that the sober sections of the Pandits did not realise that in the solution of their problems a large-scale agitation involving communal tensions would not help in the least. The terms of settlement of the agitation announced by Chavan on September 3 were offered more than once by Sadiq and his colleagues to the Hindu Action Committee right from the beginning of the agitation. Why then did the leadership of the Pandit agitation take to the path of direct action?

It is in this context that the Jan Sangh's role assumes significance. More precisely, the RSS elements are reported to have provided the aggressive communal pep to the entire agitation. The Hindu Action Committee as such has been trying to say that it has no specific political affiliation, but there is known to be a strong Jan Sangh faction in it; the President of the Committee, P.N. Ghasi (incidentally, a Bakshi associate), is believed to be leading this faction.

There are also reports about the mysterious doings of a seemingly social organisation Anand Marg which, according to responsible Bihar sources, had taken a prominent part in the communal happenings at Ranchi.

Against this background, Balraj Madhok appeared. Madhok officially came as a member of a parliamentary delegation, but as a sideline, he intervened in the Pandit agitation. When he met the Chief Minister, he gave the impression of being anxious to help in calming down the excitement, but the impact of his address at the public meeting had just the opposite effect. He exhorted the Pandits not to consider themselves as a minority, but to realise that the entire Hindu India would back them; and naturally enough, he warned the Muslims that the Jan Sangh was the emerging authority in the national scene: it had all the smackings of a retaliatory mind.

This provocation had its inevitable impact. Two days later, on August 24, a lakh-strong Muslim procession was out on the streets denouncing Madhok's speech. Obviously the pro-Pak elements took advantage of the situation—since Madhok almost proved their thesis about the incompatibility of coexistence between the Hindus and the Muslims—but the Congress leaders claimed that by joining in this demonstration, they could prevent it from taking a violent communal turn: it was confined to angry gesticulations against Madhok.

Next day, the Hindu Action Committee retaliated by

bringing out another procession: tensions began to mount and the zero hour was fast approaching. The Government clamped down the curfew. But one an hardly say that the Government acted with the necessary firmness: for instance, seven thousand curfew passes were issued, and the next day, the authorities, in such an atmosphere surcharged with communal tension, were complacent in permitting a full-scale procession with the body of one of the Hindu demonstrators who had died in hospital as a result of police lathi charge. This procession became violent and there were clashes with rival groups; the result was arson on some of the shops and premises, in which both communities suffered. This was the only fatal case involving the Hindu community: against this, Muslim circles have complained that hardly any notice was taken of the death of two Muslims in the disturbances.

Incidentally, one could hear in Srinagar of charges of communal bias against the Central Reserve Police and the Punjab Police, while the Hindus criticised the Kashmir Police for lathi charging women in a Pandit demonstration.

After this, there has been no disturbance in Srinagar, barring a little rowdyism by student groups a few weeks later, on September 20. At the Women's College, a statement signed by students had been drawn up repudiating the hair-raising stories of insecurity of the lives and honour of Hindu women, whipped up by communal elements outside the State: this had a particular reference to Ghasi's public allegations in New Delhi and also to virulent writings in the north Indian press, particularly some of the Indian language dailies. This was picked up by some Hindu students of another college as an item to be objected to, on the ground that the signatures to the statement had been secured under duress: and fifty of the boys went on a dharna for hours in front of the Women's College gate in one of the busiest thoroughfares in the city. The police was present throughout but with amazing ineptness let this provocative demonstration go on for hours, instead of removing the boys at least under Section 144, which was supposed to be strictly in force. Three hours later, an equally bellicose Muslim students' procession came out with provocative slogans. Then the police woke up and lathi charged both sides to disperse them.

It is to be noted that two members of the Hindu Action Committee actively tried to dissuade the group of Hindu boys from demonstrating, but they were brushed aside.

The Hindu Action Committee attacked the Sadiq Ministry for having warned the Government employees that any of them found to be guilty of violating the law would not be reinstated after any police action against them. But what the Hindu leaders have refused to take note of is that last year Muslim employees, involved in a demonstration brought out by Maulvi Farooq's men, were immediately suspended and some are still in prison, and none of them has been reinstated. This time, in contrast, the Government employees engaged in the Pandit agitation have not been punished, but only charge-sheeted, and as far as could be made out, no action has been taken against them.

How hideous is the nature of communal propaganda let loose in Kashmir could be seen from many of the inflammatory material sent into the Valley from outside. On August 31, for instance, the police seized a parcel at the Indian Airlines office at Srinagar: it had been despatched from Amritsar, where the leaflets had been printed. The leaflets contained straight inflammatory calls to Hindus to fight the Kashmir Government, Sadiq himself being branded as a regenerated Aurangzeb.

Another leaflet which got fairly wide circulation attacked Sadiq for being worse than President Ayub who, according to this version, had shot a Muslim doctor in East Pakistan for having coerced a Hindu girl into marriage, and sent her off along with her father in safety to India. "He (Sadiq) should have settled the issue as a statesman like General Ayub of Pakistan who settled the issue as a soldier." There are reasons to believe that the origin of this leaflet could be traced to pro-Pakistani circles which are naturally fishing in the troubled waters of Kashmir.

This is but one of the many evidences of how the Pandit agitation is providing good meat for the pro-Pakistani elements, which, after the grievous setback suffered in 1965 with the failure of Pakistani forces in capturing Kashmir, had been largely demoralised and had to lie low. Recently with the unearthing of a key Pak spy-ring in Kashmir, these suffered another severe blow. But now, with the Pandit agitation fanned by the RSS elements, the pro-Pak agents have received a shot in the arm. Their activity is conspicuous in tension-charged Srinagar.

The key point which the Pak propaganda has made so long in Kashmir is that it is impossible for the Hindus and the Muslims to coexist. For nearly three decades, the Kashmir leadership has by their word and deed been consistently refuting this Jinnah thesis. Today, the Pandit agitation, made into a catspaw of extreme Hindu communalism, is trying to sabotage the crusade by the Kashmir leadership against Pakistani communalism. "Our unity has been our strength in many a grave crisis we have been called upon to face during the last two decades," Sadiq appealed in the Assembly. "This unity we must preserve at all costs." This was reiterated before Chavan by a group of Kashmiri Muslims in a written memorandum: "We are proud to claim that we have resisted our co-religionists from across the border and protected the life and property of other communities and have not at any stage hesitated to sacrifice everything dear to us to achieve this end."

This was no empty boast even today. In the very week when Balraj Madhok was delivering his passionate oration exhorting the Pandits to look upto the Hindus in India as their protecting angel, a congregation of fifty thousand Muslims at Hazratbal mosque took the pledge of defending Hindu-Muslim harmony at all costs. Mirza Afzal Beg, founder President of the Plebiscite Front, defying the internment restrictions on him, boldly came out in defence of the Hindus and never let communal hatred pollute the air of his home district, Anantnag.

What is very often missed by outsiders is that the communal passions never spread beyond the city limits of Srinagar; and there too, it caught on for short periods in localised areas. Even at Srinagar there was not a single case of stabbing, the very first sign of communal clash judging by the yardstick that one has come to follow in the rest of the subcontinent.

Through the entire countryside, the picturesque hamlets stretching from Baramulla to Pahalgam, from Gulmarg to Kokernag, have at no time been disturbed of their idyllic peace and warmest communal amity. It was not for nothing that Chavan in his Srinagar press conference said: "In Kashmir there were no communal riots, Hindus and Muslims as such did not clash with each other." And this he considered to be "the basic difference between Ranchi and Srinagar". This by itself provides the finest commentary on the robust secularism of the Muslim peasantry of Kashmir and constitutes the bedrock of their resistance against the onslaught of communalism, whether of the Pak or the RSS variety.

At the same time it would be incorrect to assume that nothing has been lost in the short-lived tension generated in Srinagar by the Pandit agitation. The tension has no doubt subsided, but a climate of mutual alienation has set in: for the first time, since Independence, many in Kashmir have begun to think in terms of their community affiliation.

The stifling frustration at being unable to hold the communalists in the leash has further embittered relations. Even comrades-in-arms of the Quit Kashmir days have started suspecting each other of communal bias. At Srinagar, one felt this most acutely when going round meeting old acquaintances: there has grown the very perceptible tendency of looking inward—towards one's own community—instead of trying to build bridges between the two communities.

It is in this background that one would not be surprised if this was magnified through whispers by those having a vested interest in communalism, the RSS elements on one side and the Pak agents on the other.

But when I met Mir Qasim, one of the first things he asked me was why only Balraj Madhok could come to Kashmir and no MP from any of the secular parties with the sole exception of Raj Narain. He was most insistent that democratic forces in India should come forward in the common struggle to drive out communalism from Kashmir. This obviously is not the voice of a communalist.

One could feel a sense of agony as one listened to his very just complaint that the job of fighting communalism could not be left to the people of Kashmir alone. If in despair some elements got cooped up in the shell of their own community, the blame should fall squarely on the democratic forces in India as a whole.

Equally distressing was it to hear some friends talking of D.P. Dhar as if he had become an ardent Pandit. Dhar, actually, was the target of attack in the Pandit agitation, and he was one of those who earnestly tried his best to bring it to an end. He reinforced the plea for democratic intervention by secular forces from India.

More important than all the mutual misgivings, I found a surprising consensus among all these leaders about the basic cause of the Pandits' unrest. All these years, when the supreme task facing the Kashmir leadership has been to combat the anti-India forces, the Pandit community had been left unattended. On the question of integration with India, the Pandits naturally were taken for granted, and no political work was done among them to educate them and bring them into the mainstream of the secular democratic movement. Barring a few—not counting more than a hundred—the Pandits as a community did not participate in the freedom struggle against the Maharaja rule. And when freedom came, they came into the new world without the baptism of fire which large sections of other communities in Kashmir had to go through.

It was in this political vacuum, communalism stepped in to cash in on the economic unrest. It is no accident that one of the first speeches that incited the Pandit community into action this time was delivered by S. N. Fotedar (the former MP and now the Chairman of the State Legislative Council), the very same person who had led a black-flag demonstration against Nehru in 1946 when he had rushed there to stand in solidarity with the Quit Kashmir movement and courted arrest defying the Maharaja's ban on entry into his state.

There were no doubt certain lags in the functioning of the Kashmir leadership, which any honest reporter can hardly overlook. The Congress as an organisation was almost petrified by this agitation. I could hardly get any evidence of an all-out bid on the part of any democratic, secular organisation to combat the communal menace. There was much that the all-India Congress leadership itself could have done to help; the Kashmir leaders: not even a line of condemnation of the Jan Sangh depredations in Kashmir came from the Congress President, though less than a year ago, he himself was the victim of communal vandalism in New Delhi. While Indira Gandhi commands support in most sectors of public opinion in Kashmir, there is universal complaint about the Centre's indifference—not a single Central project is located in Kashmir, and the rail link with Jammu is put off from year to year.

The complaint against the Left parties that one heard from the Kashmir leaders was not confined to their silence or inaction in combating communalism generated by the Pandit agitation alone. A long chain of events of the last six months has created a sense of estrangement between the Kashmir leadership and the Left parties, particularly the Socialists and the Communists. The stand taken by the Left parties in opposing Dr Zakir Hussain's election as President was resented by the Kashmir leaders: for them, it is a very big thing to be able to tell the masses in the Kashmir Valley—so much under constant Pakistani propaganda—that an eminent Muslim has been elected to the highest office in the Republic, a true sign of secularist outlook; and they feel that by opposing this choice, the Left parties have weakened the sense of reliance in them that the Muslim masses generally repose in anti-communal forces.

The forming of coalition Governments with the Jan Sangh as a partner is another point on which I found the Kashmir leaders very much agitated. Their point has been that such a strategy would at least weaken the scope and capacity of the Left parties in combating the communalist menace. The Jan Sangh's spectacular success in the election to the Delhi Metropolitan Council and the equally poor show of the Left parties also had an adverse reaction in Kashmir.

On top of it all, the Ranchi riots—and the gruesome slaughter at Hatia—followed by the spate of communal outbursts from Ahmednagar to Gorakhpur could not but accentuate the worry of the leaders in Kashmir at the rising menace of communalism; and one could understand their resentment at the Left parties not taking up the struggle against it as a sacred crusade: in a sense, this resentment itself is the testimony to their long-nurtured faith in the democratic parties. There is no doubt that the rise of Jan Sangh in north India has perturbed the Kashmir leaders; and as one of them put it to me: "Perhaps we would have felt secure if Kashmir had been situated in South India."

It is not that the present leadership in Kashmir has a poor record to its credit—an impression which one often comes across in India. After the fiasco of the Pakistani attack in 1965, the section of Muslim opinion, which was under the spell of Pak propaganda, was gradually getting reconciled to finding a solution within the four corners of the Indian Constitution. This was further facilitated by the Government's impressive record on the food front, particularly this year: and food, as is known all over India, is the main source of mass discontent. The food production in the State went up from 4,50,800 tonnes in 1965-66 to 5,83,365 tonnes in 1966-67, and this year's returns would show a further spurt without doubt.

From even casual enquiries, one could not but be struck by the effective measures taken by the present Government on the agrarian front: all forms of eviction of sharecroppers are banned by law, while Kashmir is one of the first States to go in for the abolition of land revenue for the small cultivator. One of the main reasons for the very good harvest this year is the liberal distribution of fertilisers. For the current year, the target of distribution has been fixed at 1.04 lakh tonnes, while in the entire five years of the Third Plan only 30,095 tonnes were distributed. In the crash agricultural programme undertaken this year, as much as Rs 2.28 crores would be spent on fertilisers out of the total outlay of Rs 3.71 crores for the programme. The cultivator is given fertiliser on credit and the loan is to be repaid after harvest in kind to the Government. This year, Kashmir has abolished all trade, both wholesale and retail, in foodgrains, and I found D.P. Dhar, the Food and Finance Minister, quite confident of the success of this experiment. Rationed rice is sold at 35 paise per kilo—subsidised by the State Government and not by the Centre. In blackmarket, it is available at Rs 1.20 paise per kilo.

There are thus many items in the Kashmir Government's record which the progressive forces in the new United Front Governments in different States may emulate with profit. To take one more example, the last session of the

Kashmir Assembly passed a bill disqualifying from standing for election for ten years any person found by a court or commission presided over by a Supreme Court judge "to have illegally or by corrupt means or by otherwise abusing or misusing" his position as a legislator or holding any office thereof. This is one of the concrete steps by which corruption in public life could be fought.

In this connection, one has to refer to the dwindling prestige of Bakshi Ghulam Mohammed. After the publication of the voluminous Ayyangar Report spotlighting his versatility in irregular practices, Bakshi had gone down in public esteem. He is trying to salvage his public life by desperate means: reports are current about encouragement given by his side to the Pandit agitation, while there are other reports about his links with the Muslim extremists. But the overall impact of such multifaced intrigues has been that his political image has been tarnished for good.

Braving the constant barrage of Pakistani propaganda that Muslims would not be safe in "Hindu" India, the present leaders of Kashmir have undeviatingly stood upholding the cause of secularism, trying to convince the Muslim masses in Kashmir that the secularist forces in Indian democracy would defend them from communalist domination. The disturbing developments of the last few months—the rise of the Jan Sangh—could not but come as a threat to their political campaign against Pakistani propaganda among the Muslim masses in Kashmir. In the arduous battle for winning over the bulk of the Kashmiri people, the Jan Sangh's ominous debut in the Kashmir politics will naturally help to undermine the strength of the pro-India forces and come as a god-send for the Pakistan propaganda.

It is but natural in this context for the Kashmir leaders to demand that the secular forces in India should make common cause with them. "In 1965, we fought the infiltrators, but the Indian Army also came and fought by our side to ward off the invader," one of the senior Kashmir leaders told me. "Today, political infiltration has begun, and are we not justified in expecting India's secular forces to come and fight these shoulder to shoulder with us?"

The battle for secularism has to be fought in all earnest in the Valley of Kashmir. Breaking the narrow horizon of the Pandits' agitation, it is time that the democratic forces all over India caught the wider perspective of the struggle in Kashmir. One must not get bogged in the weeds of the Dal Lake and miss the majesty of the Chinar in the Shalimar Gardens.

(September 30, 1967)

9

Sheikh Abdullah, What Next?

Perhaps no other issue has persisted throughout the two decades since independence as a challenge to Indian statesmanship as the question of Kashmir. No other item has been discussed so often and so intensely at home, and none has provoked so many questions abroad, both among India's friends and detractors, among allies and adversaries.

And at the centre of this issue stands the question of Sheikh Abdullah. At one time he was taken as the very symbol of secularism: his leadership together with the team that rallied round him was regarded as the advance guard of radicalism at the Governmental level. But within six years of Independence, he was imprisoned in a dramatic overthrow: was he selling out Kashmir to Pakistan? At least that was what the Indian public was made to believe, and yet not a scrap of evidence was produced to prove the charge: and so he was detained and not tried. After a brief spell outside prison in 1958, he was again kept in detention. This time an elaborate conspiracy case was launched against him—lakhs of rupees were spent, and the case dragged on from year to year. And yet in

1964, the, conspiracy case was dropped and Sheikh Abdullah was released and Jawaharlal Nehru himself played the host to him in New Delhi—no trace of the conspiracy could be seen anywhere.

In fact, his confidential talks with Nehru were sufficiently important for him to be entrusted by Nehru to go to Pakistan for arranging an Indo-Pak summit on Kashmir. And yet about a year later he was again detained. Once again after a protracted period of detention, today he is on the threshold of being released. An extraordinary record indeed of a Government repeatedly shifting its position in one of the most important political cases baffling settlement for fifteen years.

And it is not only the Government but the Opposition as well, particularly the Left Opposition, that has shifted its ground repeatedly in its attitude towards Sheikh Abdullah. This could be seen from the fact that the very parties which endorsed his imprisonment since 1953 are insistent on his release today.

Barring the Jan Sangh and those in the Left who coined the catchy but unreal slogan that Kashmir is not a dispute but a situation, practically every party from the Congress to the Communists, from the Socialists to the Swatantra, are faced today with the question of what to do next with Sheikh Abdullah. This is a question which can no longer be shelved. With his impending release in the next few weeks, it is time that a sober and realistic approach towards Sheikh Sahib—that inevitably means towards the Kashmir tangle—is hammered out by all the secular forces together, an approach which harmonises the self-interest of the nation as a whole with the aspirations of the Kashmiri people.

Talking to leaders of different sectors of Kashmir opinion

during a brief stay there recently, I could sense a common desire on the part of all—from G.M. Sadiq to Mirza Afzal Beg, from Syed Mir Qasim to Dr Karan Singh—that the present drift with regard to the overall settlement of the Kashmir question must end once and for all; that it must no longer be treated as a chronic case of stop-gap emergency But the very first step towards any serious national effort in that direction has to be a well-thought-out approach towards Sheikh Abdullah with the earnest desire for a stable understanding with him.

As a senior Kashmir leader put it to me, there are two misconceptions about Sheikh Abdullah: that he has changed radically in his views during his long period of detention discarding many of his old views; and the contrary view that Sheikh Sahib has learnt nothing and forgotten nothing through all these years of political hibernation and so cannot be trusted. The first is based on wishful thinking and the second is based on blind prejudice. For there can be no political leader who does not reappraise political digits with the changing circumstances, while no leader can afford to totally disown his stand while kept in forced isolation from his movement.

What does Sheikh Abdullah want? Many interpretations have been put to many of his utterances during his brief spells of freedom in the last fourteen years. Quite often these utterances have been torn out of context or made under a barrage of calculated provocations; sometimes, it is to be admitted, Sheikh Abdullah's words and deeds perplexed even some of his genuine friends.

In this context, a long session with Mirza Afzal Beg amidst the warm hospitality of his Anantnag home was found to be rewarding. The prevailing police restrictions on him debarred his giving any press interview, but an off-the-record discussion could show how the mind of this close lieutenant of Sheikh Abdullah has been working. Beg is recognised as being closest to Sheikh Sahib; while, according to the current Srinagar assessment, he represents perhaps comparatively the extremist wing in the Sheikh camp, my own impression from this frank and friendly talk was that he can hardly be regarded as intractable. It is not unnatural to be bitter after the long years of detention and the upsetting experience suffered by his followers, but even then I could not see that the iron has entered into his soul. He talked without rancour and was eager to dispel many of the impressions—which he thought were misconceptions—that are current about Sheikh Abdullah and his supporters in this country and abroad.

It is worth noting that Sheikh Abdullah's camp is not monolithic in its views or activities. It is a huge conglomerate of protest—the common tie that binds them all is a rankling feeling that they have got a raw deal from the Government of India. Naturally, pro-Pak elements are to be found in his crowd, but one has to take note of the fact that very often it was Sheikh Abdullah and his closest lieutenants who had to combat pro-Pak elements even during his last period of freedom in 1964-65. Maulvi Farooq's band could never be reconciled to Sheikh Abdullah's and the showdown between the two was imminent had Sheikh Abdullah himself not been whisked off to detention to South India in the summer of 1965.

In the present round of tension also one could notice the difference between Sheikh Abdullah's followers and the avowedly pro-Pak elements in the Valley. Mirza Afzal Beg defied the internment restrictions on him to boldly campaign for communal peace in his district—an action for which Sheikh Abdullah himself wrote to him commending it. In contrast, the pro-Pak elements today are going in for communal disturbances to bring grist to the propaganda that Hindus and Muslims cannot live in peace.

Meeting a number of others, I got the impression that Sheikh Abdullah himself represents what may be called the consensus in this protest camp. He is likely to work out his line of action by sensing the mood of the overwhelming section of his present followers. In this respect, the views of the Plebiscite Front assume great importance; since it is the Plebiscite Front which is the most organised body in the Sheikh's camp. The Plebiscite Front was formed by Mirza Afzal Beg in 1955 and he continues to be its Founder President. Without going into the controversy whether it is today the biggest political organisation in the Valley, one cannot escape the conclusion that it is an organisation whose views carry the most significant weight in Sheikh Abdullah's camp.

This point is important since there was a tendency in the past to try to demarcate Sheikh Abdullah (who is formally not a member of the Plebiscite Front) and the Plebiscite Front itself. But it is doubtful whether anybody in the Sheikh's camp can deliver the goods without the consent of the Plebiscite Front. In recent times it is clear that Sheikh Abdullah has kept the closest contact with Mirza Afzal Beg even in detention although they have not been allowed to be kept together. In fact, I found one of the minor irritants which has annoyed Beg recently was that despite several appeals to the authorities, he was not allowed to have an interview with Sheikh Abdullah during his stay in the Medical Institute in New

Delhi and he was removed from there only a few hours before Sheikh Sahib's arrival.

While it is not possible to record Beg's views as an interview one could get an idea of the mind of the Plebiscite Front by talking not only to him but to his other associates. One of the things which was of topical interest during my visit to Kashmir was Sheikh Abdullah's letter to President Ayub correcting some of the points made about his talks with the latter in the recent biography of the Pakistan President. (Incidentally Sheikh Abdullah's letters to President Ayub on this subject seemed to displease the pro-Pakistani camp in Kashmir and for some-time there was a feeling among them that Sheikh Sahib was letting them down. Some of these leaders could pacify their followers with the explanation that while Sheikh Abdullah has corrected President Ayub on some of the points, he has not touched specifically the point in President Ayub's biography that ultimately the Kashmiris will have to find their place in Pakistan.)

No section of the Plebiscite Front claims that the idea of a confederation was ever suggested by Nehru. What Nehru seemed to have been bent upon was that Sheikh Abdullah should persuade President Ayub to agree to an Indo-Pak summit meeting when the question of Kashmir itself could be discussed; and it was to the credit of Nehru that he laid down no precondition for such a summit meeting: all proposals would be taken up and discussed threadbare in the light of the experiences of the two countries since the Partition.

It was during the course of Sheikh Abdullah's talks with President Ayub that many of the proposals which had come up—whether from the Security Council representatives or from eminent individuals from both countries—

were referred to while no particular proposal was taken up as the agenda for the projected summit. Later on, I came to learn that the idea of a confederation between India and Pakistan with Kashmir figuring as a third partner was actually suggested by Acharya Vinoba Bhave but it was not pursued because Nehru did not seem to be in favour of it, and as President Ayub's biography indicates, Pakistan was also opposed to it.

There is an impression in many quarters in this country that the idea of an independent Kashmir has all along been opposed by India. In fact, while many would concede that plebiscite was accepted by India in all seriousness at one stage—and later given up on the ground that Pakistan had not fulfilled her part of the pre-condition for such a plebiscite—the question of an independent Kashmir is ruled out as if it had never had the sanction of India. Against this, the Plebiscite Front people quote the following passage from Sir Gopalaswamy Ayyangar's speech in the Security Council on behalf of India on January 15, 1948:

> "The question of the future status of Kashmir vis-a-vis her neighbours and the world at large, and a further question, namely, whether she should withdraw from her accession to India and either accede to Pakistan *or remain independent, with a right to claim* admission as a member of the United Nations—all this we have recognised to be a matter for unfettered decision by the people of Kashmir after normal life is restored to them."

Since then much water has flown down the Jhelum and it will be naive to think that seasoned veterans in Sheikh Abdullah's camp do not recognise the changing reality. What they emphasise today is that Nehru in his wisdom, despite all that had happened from 1953 onwards, could keep an open mind in his last days; and they seem to have an implicit faith that if Nehru's proposed summit with President Ayub had taken place—as it was planned within a month of Sheikh Abdullah's visit to Pakistan in May 1964—probably a way-out could have been found; at least a serious groping towards a way-out would have begun. The tragedy of Nehru's passing away, within two days of Sheikh Abdullah's success in persuading President Ayub to agree to the summit, blighted all chances of any improvement of Indo-Pak relations vis-a-vis Kashmir.

Theoretically, Sheikh Abdullah's followers, particularly the Plebiscite Front leaders, refuse to accept that the concept of an independent Kashmir is untenable. The argument that such a state placed at the crossroads of world-power politics would not be able to retain its independence does not convince them and they point to the example of smaller states, such as Cambodia, maintaining their independence despite sandwiched between the Great Powers' spheres of influence. Rather, they seem to feel that an independent Kashmir in the present context of power relations in this part of the world need not be subservient to the dictates of any foreign power. The fact that the present foreign policy of Pakistan has shown signs of asserting itself even in relation to America despite the massive dependence on American military aid is taken by some section of Kashmiri leaders as vindication of their points.

However, I did not find that Mirza Afzal Beg or any of the other leaders in Sheikh Abdullah's camp today have got an *idee fixe* about an independent state of Kashmir. What they are determined to have is that whatever be the settlement of Kashmir, it should have the sanction of the people of the Valley, and that no settlement will be lasting unless it is also based on an understanding between India and Pakistan. As one of the leaders put it to me, "Even if Sheikh Abdullah and his entire followings come to a total agreement with the Government of India and the Indian people, we must not forget that this State is placed geographically in the closest proximity of Pakistan, and the mishandling of the Kashmiri leaders by India during these years, has provided political and propaganda ammunition for Pakistan to influence the people of this Valley."

They also point to the economic bonds that bind Kashmir to Pakistan. In this connection I was given to read a passage from an article written not very long ago by N.C. Chatterji, MP who can by no means be accused of being pro-Pak:

> "The geographical situation of the State was such that it would bounded on all sides by the new Dominion of Pakistan. Its only access to the outside world by road lay through the Jhelum Valley road which ran through Pakistan, via Rawalpindi. The only rail line connecting the State with the outside world lay through Sialkot in Pakistan. Its postal and telegraphic services operated through areas that were certain *to* belong to the Dominion of Pakistan.
>
> "The State was dependent for all its imported supplies like salt, sugar, petrol and other necessities of life on their safe and continued transit through areas that would form part of Pakistan.
>
> "The tourist transit traffic which was a major source of income and revenue could only come via Rawalpindi.

> The only route available for the export of its valuable fruit was the Jhelum Valley route. Its timber could mainly be drifted down only in the Jhelum river which ran into Pakistan."

The overall impression I got was that Sheikh Abdullah's trusted lieutenants today are not insistent on any particular formula or plan to be accepted before any rapprochement could be reached between them and the rest of Indian political opinion. They are making no pre-condition for any discussion, rather they are keen that Sheikh Abdullah himself should have the opportunity of meeting as many sections of Indian opinion as possible; and that the Prime Minister herself should take the initiative in having purposeful talks with him and follow the lead of her father in utilising Sheikh Abdullah's services for a better understanding with Pakistan itself.

In this context I found an interesting reference from an article by Sheikh Abdullah in the American quarterly review, *Foreign Affairs* (April 1965), published only a few weeks before his arrest in 1965. After quoting two of Nehru's speeches in 1952, reiterating India's pledge that a settlement in Kashmir has to be in accordance with the will of the people of Kashmir, Sheikh Abdullah wrote:

> "These words of the great departed leader inspire and fortify me, and I do indeed hope that his successors will rise to the occasion and by a great act of faith seek to resolve this question which has bedevilled the relations between India and Pakistan."

But soon after, when he returned from his foreign tour, he was immediately detained. The reason for this—as could be made out from official statements at the time—was that he had during his tour hobnobbed not only with Pakistani diplomats but even had an unscheduled talk with Chou En-lai at Algiers. When I raised this point, Beg, who had accompanied Sheikh Abdullah, told me that a visit to Algeria was sanctioned by the passports New Delhi had granted them. While in Algiers, Premier Ben Bella without prior notice came to their hotel and urged them to meet the Chinese Premier; there was no prior appointment nor was the talk anything more than a courtesy call where Sheikh Abdullah said nothing that he had not said before the world. Beg added that they had wanted on their return to report on their entire experience during the tour abroad to the Indian leaders; instead of that, they were packed off to South India the moment they landed at Palam.

The repercussions of the Indo-Pak conflict in 1965 on all sectors of opinion in Kashmir can hardly be overlooked. There are two significant reactions which I could not fail to notice. On the one hand, the avowedly pro-Pakistani elements have suffered a setback—at least in their capacity to influence mass opinion in a decisive way. The propaganda that Pakistan can come and "liberate" the Kashmiris by force of arms has lost its efficacy considerably: the experience of the 1965 conflict has made people wiser. On the other hand, there is also the tendency to emphasise the danger of letting Indo-Pak animosity over Kashmir continue since it could spark off even a full-scale military showdown. Obviously, both these reactions represent different facets of the reality.

A groping towards realism is not absent in the Plebiscite Front circles. When the difficulties and dangers of holding a plebiscite are posed, they do not take the stand, plebiscite-or-nothing. Rather, they say that any proposal which takes into account the general will of the people of Kashmir can solve the present impasse. One of them even said that if there was a "free and fair" General Election in the Valley, that could work. With regard to this year's General Election, they say that even Gandhiji never accepted any election as reflecting popular will while political leaders were kept in prison; and with Sheikh Abdullah and his band in detention, they are not prepared to concede that this year's General Election could reflect the true state of public opinion in Kashmir. It is interesting to note in this context that the Plebiscite Front leadership is more critical of the electoral performance of the Congress in Kashmir than in Jammu. Apart from Sheikh Sahib and his supporters being denied civil liberties to contest the General Election, they also point to the unusually large number of uncontested returns in the Valley constituencies as confirming their misgivings about a fair and unfettered election campaign.

The Plebiscite Front leadership refute the charge that in case of any plebiscite being granted, they would willy nilly acquiesce in Kashmir going to Pakistan. One of their topmost leaders told me that once a mechanism was decided upon to determine the will of the Kashmiri people, they would immediately disband the Plebiscite Front and then "we shall get the leaders of Kashmir to put their heads together to advise the people".

The impression is inescapable that if many of these leaders are embittered with India, they do not necessarily entertain rosy hopes about Pakistan. The neglect to which the Azad Kashmir area has been put—both with regard to the political set-up and development programme—has not been overlooked by them. One has also to recall that when Sheikh Abdullah and his team went to Pakistan in the summer of 1964, he emphasised before the Kashmir leaders there too the need for demanding that the will of the Kashmiri people in that sector also must be heard; and following his visit, there was largescale attack by the Pakistan Government upon the Azad Kashmir leadership.

Mirza Afzal Beg's people talk of a "phased programme" for settlement of the Kashmir problem. In this connection, they are particularly bitter on two counts. They complain that even the Delhi Agreement of 1952 has been allowed to be eroded. If some of the special facilities granted to Kashmir under that agreement have been abused by those in authority—the obvious reference is to Bakshi Ghulam Mohammed's *badshahi—that* was not the fault of the Kashmiri people, since such leaders, they say, were chosen by New Delhi itself. Secondly, they complain that Kashmir's borders were so tightly sealed up—even before the 1965 conflict—that it brought economic ruin to a large section of the people including fruit growers and carpet weavers. The limited trade transactions permitted between East Pakistan and Assam or West Bengal has never been permitted across the Cease-Fire Line. "If this was done to keep out spies and mischief-mongers from across the border," one of, them cynically asked, "has it all worked? With all the sealing up of the border, infiltrators came." The real defence of the frontier does not lie in keeping up a wall of hostility.

Normalisation of trade routes to Pakistan is dictated by the compulsions of Kashmir's economy and, no doubt, the denial of this embitters those who are hard hit in the Valley and provide fruitful soil for Pakistani propaganda about India being callous about the hardships of the Kashmiri people.

(October 21, 1967)

10

Wanted: Not Drift but Statesmanship

The question of dealing with Sheikh Abdullah is today the key point in any effort at stabilising the Kashmir situation. This proposition is accepted by practically all sections of opinion in the State of Jammu and Kashmir.

Sheikh Abdullah's camp seems to have a tendency to take this as a bargaining counter; that is, unless the Sheikh is installed back in power, there could be no stable peace in Kashmir. This viewpoint is challenged by others. According to the Sheikh's critics, the fact that India could ward off a full-scale military attack by Pakistan for the capture of the State of Jammu and Kashmir in 1965 has itself undermined the Sheikh's importance. The realisation by the pro-Pakistani elements that a military solution of the Kashmir question can no longer be forced and that India would not hesitate to take up arms again in defence of the Valley is often interpreted by a section of observers in Kashmir to mean that there need be no hurry in settling with the Sheikh, since he can no longer exploit the military threat of Pakistan as a means to wring concessions from New Delhi.

But the more careful among observers in Kashmir are

not inclined to accept such a simplified view. They seem to think that a settlement with Sheikh Abdullah, honourable to both sides, in the long run will pay dividends in any confrontation, political or military, with Pakistan. After all, India could stand up to the tribal aggression from Pakistan in 1947 mainly because of the popular resistance magnificently organised by the Kashmir National Conference under the leadership of Sheikh Abdullah. Without such a mass popular base, the aggressors from across the frontier would have almost had a walk-over in those crucial weeks. The Indian Army itself would have found it difficult to operate when it was rushed there despite all the obstacles put up by Mountbatten in those days.

Incidentally, this blows up the theory that the accession of Kashmir to India became a reality because the Maharaja signed the Instrument of Accession. What is to be borne in mind is that even with a declaration of loyalty to India by the Maharaja—which in fact was not very vocal in those days—there could have been no chance of holding the advance of armed bands into the farthest corner of the Valley, had there been no Sheikh Abdullah and his band of patriotic workers who roused the entire people to put up resistance. Perhaps in no other part of the country there was such an armed mass upheaval under a political leadership for accession to India as it happened in the Valley of Kashmir in 1947.

The need for a settlement with Sheikh Abdullah really boils down to the realisation of an urgency of a political understanding with him and his supporters. Nehru himself tried to achieve that in 1964 during the weeks preceding his tragic end; the harm done in 1953 by the deposition and imprisonment of Sheikh Abdullah perhaps would have been undone had he lived a little longer. But now again the process has to be taken up and this needs the immediate opening of a dialogue with Sheikh Abdullah and his lieutenants. And the initiative for this has naturally to come from the Central leadership in New Delhi. In political life one has to realise that nobody can open talks from a position of disadvantage, and no political leader, however eminent, could seek negotiation so long as he is under detention. It is therefore obvious that the initiative for any talk with Sheikh Abdullah—and the need for it is overwhelmingly urgent—has to come from the leaders of all other secular and democratic political parties. Those who have demanded his release, it is but meet and proper that they should at least come forward to take that initiative.

It is the lack of this initiative in today's context which comes as a matter of surprise to many observers and more the delay the more is there the chance that the opportunity might be wasted. At present Sheikh Abdullah is surrounded by people who stood by him; and right or wrong, quite a substantial section of them belong to the pro-West camp. However, I found during my round of talks both in Srinagar and in New Delhi that a large spectrum of opinion did recognise the necessity for such a dialogue; at the same time there is rather an amazing reticence for any particular section of responsible opinion to come forward and do the job. Perhaps on this score will come one of the most significant tests for statesmanship on the part of the political leadership in India.

An interesting feature of the political postures adopted by some groups in Kashmir is the raising of the demand for President's Rule in the State. According to them, the present Sadiq Ministry is incapable of solving any of the problems facing the State, that it is hopping on from crisis to crisis and that it has no political perspective and finally that it is a house divided against itself.

This is the common theme of a curious amalgam which includes not only the Jan Sangh but Bakshi Ghulam Mohammad as well; I did not find it being raised by the Socialists despite the fact that Bakshi is trying to find a niche in the SSP proclaiming himself to be a follower of Dr Lohia—at least after his death.

Against this demand for President's Rule in Kashmir, many arguments have been raised not only by Sadiq and his team but also by other elements including the CPI. First, the state of instability in Kashmir is not more acute than it is in many other parts of the country; the law and order situation in Kashmir is certainly not worse than it is in many other States where the slogan of President's Rule is not heard at all. Secondly, the ruling party has got a firm majority in the Assembly; in fact Kashmir is one of the few States in India today where the Congress Party commands a comfortable majority.

Thirdly, the allegation of rift inside the leadership of the Kashmir Government is definitely overplayed. There is practically no State in India today where the Congress leadership has not reduced itself to a motley of factions, some of them very well-knit. In contrast, one does not find such a spectacle in the Kashmir Congress even if there is a lack of personal equation at some levels among the Kashmir leaders today.

But the main objection to President's Rule in Kashmir is an essentially political one. The point has to be understood that if President's Rule is clamped on Kashmir, Pakistan will announce to the world that India despite all her efforts could not find any section of opinion in Kashmir dependable enough to run the Government of the State, that she had to close down parliamentary democracy and go in for direct Central rule without any democratic check. In fact, the imposition of President's Rule will come as a god-send for Pakistani propaganda. It is, therefore, a strange logic that Balraj Madhok and his aggressive party is following today. The very demand that they are raising goes against the interest of India and will help Pakistan and her allies more than anybody else.

What is really wanted in Kashmir today is the toning up of the administration. The ravages left behind by Bakshi's personal rule could not be repaired quickly by the present Government. Since its assumption of office there has come a series of major difficulties facing it: first came the excitement and tension with the release of Sheikh Abdullah, followed by the threat of tension following his re-arrest in mid-1965; then came the period of Pakistani infiltrators, followed by a full-scale armed conflict with Pakistan. In 1966, the Sadiq Government was able to repair quite a lot of the damage, although towards the end the preoccupation with the General Election slowed down the process.

After the General Election, a number of important reforms were introduced specially with regard to land tenure and economic rehabilitation; in fact, its record in some direction is better than that of most of the State Governments in India today including those which are led by the Left parties.

But the respite was short-lived. With the Pandit agitation and Jan Sangh's intervention a new period of worry has started. If it could go in for smooth sailing in the last few months perhaps the Sadiq Government itself would have been able to tackle the problem of Sheikh Abdullah without any direct assistance from New Delhi. In this way the Jan Sangh and the Right-wing critics of the Government have only helped to make things more difficult for the present Government to face Sheikh Abdullah and the challenge that his activities sometime pose for the authorities.

It is to be understood that the present round of communal tension in Kashmir has been taken advantage of most by the pro-Pakistani elements and for that one has to thank the Jan Sangh. And if the pro-Pakistani elements have to be again brought under control and isolated, it would be necessary for all secular and democratic forces not only in Kashmir but all over India to rally and see that communalism does not become a permanent sore in the beautiful Valley. Viewed in this context, the move for calling a convention of various political parties, which is believed to be in the offing in New Delhi, assumes significance. One would have expected the Congress leadership to take the initiative in this matter, but that was very much lacking at the recent AICC session at Jabbalpur. Kamaraj worrying about his own future as the Congress President has not yet found time to go to Kashmir although a few weeks ago there was a report that he might pay a visit to the State after the Jabbalpur AICC session. But Kamaraj himself may not carry much weight just now, apart from the fact that he still continues to be the chief of the Congress Party organisation.

In this context, it is necessary for the Prime Minister to tour round the whole State, particularly the Valley, so that the Muslim masses could be assured that there was no threat to their security. I notice Indira Gandhi's prestige among them is high since they regard her to be totally anti-communal, in the tradition of her father.

In this connection, it may be useful to make a passing reference to the situation in Ladakh where Kushak Bakula has raised the demand for a NEEFA-type administration. This has come as a surprise to many and naturally it is resented by Sonam Norbu who has come up as a formidable challenge to Kushak Bakula's political position. For one thing, a NEFA-type administration in Ladakh would mean putting the clock back: whatever may be the weakness and the shortcomings of the present set-up in Ladakh, it has at least the semblance of parliamentarianism—the elected bodies and the representative institutions. In the NEFA-type administration, on the other hand, there is very little scope of elected bodies, and it is in a way the continuation of the old system under the British restricted to tribal areas whose political activity is hardly in evidence.

In Ladakh, Kushak Bakula had a free run for nearly a decade and a half, and he was given sufficient funds to develop the area. Very little tangible proof of his administrative capacity can be found today; rather I heard serious allegations of funds being wasted or irregularly channelised. Kushak Bakula, who incidentally is no elected head of the Lama community but was just picked up as a reliable figure-head by the Kashmir Government in the old days, has continued to enjoy uninterrupted patronage. In recent years his leadership has been challenged by the new elements coming up in Ladakh's social life. Norbu represents this new element. When I talked to him, I found him an extremely modem man. An engineer by profession, he is regarded as quite a leading specialist particularly in road building. His remarkable achievement was the building of the magnificent road across the Zozi La Pass which connects Srinagar with Kargil and Ladakh for the greater part of the year. In fact, Norbu won his Padma

Shri in recognition of this engineering feat. Norbu and his group have become a headache for Kushak Bakula and, after his displacement from ministerial office, Bakula has been a totally frustrated man. So he has worked up his group and he is getting a lot of publicity because of the fact that he has raised himself against the present leadership in Kashmir.

The choice before the authorities is clear: should they prop up the obscurantist vested interest represented by Kushak Bakula; or, should they encourage the modem enlightened trend represented by Sonam Norbu and his colleagues?

(November 11, 1967)

11

Setting the Priorities

Any discussion on Kashmir can hardly afford to leave out the political role of Dr Karan Singh. A young man of erudition and culture, Dr Karan Singh in his personal life has little semblance of the feudal stock from which he comes. With his doctorate thesis on the philosophy of Aurobindo, Dr Karan Singh appears to be cut out more for academic life than the hectic strain of a political career. However, eighteen years as Governor of the State, he has come to acquire a knowledge and assessment of Kashmir politics which is very much his own and he seems to be conscious of it.

During his last tenure of office as Governor, there was quite a lot of excitement because of an interview that he had granted to *London Times* elaborating his views on the constitutional set-up of Kashmir. The interview itself was frowned upon by the New Delhi authorities at the time since it seemed to infringe upon the constitutional propriety that a Governor is expected to maintain.

However, the political repercussions to the Karan Singh plan, as it has come to be known, flowed from the plan itself. He suggested that the Valley should be made into a separate State and Jammu and Ladakh should be merged in the contiguous Himachal State forming a Vishal

Himachal.

The moment the plan was released, it produced very adverse reactions. Sadiq himself characterised any proposal to slice off the Kashmir Valley as a move inspired by the Western powers. What was meant was that Sir Owen Dixon had made this suggestion with regard to the proposal to hold the plebiscite: he had restricted the idea of plebiscite only to the Valley saying that this alone was the disputed area; the fate of the other areas could be settled by negotiations, according to the Dixon Plan. The critics of the Karan Singh plan say that once the Kashmir Valley is made into a separate State, it would embolden secessionists and turn it into a stepping stone to the dislinking of the Valley from the Indian Union.

After this hostile welcome, the Karan Singh plan did not get much publicity in this country. In a sense it was shelved but it has never been buried. Talking to Dr Karan Singh, I could gather the arguments that he has in support of this plan. (It is to be noted that although Dr Karan Singh himself has not been active in publishing it openly, he has not abandoned it and is eager that it should be given a trial.)

First, he seems to hold that in any such complicated issue the correct way of dealing with it should be to localise the ailment; that is, restrict the area under dispute. In this way the Valley has a claim to be treated on a special plan. Secondly, it is refuted on behalf of Dr Karan Singh that the creation of a separate State out of the Valley would encourage the secessionists since such a State itself would be very much a part of the Indian Union. By this logic, Dr Karan Singh's supporters argue, the establishment of Nagaland should be considered as encouraging the Phizo-secessionists and a stepping stone towards letting the Naga areas opting out of the Indian Union.

The supporters of the Karan Singh plan—and they are quite a few particularly in Jammu—hold with certain cogency that the present State of Jammu and Kashmir, as its very name suggests, is an artificial creation. It reflected the expansion of a Maharaja's dominion and not the product of a natural evolution, nor is it based on ethnic or linguistic considerations. In fact, they say, there is no other State in India which has got so much of racial heterogeneity as the present State of Jammu and Kashmir.

I found that Sheikh Abdullah's followers are not very much worked up about the Karan Singh plan. According to them it is based not on linguistic considerations, while Dr Karan Singh has said nothing about the status of the Pak-occupied Azad Kashmir area; should it form part of his Valley State of Kashmir or should it form a separate entity? Dr Karan Singh's reply to such criticism is that he was not actually redrawing the map of Kashmir along linguistic frontiers. If that was to be done, then there were many areas inside the present Valley such as Gurez where non-Kashmiris constitute the majority. He says that he is suggesting nothing more than a sensible constitutional re-arrangement. If in the process it helps to stabilise the politics of the Valley, it would be an additional gain and he seemed to feel that his plan would help to minimise many of the present tensions of the State of Jammu and Kashmir.

In this connection one has to refer to the recent Jammu agitation in the course of which demands for a better deal for the Jammu people were raised. This preceded the agitation of the Kashmiri Pandits. It is interesting to note that the Dogras who constitute the majority in the Jammu region are not particularly enthusiastic about the demand of the Kashmiri Pandits for a larger share in Government employment. The Leader of the Opposition in the J&K Assembly while sympathising with the Pandits having to face police repression, added a rider that his party would not be interested in backing the claims of the Pandits with regard to a higher quota in Government service. The Gajendragadkar Commission which will go into the question of regional imbalances in Kashmir will naturally have to take up the question of the Jammu people also, and it looks as if the Karan Singh plan has in a way been able to create a base for itself in the Jammu region.

Will the Karan Singh plan satisfy Sheikh Abdullah and his supporters? This is a doubtful question because what Sheikh Abdullah is demanding is not just a constitutional re-arrangement beginning with the present set-up, but essentially a political rethinking by which the Kashmiri people's sense of identification with the rest of India could be realised; and also to make it durable, an understanding with Pakistan should be worked out.

However, I noticed this time that there is much less of denunciation of the Karan Singh plan than there was when it was first mooted. Whether Dr Karan Singh's elevation to the Central Cabinet will give him an opening for canvassing support for his plan is not yet clear. The fact that he is engaged in trying to seriously appraise the situation and to grope for a way-out is considered by many as a significant indication of his readiness to participate in any negotiations for bringing about a settlement in Kashmir.

No generalisation of the Kashmir situation is possible, least of all for an outside observer. However, three points have to be borne in mind, and they should set the priorities so far as the Kashmir problem is concerned.

First, the need for a proper understanding with Sheikh Abdullah and his supporters. Instead of harbouring the illusion that a detained Sheikh has lost much of his popularity, it would perhaps be necessary for New Delhi to work out a strategy by which Sheikh Abdullah's standing and competence could be harnessed in the interest not only of Kashmir but of the country as a whole. It must not be forgotten that Sheikh Abdullah is one of the few outstanding leaders still amongst us since the days of the freedom struggle, and if he is provided a wider horizon on this side of the Banihal, it would be all to the good of the country as a whole.

This enjoins that when he is released, as he must be—the sooner the better—there should be a concerted effort to win him over and not to repeat the disastrous line allowed to be followed by Bakshi Ghulam Mohammad in 1958 in trying to provoke and corner him. And in this task, the Left forces have a special responsibility since they can help to bring Sheikh Abdullah back into the mainstream of the democratic movement.

Secondly, there should be an attempt to offer to the Kashmiri people the maximum amount of autonomy in consonance with their remaining within the Indian Union. If such terms could be offered to the Nagas, there is no reason why a similar treatment should not be meted out to the Kashmiris. Actually, the principle of maximum autonomy was writ large in the Delhi Agreement, which even conceded a separate State Flag for Kashmir. But the Delhi Agreement was envisaged as a tentative understanding and it is time that the principle of autonomy for Kashmir is worked out in detail through free and frank negotiations with the leaders of Kashmir. Perhaps a round table with leaders representing all shades of Kashmiri opinion may help.

In this connection, one has to recall what Nehru had said in 1952 in all solemnity in Parliament:

> "So while the accession was complete in law and in fact, the other fact which has nothing to do with the law also remains, namely, our pledge to the people of Kashmir—if you like, to the people of the world—that this matter can be reaffirmed or cancelled or cut out by the people of Kashmir if they so wish. We do not want to win people against their will and with the help of armed force; and if the people of Jammu and Kashmir State so wish it, to part company from us, they can go their way and we shall go our way. We want no forced marriages, no forced unions like this.....
>
> "So, we accept this basic proposition that this question is going to be decided finally by the goodwill and pleasure of the people of Kashmir, not, I say, by the goodwill and pleasure of even this Parliament if it so chooses, not because this Parliament may not have the strength to decide it—I do not deny that—but because this Parliament has not only laid down in this particular matter that a certain policy will be pursued in regard to Jammu and Kashmir State but it has been our policy.... But whether it is a pain and a torment, if the people of Kashmir want to go out, let them go because we will not keep them against their will however painful it may be to us. That is the policy that India will pursue, and because India will pursue that policy the people will not leave her, the people will cleave to her and come to her. Because the strongest bonds that bind will not be the bonds of your armies or even of your Constitution to which so much reference has been made, but bonds which are stronger than the Constitution and

laws and armies—bonds that bind through love and affection and understanding of various people...."

While the context changed since 1952, the need for winning back the confidence of the Kashmiri masses cannot be minimised. And if this is done boldly and with imagination there is little ground of pessimism about the possibility of solving the Kashmir problem. In fact, this would help to consolidate better relations with Sheikh Abdullah and his followers, just as a rapprochement with them will help to win back the confidence of the Kashmiri people.

Thirdly, in dealing with the Kashmir question there should be more determined efforts to establish better relations with Pakistan. If the cold war between the super-powers could be reduced, there is no reason why the cold war between India and Pakistan should be kept up, and in this respect the responsibility of India for trying to reduce the cold war tension is as much as that of Pakistan. In some respects, one is tempted to say that India, as the senior partner in the subcontinent with greater command of resources and experience, is expected to show a greater degree of statesmanship than perhaps is possible for Pakistani leaders continuously cooped up with a sense of complex in dealing with India.

Such a move itself would help to settle the Kashmir problem just as much as the solution of the Kashmir problem itself will in its turn help strengthen better relations between India and Pakistan. However, the wider question of Indo-Pak relations has to be dealt with in greater detail and can be the subject of another round of discussion not necessarily to be tagged to any report on Kashmir.

(November 18, 1967)

12

Pakistan : View from the Capital

After the initial shock at the dramatic denouement in Pakistan climaxed by General Yahya Khan's seizure of power, New Delhi is now in a position to sort out the implications of these unprecedented developments across the border.

In any consideration of Indo-Pak issue, Kashmir inevitably holds the pride of place. During the four months of upheaval, ominous voices were heard particularly in West Pakistan of some Army officers and politicians, including Bhutto and Akbar Khan, sabre-rattling against Kashmir. However, the turn of events in Pakistan has led to a situation in which the Army seizing power is now pinned down to the task of suppressing internal unrest, with little scope for any external adventurism. In other words, General Yahya Khan would be so busy putting his own house in order that it will be the height of folly on his part to think of any armed confrontation with this country. It is significant in this context that the Pakistan Ambassador turned up along with his Chinese counterpart in the official receptions in Rangoon during Indira Gandhi's recent visit to Burma.

A noteworthy feature of the entire political churning up in the last few months has been the conspicuous absence of any frenzy against India. While this has become the normal characteristic of all mass movements in East Pakistan during the last two decades, what is significant is that this time even in West Pakistan there have been hardly any anti-Indian tirade; whatever anti-Indian outbursts could be heard were rare exceptions rather than the rule. From available indications it is clear that there has been no military concentration on the Pakistan side of the Kashmir border.

Secondly, the ignominious collapse of the Ayub regime and its desperate last-ditch struggle against democratic forces, as evidenced by the handing over of power to the Army Chief, had its political repercussion on the Kashmiris, including those belonging to Sheikh Abdullah's camp. The contrast between the normal functioning of a stable democratic order in India with the mess in which the military dictatorship has landed Pakistan could not possibly be missed by the average Kashmiri, however disgruntled he may be with the present set-up in his State. It is also significant that the victory of the United Front in West Bengal and the setback suffered by the Jan Sangh in the mid-term elections have been noted very carefully in Kashmir; in fact, this brings to the average Kashmiri a sense of security that the Hindu communalist forces have not been able to get the upper hand in political life and the staunchly secular anti-communal Left, as demonstrated by the West Bengal United Front, has begun to show the possible alternative to the present order in New Delhi.

As against this, the exploding of the myth of stability and prosperity in Pakistan under Ayub cannot but have its impact on the Kashmir public opinion. The very organ of Pakistani propaganda on Kashmir, namely, the Pak Radio, has inevitably become the vehicle of all the news of the turmoil prevailing in that State. The engine of repression trying to crush democratic forces in Pakistan did not leave Azad Kashmir untouched; there too some of the Kashmir leaders had to face police repression in the general attack on civil liberties during the last days of the Ayub regime.

It is in this background that one has to notice the change in temper and attitude of even the recalcitrant Plebiscite Front: the decision of the Front to contest the by-elections this summer is regarded as very significant because this is the first time that Sheikh Abdullah's followers would be entering a trial of strength in a battle for the ballot, instead of going in for endless rounds of angry denunciation of Kashmir's accession to India, alongwith the demand that Pakistan should be made a party to the settlement of the Kashmir affairs. Despite the unfortunate wrangles in the ruling circles in Srinagar, as evident from Syed Mir Qasim's threatened withdrawal from active politics, one cannot help feeling that the overall situation in Kashmir is fast reaching a healthy turning-point. The shambles in which Pakistani politics has reduced itself has considerably weakened its attraction for even the most truculent Kashmiri.

More important than the impact on Kashmir is perhaps the repercussions of Pakistani developments in the East. New Delhi observers concede that Rawalpindi is facing the biggest crisis in its career in East Pakistan. There have been many mass upheavals in East Pakistan in the last twenty years; at one stage in 1954, when the Muslim League was swept out of existence in the only full-fledged

General Election in Pakistan, the forces of Bengali nationalism asserted themselves to a point which struck terror in the hearts of Pakistan's rulers. Soon after, on the plea of certain unbalanced utterances of Fazlul Haq and by engineering a spate of riots, the Central Government clamped down Martial Law on East Pakistan fifteen years ago.

Since then, there have been many more demonstrations, some even a few years ago, in which the demand for autonomy was universally voiced, and in the crest of the popular upsurge could be seen Sheikh Mujibur Rahman and leaders of the Awami League. It was out of fear of that mass upsurge that the Ayub Government trumped up a conspiracy case against Mujibur Rahman and his associates charging them with a plot to take East Bengal out of Pakistan.

In fact, the talk of independent East Pakistan has been loosely used both by Pakistani politicians and foreign commentators in the last decade. The persistent East Bengali bitterness at the denial of a place in the Pakistani sun has been accompanied by the growing imbalance between the two wings in the developing economy of the country; even West Pakistani observers have not been able to minimise the strength of the East Pakistani complaint that their province has been treated as a sort of semi-colony, whose wealth has been exploited for the benefit of capital accumulation for the West Pakistani big business.

In such a situation the rulers in Rawalpindi could never whip up a large-scale anti-India frenzy in East Pakistan as a diversionary move to stifle popular discontent with the growing economic hardships and political disabilities. Even during the 1965 war, there was no evidence of any anti-India frenzy anywhere in East Pakistan—a development which was considerably helped by the statesmanlike attitude of New Delhi as embodied in Shastri's declaration at the height of the conflict that India had no quarrel with the people of East Pakistan.

In recent times the Ayub regime tried to whip up anti-India sentiment in East Pakistan not only by staging a mock conspiracy trial against Sheikh Mujibur Rahman and others but raising the bogey that East Bengal's agrarian economy would be in ruins if the Farakka Barrage is constructed by India. But even this proved to be a propaganda damp squib. Whatever the genuine points of discussion and clarification that Pakistan should have over the question of the Farakka Barrage, there is little evidence to show that with all the official propaganda emanating from Rawalpindi the common mass in East Pakistan could be poisoned against India through this campaign.

During the current upheaval in East Pakistan, one could not miss the very healthy attitude of the anti-Ayub mass demonstrations in regard to India. Although little news has been allowed to trickle across the frontier, observers in this country have not failed to notice the unequivocal East Pakistani approach of friendship towards this country. This has been very clearly underlined with special emphasis in most of the pronouncements of Sheikh Mujibur Rahman in particular. A shining example of Hindu-Muslim fraternisation came from Mymensingh where at the height of the mass upsurge, the authorities opened the prison gates for the Muslim prisoners who, however, refused to budge until the Hindu prisoners were also released alongwith them. Throughout the disturbances in East Pakistan, the minority question has never figured at all. Despite lurid stories of lawlessness, there was not a single report of any attack on Hindu minorities or any whipping up of anti-India feelings.

It is in this context that New Delhi has been wondering almost with bated breath how things are going to shape in East Pakistan. The advent of the military regime can only exasperate the East Bengalis, for the Army itself is known to be overwhelmingly dominated by West Pakistan with East Bengalis having no voice at all. General Yahya Khan's batallions in Dacca will face a situation ten times worse than the US in Vietnam if it really comes to a show-down with the Bengali peasantry spread all over the riverine districts.

In this situation there is therefore an uneasy feeling in New Delhi about the final outcome of the political developments in East Pakistan. Could the Bengalis across the border be possibly trying to carve out a Pakistani Biafra? The only difference with the Nigerian parallel is that the Central authorities in Pakistan can never launch a full-scale military attack on a people in revolt nearly two thousand miles away from the centre of power with no direct line of communication in between. The very logistics of any large-scale military operations in East Pakistan should scare Rawalpindi away from such a suicidal venture. At the same time, the loss of East Pakistan would mean to a very large measure the ruin of Pakistani big business as it has developed in the last twenty years. Whether General Yahya Khan would be able to retain East Pakistan for his money-bag patrons in the West is anybody's guess today. What is of relevance to New Delhi is that such a situation might land it in a very uncomfortable predicament.

On the one hand there is a considerable volume of

sympathy and goodwill for East Pakistan's democratic movement in this country. This was reflected in the very welcome statements made by United Front leaders in West Bengal soon after their installation in office, the statements which were sought to be exploited without any degree of success by professional commentators who earn their living by anti-communism. The West Bengal United Front leaders said that the cultural and trade barriers between the two Bengals should be lowered, if not altogether eliminated. Actually nothing more was said and nothing more was expected.

However, with the dramatic unfolding of events in East Pakistan, a new stage is almost reached when the question is posed: what should be the role of India in the event of an independent state coming to birth in East Pakistan? This is a question which New Delhi has always been fighting shy of facing openly. Rather, there has been a perceptible cooling off in official circles at the prospect of an independent East Pakistan.

Theoretically India is opposed to any politics of secession. This, it is claimed, is in keeping with the traditions of India's national movement which resisted, though unsuccessfully, the very idea of partitioning the country. In contemporary times, a new dimension has been added to India's staunch allergy to the politics of secession, whether it is raised in Kashmir in the north, Nagaland in extreme east or in Tamil Nadu in extreme south. The danger of secession of any territory from the parent state has always been emphasised by New Delhi and consistent with this stand, it is not likely to express appreciation or sympathy that may be construed as encouraging secessionist trends in Pakistan.

In terms of internal political alignments, it is said that

communal forces like the Jan Sangh with their unadulterated hostility towards Pakistan, might try to politically exploit the situation, claiming that Pakistan as a state is about to be destroyed. Despite all this official resistance, there will be a genuine spate of sympathy and an eagerness to extend the hand of friendship to the democratic struggle in East Pakistan on the part of the people of the eastern region, particularly in West Bengal.

There is also another aspect to the problem which worries New Delhi. A new state perched on the strategic cross-roads of eastern India may pose problems of foreign policy and defence. Because, there is every danger that a new born independent state entity in East Pakistan might fall under the spell, if not domination, of one of the Big Powers, particularly China (with Maulana Bhashani's admiration for it) or America which after its debacle on the banks of the Mekong might try to fish in the troubled waters of the Padma.

The developments in Pakistan are therefore being watched in New Delhi with mixed feelings of great expectations and intense anxiety. The old simplified logic that a setback for Pakistan is a gain for India hardly holds good in the present situation. The realities of the present-day power-politics are too complex to offer simplified solutions. In any event the developments in Pakistan pose a formidable challenge to India's statesmanship and diplomacy in which not only the Congress leadership but others, particularly those of the Left, have to prove their mettle.

(April 5, 1969)

13

Politics behind Skyjack

The skyjacking of an Indian Airlines plane by two hijackers styling themselves as members of the "National Liberation Front" only highlights the seriousness of the challenge that Kashmir faces today, qualitatively different from the ones faced by the State in the past.

Even though popular reaction to the externment of Sheikh Abdullah has been unprecedentedly quiet in the Kashmir Valley, the dramatic developments in consequence of the plane hijacking may force changes of far-reaching significance in the fortunes of the State. Looming large on the State's political horizon now is the threat from Pakistan, not only as a counter-blast to the recent action against the Plebiscite Front and its leaders, but also as an imperative of internal Pakistani developments, which do not seem to be conducive to detente and eventual friendly settlement of issues dividing India and Pakistan.

In the new power-structure in Pakistan, between the Army, President Yahya Khan and Bhutto and Mujibur Rahman, it is Mujib who has come to represent a healthier trend in favour of Indo-Pak amity, while in the opinion of observers both in New Delhi, and Srinagar, the younger section of the Pak Army, Yahya Khan and Bhutto share a common stake in resisting Mujib's demands. With the talks between the east and west wing leaders in Pakistan having reached a dead-end, the prospects are that the work of Constitution-making in Pakistan may again be scuttled, providing another opportunity to militarist sections to reverse the clock back there.

It is in this context of possible developments in the neighbouring country that authoritative circles in Srinagar and New Delhi assess the nature of the threat to Kashmir, as a lever with which the Pakistan leadership, especially in the western wing, might whip up frenzy and an atmosphere of confrontation with India to divert popular attention from the intractable problems of framing a Constitution which provides an answer to the democratic urges in Pakistan.

In fact, observers in New Delhi, basing themselves on the analysis of the reports reaching them from sources in Pakistan, have gone to the extent of fixing a deadline when the threat from Pakistan in the form of an armed adventure against Kashmir might materialise. Their calculation is that by next spring, after the crisis in Pakistan would have reached a fever pitch, the militarist circles in Pakistan would most likely resort to armed action against Kashmir depending, of course, on the measure of support they are likely to get from the West and China.

What has strengthened this belief is the new evidence available about the Pakistan Army having trained its personnel in the use of new weapons and aircraft available to it from the West, especially the USA, in Turkey and Iran. The earlier assessment that it would take longer for Pakistan to train its armed personnel in the use of new weapons and aircraft from the USA—thus providing India an edge over Pakistani armed preparations—has been abandoned.

Pakistani militarist and extremist circles, in addition to their internal compulsions, have another reason to feel emboldened to plan armed confrontation against India. This is the fluid internal situation in Jammu and Kashmir, marked by inroads made by Pakistani espionage and subversive organisations in the State, particularly in the Kashmir Valley and Doda. Pakistan, it appears, has been operating in the State through different layers, each one having been assigned a specific role, in expectation of utilising and coordinating their potential in the event of a confrontation with India. The underground organisations like Al-Fatah, National Liberation Front, Al-Burq and Red Kashmir, which have gained prominence in the wake of recent crackdown on the Al-Fatah gang and skyjacking of Indian Airlines plane, are to be regarded as evidence of the rapid build-up of the Pakistani subversive set-up in the State. Qualitatively, the growth of these organisations, mostly of educated youth drawn from educational institutions and professional colleges, with a flare for adventure and a measure of indoctrination, represents a new facet of the lengthening Pakistani shadow over Kashmir.

In the past, Pakistan used to rely mainly on personnel from traditionally open political forums with secessionist slant, like the Plebiscite Front and the Awami Action Committee. But the experience of the 1965 armed conflict, enforced a new strategy with emphasis on concentration on students and youngmen ready to undergo sacrifices and hardships of combat groups against India. As part of this strategy, the young recruits were required to fend for themselves, create their own resources and bases through careful utilisation of their own talents under the direct overall guidance of specialised centres based in Pakistan. Pakistan was to provide these recruits training in the use of weapons and the art of espionage and subversion.

More important, the steady growth of these organisation, facilitated by frustration among the unemployed educated youth in the State, was a handy weapon to keep the leadership of the secessionist organisations with mass appeal in the right spot and beat down their vacillations in the event of their linking up their effort with the progressive-democratic mainstream in India.

What brought success to the Pak efforts was the extremist hold on the Plebiscite Front whose grip on the secessionist camp was the guarantee that, in the ultimate analysis, Sheikh Abdullah would be made to toe the Pakistan line. Early in 1966, documentary evidence was available with the Government establishing full complicity of the Plebiscite Front leadership in the execution of Pakistan's plans of subversion in Kashmir. The crackdown on the hideout of a Pakistani agent, Sheikh Bhadrawahi, soon after 1965 war, had revealed all this.

With the liquidation of the Bhadrawahi gang, the State Government almost lulled itself into complacency thinking that it had smashed the last remnants of Pakistani underground which had been built up as preparation to massive armed infiltration into the State that had preceded the war in 1965.

In another direction, the results of the 1965 war, the ouster of Ayub Khan in Pakistan and later the open split in the Congress leadership in India, enforced rethinking in Sheikh Abdullah's camp, which was steadily facing erosion as a result of the split in the combination of parties that had come together in the wake of the holy relic agitation in 1964.

The first signs of this rethinking were available as Sheikh

Abdullah began a prolonged series of discussions with different groups and leaders of both pro-Pak and pro-India opinion with a view to finding out a solution of the Kashmir issue through a dialogue and consensus between the contending viewpoints in Kashmir. While the Kashmir Chief Minister, G.M. Sadiq, adopted a positive response towards this new developing trend within the Sheikh's camp and allowed it to grow unhindered, this was looked upon with concern by other sections of opinion both in Srinagar and New Delhi. The ensuing phase was marked by an internal split in the Congress in Kashmir, with the opposing wings of the ruling party in Kashmir taking divergent positions and in the process dissipating their strength in a long-drawn internal party strife. The split in the ruling party in Kashmir, far from consolidating forces of stability and progress in the State, came as an expected windfall to the extremists in the Sheikh's camp.

It was in this context that the Sheikh endorsed Mirza Afzal Beg's decision to end the phase of boycott of the elections and to gear up the party for a trial of strength at the polls. This new strategy adopted by the Plebiscite Front, however, did not mark any basic change in the attitude of the Plebiscite Front; on the contrary it was a bid for taking over the administration through normal constitutional channels for a final confrontation with New Delhi with the aid of Pakistan and Western countries.

These fears were confirmed as Sheikh Abdullah's bid for dialogue in search of a consensus on the solution of Kashmir's future attracted attention from various agencies. During the second session of the State People's Convention (October 1970), where the extremist Pakistani viewpoint found little support, Sheikh Abdullah threw his entire weight in favour of independent Kashmir, a solution which found its strong advocates from the Front sympathisers abroad known for their pro-West leanings and contacts. Reports now available indicate that most of the papers sponsored at the Convention by the Front leadership were prepared in consultation with Western agencies who had earlier contacted the Front's men through their links in London and New York.

The outcome of the Convention and the Sheikh's opting for independent Kashmir deepened concern at the situation in Kashmir and brought about a re-orientation of the policy of liberalisation.

The Plebiscite Front strategy of utilising the elections with the possibility of their ganging up with, Right Reaction for mounting an offensive again Indira Gandhi underlined the need for bringing together the warring factions inside the Congress in Kashmir to close up their ranks. The efforts in this direction did not bear much fruit, at first.

The controversy was finally clinched in July 1970 when Indira Indira Gandhi during her visit to Srinagar publicly warned Pakistan that India would resist any armed mischief in Kashmir. The Prime Minister also made it clear that no Government in New Delhi could afford to see the reversal of history as far as Kashmir's accession to India was concerned. The Prime Minister's declaration, it appears, not only served to warn against the hard-line approach towards the secessionist challenge in Kashmir, but was also meant to discourage militarist sections in Pakistan preparing for a policy of confrontation against India on Kashmir.

About this time, a series of mysterious fires all over the Valley brought about ominous developments. While the fires were raging in the Valley, the Plebiscite Front led by Beg had been quietly building up resistance groups in the rural areas rousing the villagers to resist "outsiders". In a matter of weeks, the villages, where previously the Plebiscite Front had no organisational basis, turned into centres of resistance with militants dividing the areas sector-wise and determining who should enter and go out of the villages. They even resisted the entry of local police to some of the villages. While this secessionist build-up was going apace, under the pretext of defending the villages, the ruling Congress and the administration remained completely paralysed unable to overcome the menacing situation.

What added a new dimension to the resistance campaign by the Front leaders was the sudden eruption of clashes with the authorities. In the urban areas, particularly in Srinagar, Sopore and other towns, clashes took place between the Army and Border Security Force on the one hand and the Front's resistance groups of students. At Sopore, a platoon of the CRP was waylaid and deprived of its provisions. In Srinagar during a series of clashes, a number of Army personnel were injured and their vehicles damaged. Meanwhile, as the evidence on the build-up of Pakistani underground inside the State began mounting, efforts were renewed to bring back Mir Qasim to active party fold. As a grand strategy to contain the secessionist challenge, it was also decided to bring back Bakshi Ghulam Mohammad, lest his ouster from the pro-India camp could in any way help the secessionists.

In pursuance of this new initiative on Kashmir—which began with Indira Gandhi's visit to Srinagar in July 1970—a fresh reassessment was made of the situation in the State and a new set of policies evolved to face the secessionist challenge. Thereupon Sadiq held a series of parleys with Mir Qasim and the two together went round the Valley addressing public meetings in which the Chief Minister attacked the Plebiscite Front campaign for utilising the Constitution to subvert the integrity of the State. Sadiq also warned that the Government would not take it lying down if the Front leaders failed to return to the path of realism. Beyond this, however, the political campaign to curb the Plebiscite Front was not taken up. The result was that the ruling party again went into slumber after a spurt of activity lasting about a month beginning from mid-September to the first fortnight of October. With administration shifting to Jammu for the winter, the prospect was that the proposed campaigning in Kashmir against the secessionists would have to be postponed till May when life in Kashmir took to the busy routine of the summer days.

These ominous developments in Kashmir almost coincided with Indira Gandhi's decision to go in for a mid-term poll. That the secessionists were not interested in utilising the elections for a normal trial of strength with the ruling party was evident from Mirza Afzal Beg's campaign speeches in which he enjoined upon his followers to take to bloody reprisals against those officials and the men in the ruling party whom they might suspect of rigging the poll in favour of the ruling party. What, however, imparted a sinister dimension to his campaigning was an appeal to the Jan Sangh for a joint front against the ruling party, indicating the secessionist readiness to share the effort for bringing about communal polarisation in the State under the garb of election campaigning against the ruling party. Such a situation would have ideally suited the plans of Western agencies including the CIA who lay great store by potential building up in Kashmir to create a grave situation in the country during the elections.

What finally appears to have forced a decision in favour

of punitive restrictions against the Front and its leaders was the summons to Sheikh Abdullah and Mirza Afzal Beg from the Pak High Commissioner to reach New Delhi for consultations.

Reports of what transpired between Sheikh Abdullah and Mirza Afzal Beg and the Pak High Commission indicated that Pakistan was preparing to unfold its grand design of scuttling elections in Kashmir. These reports said the Pakistani authorities had cleared the secessionists' plan to join the elections on the condition that they would later ensure Pakistan's presence on the scene in Kashmir. While Pakistan would man the execution of their operation scuttle, the secessionist leaders were required to initiate a mass upsurge.

It was in this background that Sadiq from his sick bed in Bombay issued the first public statement alerting against the Sheikh's meeting with the Pak High Commissioner.

The action against the Front, Sheikh Abdullah and Mirza Afzal Beg which deprived Right Reaction and its Western mentors of an explosive potential which could be used against Indira Gandhi and the progressive forces in the country came in for strong criticism by the Right reactionary parties terming it as another election gimmick by the Prime Minister. But their propaganda advantage was short-lived as the State Government uncovered the ramifications of the so-called Al-Fatah gang in the Kashmir Valley. If any doubts still persisted about the Pak design to scuttle the elections in Kashmir, the hijacking of the Indian plane and its consequent destruction in Lahore dramatically brought into focus Pakistan's bid to escalate the war hysteria on Kashmir.

The aftermath of the hijacking and the retaliatory steps by India have posed a knotty question before the observers both in New Delhi and Srinagar. If the Pak plan was to drown the elections in blood in Kashmir and thus initiate a phase of confrontation leading to possible armed conflict between the two countries, then why should Pakistan prematurely raise its hand by plotting the hijack?

The answer lies partly in the choice of personnel assigned to carry out the hijacking. Hashem Qureshi, the star performer in the hijacking bid, is known to have been acting as a double-agent. In fact, the Central intelligence agencies came to know months back about the plans to hijack the Prime Minister's son. Contrary to general belief that Qureshi was a dedicated liberation fighter, it appears now that the hijacker was a mercenary who had worked in close cooperation with many intelligence agencies. If he finally decided to undertake the risky operation it must have been under great pressure from Pakistan.

The hijacking assignment to Qureshi could not have possibly been carried out smoothly without Western intelligence agencies lending their good offices to coordinate the efforts at the sub-continental level. The hijacking, followed by dynamiting the airliner, has not only established Pakistani complicity in the anti-Indian provocation, it has also indicated the Pakistan Government's readiness to play its hand at bringing about an anti-Indira shift in the country on the eve of the elections.

To militarists in Pakistan, the hijacking marks the beginning of a new phase of active confrontation with India by step-by-step escalation of the hate-India campaign with a view to beat down Mujibur Rahman and take away the election gains of the progressive forces in Pakistan.

(February 13, 1971)

14

Bangladesh: Six Months

Six months of Bangladesh struggle has been an unprecedented experience as well as back-breaking strain for both the Government and the people of this country.

Although there has always been a fund of goodwill and sympathy in this country for the struggle of forces inside Pakistan, it is to be noted that there has never been any preparation to meet the type of contingency which developed in East Bengal after the massive victory of the Awami League in the December 1970 poll. Rather, there was a gross under-estimation of the real danger posed by a military junta devoid of popular support, a danger which could engulf its neighbours as well.

After Yahya Khan's perfidious attack on the political elements in the days following March 25, there spread throughout this country not only a sense of horror but an understandable urge to go in all-out support for the victims of military butchery in the neighbouring Bangladesh. It was at that stage that the Government while attuning itself to the popular mood was able to maintain remarkable restraint in not permitting itself to be involved in an armed conflict with Pakistan, and thereby let Yahya Khan declare before the world that the Bangladesh freedom struggle was engineered by India.

Then came the next phase when refugees in lakhs began to pour across the border, first the political elements and next the victims of a systematic pogrom by the Pak Army. This was the phase when the Government worked out its line for the world comity with regard to Bangladesh: The focus on the unbearable strain caused by the influx of refugees, together with a demand for political settlement inside Pakistan so that credible guarantees could be ensured for the return of the millions who had to leave their hearth and home, was raised at the official level. The Prime Minister wrote to most of heads of Government and it was in that round that the letter to Premier Chou En-lai was also sent. Side by side, senior Ministers of the Government toured different countries enlisting the support for the stand that India had taken. Only from the Soviet Union came official condemnation of the brutalities and in a forthright manner President Podgorny urged the Pakistan President to go in for a political settlement

This was the phase when, after the initial euphoria generated by the spectacular push-back of the Pakistan Army by the East Pakistan Rifles and other Bengali armed units in revolt, the first organisation of the guerillas was taken up seriously. The monsoon had just set in and with that came the breathing space for the partisan groups to organise themselves.

This phase has continued so far. The Mukti Bahini training has grown from the incipient stage to a regular organised level and it will not be surprising that within a month's time they would be able to work as a real guerilla force with their established bases inside Bangladesh. Away from the limelight of publicity, the training of the Mukti Bahini has been facilitated by the irrepressible patriotism of the dedicated youth of Bangladesh drawn from practically all political affiliations which refused to compromise with Yahya Khan. It is to be noted here that the consciousness and determination of the ranks of the Mukti Bahini have far outstripped those of its leadership. Colonel Osmani is known to the outside world as the Defence Minister but it would be unfair to judge the mettle of the Mukti Bahini by Colonel Osmani's personality alone. Much more advanced in outlook and activity are the young officers and the ranks with their unbounded enthusiasm.

At the political level, the first important landmark came in mid-April with the announcement of the formation of the Bangladesh Government in which two of the close lieutenants of Sheikh Mujib, Acting President Nazrul Islam and Prime Minister Tajuddin Ahmad, were placed at the helm of affairs. This was a signal for the widespread demand from many parties in this country for the recognition of the Bangladesh Government. While the juridical implications of recognition are hardly understood by those who raise the demand, it is to be noted that this is raised mainly as a mark of abiding solidarity with the freedom-fighters of Bangladesh.

This is the period when Indian public opinion has come to know more and more clearly the fullest implications of the Bangladesh struggle. Broadly it has recognised that this struggle is a struggle for self-determination for a national group inside Pakistan. It is also to be noted that if this struggle is successful, then other fighting nationalities inside West Pakistan, the Baluchis, the Pathans and the Sindhis, would also assert the right of self-determination and thereby undo the mischief created by the British with the setting up of the artificial state of Pakistan.

Thus the Bangladesh struggle has reached a crucial point. It is on the threshold of a determined struggle, no more depending on a spontaneous upheaval. On the one side, the Pakistan Army is getting ready for the dry season to set in after the end of the monsoon, and on the other, the armed guerilla forces are getting prepared for a long and protracted struggle in which no quarter would be given to the enemy.

This is one picture of the Bangladesh developments. There is another aspect of the reality which can hardly be ignored. East Bengal has long been the political storm-centre inside Pakistan. It has long been a headache for American imperialism since it established its hegemony over Pakistan in the mid-fifties. While the US Government went on arming the West Pakistan authorities and keeping up the military junta in power, it also realised that East Bengal might not remain under the heels of Islamabad for long. As the movement for autonomy grew in strength in the sixties—particularly after the 1965 Indo-Pak conflict, when it was found that no amount of whipping up of communal frenzy could move East Bengal into hatred against India—the American imperialists, specially the farsighted elements among them, began to cultivate political elements inside East Bengal, posing to be sympathetic towards the aspirations of the Bengali people. At one stage, they even tried to sell the idea of an independent state in the entire eastern region of the sub-continent thereby stirring up difficulties in neighbouring India as well. What is to be noted, however, is that a large section of the intelligentsia and quite a substantial section of the political leadership were sought to be corrupted by the inroad of the dollar in East Bengal in the late sixties.

After Sheikh Mujibur Rahman's spectacular victory at the poll, the US policy-makers were taken aback. They found themselves on the horns of a dilemma. The reality of an emerging autonomous state in Bangladesh ultimately going over to independence could hardly be ignored by them; at the same time, they could ill-afford to alienate the armed stronghold of West Pakistan that has been mainly their own handiwork.

In the subsequent period of Yahya Khan's brutalities in Bangladesh, this duality of American policy has become more evident. The US arms supplies to Islamabad continued despite all the dishonest assurances given to Sardar Swaran Singh during his visit to Washington in the summer; side by side, hordes of American agencies posing as relief workers, academicians, research organisations and philanthropic bodies descended on the periphery of Bangladesh. In the first stage, their main point of enquiry was to find out all about the potentialities of the partisan struggle inside Bangladesh. Moreover, the impoverished intellectuals from Bangladesh, uprooted and confused, were sought to be pounced upon since American authorities have always calculated, though wrongly, that a liberal dose of dollar bounty could divert people from the compulsions of partriotism.

The latest American position with regard to Bangladesh politics is to try to spread demoralisation on a large scale, to go on saying that a partisan guerilla struggle would be a long drawn-out agony of the type that Vietnam has been experiencing for two decades and a half. The idea is to demoralise the weaker sections and to prepare the ground for a political compromise in which Washington could have a major say.

As soon as the Bangladesh Consultative Committee of

several parties has been set up, the American lobby has begun to attack it. The very fact that the Consultative Committee could be formed is an indication of the realisation by the major political forces in Bangladesh that there is no way-out but to carry on a determined armed struggle for independence. And it is precisely to discredit the Consultative Committee that the canard has been raised—not only by the accredited representative of the US lobby in India, Samar Guha MP—that the whole thing is Communist inspired. What is carefully suppressed in this propaganda is that the Consultative Committee has been formed at the initiative of the Prime Minister of the Bangladesh Government, and is fully participated in by the Awami League. From Papanek to Galbraith, a long procession of American egg-heads claiming to be independent authorities have done their best to divert the attention of the Bangladesh political leadership from the arena of determined struggle to that of compromise and confabulations under the American aegis.

At the other end, the American authorities have been trying to bring sense into Yahya Khan's head, advising him to make certain gestures to confuse world opinion. Tikka Khan, who had earned the title of being a butcher even by the American press, has been removed and in his place the mild-mannered Dr A. M. Malik has been made the Governor of East Bengal; a phoney amnesty for Awami League leaders has been announced; and Sheikh Mujibur Rahman's trial has been indefinitely postponed. This so-called "peace offensive" is meant to show to the world that return to civilian rule is being planned for East Bengal.

It is in this background that one has to understand the meaning of U Thant's recent report on the East Bengal developments. While our Foreign Office has unnecessarily gone out of its way to express appreciation about it, the real meaning of U Thant's move is to create a case for the Security Council intervention on the plea that there is a threat to peace in the Indo-Pak subcontinent. If such an intervention could be put through, it will mean the freezing of the situation in favour of Yahya Khan and the scuttling of the Bangladesh freedom struggle.

It is no secret that the Americans are trying to sell the idea of a confederation. Sometime ago it was reported that the US Ambassador in Pakistan had moved in the matter, suggesting that East Bengal could be a sovereign unit but part of a Pakistani confederation. This was not acceptable to Yahya Khan. The latest model circulated from the American sources is that a confederation, with Defence alone in the hands of the Central Government, could be set up, thereby meeting Sheikh Mujib's six-point demand. There is little doubt that in the UN lobby during the current session of the General Assembly, one of the variants of this confederation idea would be canvassed for by the Americans. This canvassing might be done even through other powers friendly to both America and Pakistan, among them Iran is very often mentioned.

The American strategy seems to be to break the back of the Bangladesh resistance through sheer demoralisation, holding out the prospect of a protracted struggle; and on the other hand, to sell the idea of a compromise in which East Bengal would stay inside Pakistan, at least for the time being. Washington looks upon the prospect of the disintegration of Pakistan with great trepidation. Dr Kissinger during his visit to this part of the world aired views which are very significant: while he could not vouch for the future of Pakistan, he emphasised over and over again that Pakistan as a regional entity would play a significant role. That is, the Americans would see to it that West Pakistan is never allowed to disintegrate; and if that has to be ensured, then the Bangladesh struggle for independence has to be halted, for the time being.

There has thus come up in the course of these six months two distinct vistas for Bangladesh—on the one hand, the militant patriotic sections including the youth wing of the Awami League and the Left forces are determined to carry on the struggle for independence; on the other, the American machinations are banking on injecting demoralisation and winning over the vacillating elements for a patch-up settlement in which the facade of Pakistan's integrity could somehow be maintained at the moment.

It is in this background that India's policy with regard to Bangladesh has to be carefully worked out. It will not be sufficient to emphasise only the aspect of the strain of refugee influx—however serious that may be—while appealing to the comity of nations for intervention in favour of Bangladesh. This has been the weakness of our official stand as seen from the experience of the recently-concluded meeting of the non-aligned group in the UN. T.N. Kaul cannot be personally blamed for having put across that line since this has been the official line which New Delhi has so long pursued. What is important to emphasise is the element of the struggle for freedom, for national self-determination involved in the Bangladesh developments. Indira Gandhi's talks in Moscow and Washington as also in other capitals can hardly afford to bypass this aspect of the Bangladesh problem.

Bangladesh poses the most formidable challenge that India's foreign policy has so far had to face, and on the successful facing up to this challenge will depend the effectiveness of our foreign policy to a large measure.

(October 2, 1971)

15

The Twilight Hour

This is like the twilight hour. We are passing through these days in which we are not at war nor at peace. Our soldiers are destroying tanks and our men sabre-jets, but we have still our High Commissioner perched at Islamabad, loose talking in a manner that makes the world wonder which country he is really serving.

Many a time in the past few months it was said that the crucial phase had been reached in the Bangladesh struggle. But never before has it been so true as it is today. In fact, the crucial phase started when the Prime Minister returned from her Western tour with the realisation that the utmost that the Western Powers would do would be to appeal to President Yahya Khan to come to a settlement with the Awami League leaders, and beyond that they would not be prepared to do anything which would usher in an early political settlement so that the millions of refugees could go back to their homeland. It is no secret that hard experience has told New Delhi that the only world power which has stood by India's position is the Soviet Union despite the fact that in the present alignment of world forces this has caused almost a total erosion of Moscow's political leverage in Pakistan.

The diplomatic aftermath of Indira Gandhi's Western

tour could be seen in the Belgian move to raise the Bangladesh issue as an Indo-Pak confrontation in the Security Council—a move which could only have been inspired with the connivance, if not the initiative, of Washington. President Nixon's latest proposal has not been very different from what the US authorities have been saying for the last two months, namely, the defusion of the tension by the withdrawal of troops from the frontier. Even what President Yahya Khan tried to sell to J. K. Atal was a variant of the same Western brand, namely, the so-called civilian set-up, and not Yahya Khan, could negotiate with the Awami League leaders—and Atal, if one goes by indiscreet press interviews, almost fell for it.

Incidentally, this is not the solitary instance of mistaken judgement in Atal's diplomatic career. One has merely to recall his insistence on Nehru visiting Turkey, only to find himself in the midst of a political coup. Atal, however, showed distinction at Addis Ababa as an excellent connoisseur of polo horses.

In a nutshell, the basic issue in the Bangladesh crisis, namely, an immediate effort at settlement between the Pakistan Government and the Awami League leadership is being meticulously evaded by Washington and its entourage powers. This is obviously not due to the reason that Washington has lost its weight in Islamabad but because Washington does not want to do anything which might jeopardise the stability of the military junta at Islamabad. For, it is part of the global strategy of the Pentagon to prop up the Pak military junta by all means.

One should not forget the strategic location of West Pakistan as a soft underbelly of Soviet Central Asia—the very reason why both Washington and Peking are equally interested in backing Islamabad to the hilt. The additional reason for these two to stand solid by the side of Pakistan is to mislead the Arab world into believing that these two powers are the friends in need of the biggest Muslim state existing, that is, Pakistan.

There is a sizable body of opinion in New Delhi which has for sometime been thinking that China would not come to the side of Pakistan in the event of a military confrontation with India. This school of thought does concede that China would be making a lot of noise in support of Pakistan, but its calculation that there would be no military intervention on the part of Peking is more in the nature of intelligent guesswork than based on solid intelligence data.

However, this calculation may not be very wide of the mark because of three reasons: first, the Chinese leadership with all its big-mouth revolutionism in the UN does not want to expose its own military limitation; a full-scale intervention against India might lead to logistic difficulties which might show up the weaknesses of its Army, already in the throes of a political crisis. Secondly, Peking must have read carefully the terms of the Indo-Soviet Treaty and any armed move against India might land it into a situation where it might have to face counter-pressure on the Soviet border. Thirdly, with the successes of the liberation forces in Bangladesh it will be more and more obvious to the astute Chinese leadership that Bangladesh as an independent entity is inevitably going to emerge, and any military intervention on its part would earn Peking the open hostility of this new emerging Asian state not far from its own border.

At this stage it is important to assess, as a long-range exercise, the various phases in New Delhi's strategy with regard to Sino-Pak relations. In the fifties just about the time when Sino-Indian understanding was being strengthened, there came the US-Pak arms pact which openly pronounced its hostility towards the Communist powers, while Pakistan on her part made no secret of her intention to use her increased arms strength with American support for the purpose of grabbing Kashmir. It was no accident that this was the time when the American moves, both subtle and open, were made to mislead Sheikh Abdullah and his group into believing that an independent Kashmir could be formed, dislinked from India. While nipping this move in the bud New Delhi not only took the initiative in consolidating the forces of non-alignment in the Afro-Asian world, but also made a definite move to come to an understanding with Pakistan: the Nehru-Noon Agreement is an example of this policy and its culmination could also be seen in the Indus Water Treaty which Nehru signed with President Ayub.

It was in this period that Pakistan, obviously at the instigation of Washington, made the suggestion that there should be a joint Indo-Pak defence arrangement against the Communist powers—in other words to inveigle India into some offshoot of the military bloc into which Pakistan herself had entered under American allurements and pressures. This was rejected outright by Nehru.

Next came the phase of Sino-Indian antagonism leading to the Chinese attack on the Indian frontier in 1962. Whatever might have been the lapses in Indian diplomacy in trying to handle this issue—Pandit Sunderlal has of late been giving publicity to this point of view, backing Neville Maxwell's thesis—there is no gainsaying the fact that the Chinese assessment in the late fifties was definitely hostile to India, branding her as having gone over to the Western camp and backed by "Soviet Revisionism". It is to be noted that about this time Peking's animosity towards the other Communist countries had already begun, evidence of which was furnished at the Moscow Conference of the world Communist Parties in late 1960, where one of the charges levelled against the Soviet Communist Party by Peking was that Moscow was backing India against China.

It is worth recalling that on the very morrow of the Chinese attack on the Indian frontier, when Nehru was under fire from the Right Opposition and Krishna Menon had to quit the Cabinet because of the mounting pressure of the US lobby, there came the proposal fully backed by the Western Powers for an Indo-Pak agreement on Kashmir on the basis of a virtual partitioning of the Valley itself. Incidentally, the pro-American elements in the Government at that time were even in favour of withdrawal of troops from the Pakistan frontier to draft them against the Chinese.

As soon as New Delhi made it clear that it could not accept such a proposal of partition of Kashmir, the Sino-Pak understanding began to be forged in a very demonstrative way. First came the demarcation of the boundary between Western Tibet and Sinkiang on the one side and the Pak-occupied portion of Kashmir on the other. This was followed by a number of other agreements leading to the Chinese military help to Pakistan even to the point of helping to the setting up of guerilla training centres in the Pakistan-occupied area of Kashmir for the purpose of organised infiltration into the Valley.

During the 1965 Indo-Pak conflict, the Chinese made no secret of their full support of Pakistan; their military experts were known to have helped in the training of the infiltrators who swarmed across the Cease Fire Line into the Kashmir Valley. And at the crucial moment of the war, the Chinese threatened to attack the eastern frontier. Their calculation at that time was that if the war had spread to East Bengal, then the Chinese would force a wedge through Bhutan and help the depleted Pakistan Army in that sector. Unfortunately for the Chinese, the Indian strategy at that time was to make it clear that there would be no military operation against East Bengal. When the Chinese move thus failed, then came the famous threat about the theft of sheep and goats by India which was made into an excuse for an angry threat of war by Peking. If the war had continued longer than it did, one would not have been surprised if the Chinese attack had materialised at least on the Himalayan frontier.

The two options which seemed to have alternated in the main in the evolution of the Indian policy are: first, whether an Indo-Pak understanding could be reached in facing the challenge of China; and secondly, whether a Sino-Indian thaw could be maintained while the threat from Pakistan has to be met.

The first trend was represented by the pro-US elements in this country: they had long thought if *detente* could be established with Pakistan then a common front could be built against Communist China. This was the basis of the so-called Indo-Pak reconciliation movement sponsored by some of the pro-Swatantra elements in this country. Unfortunately for them, the latest Nixon policy for making up with China has led to the collapse of this platform. They are now floundering and have caught on to a new slogan that there should be understanding with China as a counter to an understanding with the Soviet Union. In other words, the Indo-Soviet Treaty has become their main target of attack, thereby making it clear that in their estimate, the real Communist threat comes from Moscow and not from Peking.

The other school which thinks that an understanding with China could be possible while Pakistan is the main source of animosity against India, believes that a friendly positive approach to Peking might disrupt or at least weaken the prevailing Sino-Pak *entente*. The point to note is that in the present configuration of world forces, both the US and Chinese policies are strongly in favour of propping up Pakistan, if not the whole of it, at least West Pakistan. It will therefore be idle to think that Peking which has already shown its hand in the UN—where it has not shown any hesitation to side with US against any Soviet proposal, however reasonable it may be—will let down Pakistan in the case of an Indo-Pak confrontation. Every day more and more evidence is mounting about the Chinese stand with regard to Bangladesh. The entire attack is directed against India as the instigator of the Bangladesh freedom fighters and this is being linked up even with the Tibetan rebellion and exodus of refugees which came in the wake of Chinese repression of that rebellion. There is room for honest difference of opinion about the wisdom of not immediately answering those charges by Peking, particularly when Peking is in a position to mislead quite a large number of countries in the Afro-Asian world. Whether such silence is really golden, when New Delhi's main concern is not to allow any new advantage to be scored by Pakistan over the Bangladesh crisis, only the future will tell. But it will be rather naive to think that the Chinese could be persuaded to behave in a friendly way by such a gesture of demonstrative silence on the part of New Delhi.

The overall picture is that in standing by the side of the Bangladesh freedom fighters and standing up to the bullying tactics of the Western Powers in defence of Yahya Khan, there is no scope for New Delhi to minimise the dimension of the crisis.

The nation is placed in a state of expectancy and yet there is still a resistance to go in for all-out war because underlying all the calculations, there remains the great imponderable as to the price of a major confrontation in terms of economic, social and political liabilities. One is tempted to recall T.S. Eliot's lines that

> *"War is not a life: it is a situation,*
> *One which may neither be ignored nor accepted,*
> *A problem to be met with*
> *ambush and stratagem,*
> *Enveloped or scattered."*

Nothing better can describe New Delhi's preoccupation today.

(December 4, 1971)

16

Bangladesh: Where Lies its Strength?

The long-awaited recognition of the People's Republic of Bangladesh by New Delhi marks a qualitative advance in the direction of liberation of a neighbouring nationality into independent statehood.

This recognition is not just a formal juridical act on the part of the Government of India: it signifies a specific stage in the progress of the forces of resistance inside Bangladesh against the West Pakistan armed forces, towards a real movement of liberation of an entire people. On the part of India, this act of recognition brings upon this country not only direct involvement in a common struggle against Islamabad's military junta but its important responsibility of ensuring that this struggle of seventy-five millions in Bangladesh is crowned with success—success not only in the theatre of military combat alone but in the wider struggle for a friendly and prosperous state with a forward-looking leadership which will help to strengthen the bonds of solidarity now being forged in the ordeal of battle.

The demand for recognition of Bangladesh was persistently raised by most of the political parties in the country ever since the Bangladesh Government was formed under the leadership of Nazrul Islam and Tajuddin Ahmad. In fact, the question of recognition reflected the overwhelming national mood for some demonstrative act of solidarity with the freedom-fighters in Bangladesh pitted against Yahya Khan's military terror.

The more critical among the Opposition parties wanted to take advantage of this national sentiment for petty party ends when, knowing fully well the legal, political and moral implications of the act of recognition they started branding the Government as not only weak-kneed but even having betrayed the struggle of Bangladesh: what was revealing was that into this sweeping condemnation not only New Delhi but Moscow also was dragged, not only by the parties of the Right but some of the parties claiming to be Left.

New Delhi's timing of the formal recognition of Bangladesh has come as the logical culmination of a well-thought-out strategy which bears the stamp of mature statesmanship. For a Government to accord recognition to a state which is still going through its birth-pangs requires considerable care and circumspection and a sense of the perspective: it cannot be just the declaration of solidarity as it is often held to be in the popular mind.

Specifically, in the case of Bangladesh, the evolution of New Delhi's policy has passed through certain clearly discernible stages. At the beginning, it started as a shock and protest against Pak military brutalities coupled with a sense of solidarity with the democratic forces standing up to the military regime. Then came the unhesitating hospitality to the refugees who sought shelter on Indian soil. As the refugee influx took the form of an unending avalanche, India received them ungrudgingly despite all the formidable problems, social and economic, that this unprecedented exodus brought in its train.

Then came India's campaign before the comity of nations, through numerous representations, both official and non-official, which stressed the need for creating credible guarantees for the return of the refugees to their homeland: and it was also made clear that such credible guarantees could be provided only by a political settlement between Islamabad and the elected representatives of East Bengal. The protection and assistance to the freedom-fighters came as part of the same policy that stressed the need for a settlement with the accredited representatives of Bangladesh.

The total lack of response on the part of the Yahya junta even after the effective explanatory campaign on a world scale, climaxed by Indira Gandhi's visits abroad from late September to early November, not only opened the phase of intensified actions of the Bangladesh freedom-fighters against the Pak Army, but also of armed confrontation between India and Pakistan, which was Pakistan's version of internationalising the conflict.

It is important to note the contrast in the style of handling the crisis by the democratically elected Government in New Delhi with that of the self-installed military junta in Islamabad. One drew world attention to the crisis by means of active diplomacy on a world scale, the other through heightened military tension, finally plunging the subcontinent into a full-scale armed conflict.

In tracing these stages of New Delhi's involvement in the Bangladesh crisis one has to take into account the world forces that have contributed to this war. No one in the wide world can deny that Pakistan's war machine was the Santa Claus gift of the Pentagon, a by-product of the policy of military blocs and arms pacts which

Washington has been following as part of its global strategy.

In the case of Pakistan, the first abetment of armed provocation against India came from the British, who had to make way for the USA in the fifties. And in the sixties was added Peking's contribution towards strengthening Pakistan's armed postures, provocations and actual offensive against India. No wonder, therefore, that these two powers have joined hands in denouncing India in the Security Council debates, giving vent to their spleen against Moscow for standing by New Delhi and for warning other powers against escalating the conflict—a pointed thrust as much against Peking as against Washington.

The recognition of Bangladesh by itself does not ensure the liberation of the soil of Bangladesh. It marks a step—no doubt, an important step—towards it. In fact, it indicates New Delhi's calculation that the combined struggle of the Mukti Bahini and the Indian armed forces has made it a certainty; and as one watches the progress of this struggle, there is little room for questioning the validity of such a calculation. This is, therefore, the appropriate moment when one may with profit trace the political strength of this liberation struggle of Bangladesh.

Liberation struggles have a logic of their own. It is not a simple thing to overthrow an established state power. Dissent may enlarge into mass unrest and mass unrest in its turn may take the form of revolt or sporadic outbreak of violent attacks on established authority. But all these are qualitatively different from a liberation struggle worth the name.

It is with this understanding that one has to judge the Bangladesh struggle. There is no denying the fact that for twenty years there was the smouldering fire of active dissent among the people of East Bengal against the ruling authority of Pakistan. There was mass unrest manifesting itself in various forms, from the sweeping verdict of the electorate against the establishment to violent outbursts defying police repression. But until March 1971 nobody had thought that East Bengal would witness a full-scale liberation struggle.

Many factors contributed to this situation. The popular understanding that intensive repression works as an incentive to revolutionary outburst is as fallacious as the idealist theory that war by itself can lead to revolutionary seizure of power. The barbarities committed by the Pakistani military junta against the common peoples of Bangladesh have no doubt shocked the world and have even forced some of Yahya Khan's political mentors to shed crocodile tears.

But it would be a mistake to think that the fighting forces that are today liberating the soil of Bangladesh from the oppression of Islamabad's military junta, inch by inch, are merely the product of the revulsion to military atrocities. It is no longer necessary to recapitulate the background of Pakistani colonialism in East Bengal. It may sound a little extraordinary to characterise the Pakistan Government's neglect of East Bengal as a form of colonialism but if one has to go by the available data there is no denying the fact that the treatment meted out to East Bengal, which constituted the majority unit in Pakistan's state set-up, had many of the features of colonialism.

The export of primary commodities from East Bengal constituted the major source of foreign exchange earnings for the Pakistan Government; at the same time, East Bengal was preserved as a market for dumping the manufactured goods of West Pakistan at a price level higher than that prevailing in the west wing; in Government employment, both civil and military, the people of East Bengal were studiously kept out, while the Government outlay for development purposes and also for day-to-day civil administration was far lower in East Bengal than in the favourite regions of West Pakistan.

All these by themselves again could not possibly have brought about the political revolt which was the starting point of the liberation struggle of Bangladesh. Because, there are other areas in West Pakistan such as Baluchistan, Pakhtoonistan and portions of Sind which have been badly neglected by Pakistan Government and some of these are kept at a level of backwardness which is far below that of East Bengal.

If mere impoverishment and exploitation or military oppression of the people are the reasons behind the phenomenal growth of political revolt in East Bengal, then there is no reason why the Baluchis' struggle, for instance, has not come up to the same tempo. It is precisely on this point that one has to understand the role of political consciousness—the subjective element—which has made it possible for the liberation struggle in Bangladesh to grow to a point when their independence from Islamabad is now almost as certain as tomorrow's dawn.

In the freedom struggle against British imperialism, East Bengal's record was of militant action embracing all classes of people. In sweep and intensity perhaps no other region of the Indian subcontinent has such a magnificent record of militant struggles against British rule. The annals of practically every district of East Bengal are replete with militant peasant actions against foreign rule, and there were struggles of various other types, each of which had significance all its own: one has only to recall the long and glorious record—from the great Assam Bengal Railway strike of the twenties to the Chittagong Armoury raid of the thirties, and the Tebhaga struggle of the forties, to name only a few.

It was the inadequacy in the ideological content of our anti-imperialist struggle which made it possible for the reactionaries along with the British to create communal divergences to the point that a demand for a separate state by the Muslim community could distort this anti-imperialist urge to a point where the national leadership of both the communities agreed to the Partition of the country even without the blessings of Gandhi.

The common humanity of East Bengal inevitably became the biggest political challenge for the reactionary leadership that was installed in Pakistan ever since its birth. If by any accident of history, progressive forces had been at the helm of the Pakistan state, East Bengal today would have been its most stable prop, and the revolt against such a political set-up would have come from the feudal elements which constitute the backbone of the military junta that rules that state today.

As things turned out, the weak political leadership in Pakistan could very well be kept under the thumb of the Western Powers, first of the British and then of the Americans, and it was inevitable that such a reactionary political authority would come into head-long clash with the politically advanced sector that was represented by East Bengal inside Pakistan. And today nemesis has overtaken those very people who rule Pakistan in the shape of revolt to the point of independence on the part of the biggest bloc of Muslim population inside the State which claims its *raison d'etre* in the fact of being the biggest Islamic power.

So, when we talk of the liberation struggle of Bangladesh we have to take into account this political background that has made possible the emergence of this liberation struggle. At the same time, this enjoins certain compulsions and responsibilities regarding such a struggle.

The smart set of newspaper analysts specialising in superficialities are quite glib in their forecast about the future of Bangladesh. One section, mainly inspired by the Western commentators, have for quite some time been anxious that the Western powers should come to the rescue of Bangladesh; otherwise its leadership, that means the future wielder of power in Bangladesh, would pass on to the hands of the Left.

In fact, a few years ago when mass upheaval against the Ayub Government was at its peak, there were elements in the US Government—particularly in the CIA—which toyed with the idea of an independent East Bengal state under the aegis of the West which could serve as a useful baffle wall against the forces of radicalism which had been sweeping over this part of Asia. But the decisive voice in any policy decision in Washington regarding Pakistan seems to be still held by the Pentagon. Although the military blocs as such have lost much of their effectiveness in the age of inter-continental ballistic missiles, the idea of retaining Pakistan as a strategic jumping-off ground in any crusade against the Soviet Union still persists.

And today this idea has been reinforced by the other brand of militarism which has come to rule in Peking with its unabated zeal of anti-Sovietism. In a word, Pakistan provides the geopolitical meeting ground of Nixon's America and Mao's China. It was not just a slip of tongue that once President Ayub had boasted that he was working as an honest broker between Washington and Peking.

In this context it has not come as a surprise that despite all the powerful propaganda campaign in the press and among a section of liberal Senators in America, the policy-makers in Washington could not stand against the Bangladesh struggle.

They have, of course, tried their best to disrupt or weaken that struggle as they have done in so many other liberation struggles all over the world in the last thirty years. In grooming agent-provocateurs to sowing demoralisation and disrupting the serried ranks of freedom fighters, they are no peers of Washington, some of whom come even in the garb of innocent-looking non-official observers.

All such attempts by Western agencies to gain control over East Bengal politics in the past came to nought, and even today a shrewd and suave intellectual of the eminence of Prof Galbraith could not sell the US line to the Bangladesh political leadership. The primary reason for this is the consciousness that has percolated into practically every section of the democratic camp in Bangladesh that behind Yahya Khan and his junta stands Washington, with Peking playing the second fiddle.

As the debate in the UN continues, this consciousness grows every day, and in equal measure is strengthened the affinity between the Bangladesh freedom fighters and the world of socialist states. The interaction between the political strength of Bangladesh struggle, and this international alignment can hardly be ignored.

All this, however, need not lead one to overlook the complexity of this struggle. By its very nature, it is not a liberation struggle which has grown up entirely on its own strength. This is not to belittle its significance. For, in a sense, no liberation struggle has reached its success entirely on its own, insulated from all other supporting forces. Whether it is Algeria or Romania, Yugoslavia or China, Vietnam or Cuba, the active support and assistance of fraternal forces from all over the world have played a significant, and in most cases decisive, part in carrying them forward to victory. Lenin was never tired of emphasising this bond of solidarity and its importance for the revolution he led and for the survival of the first socialist state.

In the case of Bangladesh, placed as we are, this common front between the Mukti Bahini and the Indian armed forces is of great significance, what the Prime Minister has aptly characterised as "the partisans in the same cause". At the same time, it poses important and sensitive issues on the successful handling of which the close comradeship in arms forged today will develop into friendly partnership in the common struggle for economic and social advance. The urgency of taking these up with a clear grasp of the long range perspective can hardly be ignored. The far-reaching implications of this common struggle will unfold as village after village in Bangladesh finds itself breathing the air of freedom in the coming weeks.

Meeting this formidable challenge will demand not only a great sense of responsibility but statesmanship of the highest order for the leaderships of both the countries.

The days of hope and glory are also going to be days of toil and wisdom.

(December 11, 1971)

17

New Stature, New Tasks

It is like the end of a long night for men, women, and children of this country as Bangladesh proclaims her independence from Pakistan's military junta. The rejoicing is not merely in the feat of arms—though the military defeat of the much-vaunted war machine of Pakistan has brought no little credit to this country's armed forces, officers and men alike.

What is of abiding value is that this confrontation has demonstrated that democracy in this country has not only come to stay but has strengthened the content of our independence. The spirit of defiance that one could breathe even in the political backwaters of New Delhi as the news of Nixon's Seventh Fleet steaming up the Bay of Bengal went round, is the measure of the nation's anti-imperialist consciousness, doubly reinforced by recent experience.

What has been uppermost in the minds of many is the contrast provided by this country's statesmanship in unilaterally offering an immediate Cease Fire to Pakistan the moment its forces surrendered in Bangladesh, with the unbalanced ravings of Bhutto on becoming Pakistan's President, riding on the back of one faction of the same old military junta. One cannot help noticing how with every round of the ordeal of Bangladesh, the pronouncements of India's Prime Minister reflected the enriched wisdom of a mature political leadership while with every step in the decline and discredit of the military junta the outbursts of Pakistan's President betrayed the degeneration of a clique, bereft of democratic support.

All this is not just a passing euphoria, nor is it an irredentist jubilation at the break-up of an unfriendly state next door. What is most conspicuous in the spontaneous feelings of joy at Sonar Bangla achieving her liberation is the sense of triumph that this has been achieved by defeating a military set-up which has been reared over the years by the biggest of imperialist powers and today enjoys the backing of another military power. The fact that this nation can no longer be humiliated into submission by bullying and blackmail is at the very root of the new sense of strength and fulfilment that permeates all segments of public opinion in this country today.

The warmth with which solidarity with Bangladesh is being expressed at the Government as well as the popular level gives the lie to the reactionary communalist propaganda in this country which has tried for decades to spread the anti-Muslim poison. Equally significant is the repeated declaration by the Government and responsible leaders of democratic opinion that this country harbours no animosity towards Pakistan; the clearest proof of which was provided by the decision not to let the war continue despite the fact that the Indian forces in the west were able to occupy over 4500 square miles of West Pak territory as against less than 200 square miles of Indian territory occupied by the Pak Army in the same sector. It would have been a natural temptation for any military leadership to push ahead and teach the enemy a lesson, particularly when the adversary had been holding out threats to capture Kashmir for over twenty-five years. But a sense of realism coupled with loyalty to democratic norms could be discerned in the fact that it is the leadership of India's armed forces which has throughout refused to play the hawk in this conflict.

The conspicuous absence of a spirit of *jehad* on India's part is in marked contrast to President Bhutto's intemperate call for revenge and his mulish refusal to recognise that Bangladesh has delinked itself irrevocably from Pakistan. In fact, the process of stabilising the Cease Fire Line by an armistice to be followed by creating conditions for a durable peace, is obviously hampered by such megalomaniac antics of the head of a state which has not only to lick the wounds of military defeat but to refashion its entire economy with the loss of the very province which was so long fleeced for the benefit of West Pakistan.

The official US position—coupled with Peking's bellicosity—has been tirelessly trying to help Pakistan by getting whatever concession it could extract even on the question of Cease Fire. The fact that it is Pakistan's President that is now taking up a warlike posture—refusing to learn anything from his predecessor's fate—does not bother his mentors in Washington and Peking. In essence, the US grouse is against this country for having the impudence to flout its wishes. Nixon's pettyfogging reply to Indira Gandhi's letter brings out the contrast in the calibre of leadership at the helm of the two Governments.

Herein lies the importance of the present developments over Bangladesh. The very force which could drive out British imperialism from this country has once again emerged with all the glory of resurgence against US imperialism today. And this is not confined to the question of Bangladesh alone.

The refusal to devalue the rupee in the wake of the devaluation of the dollar is a very important political landmark. Although C. Subramaniam has not changed his spots and is ready to plead for the devaluation of the rupee with the same vehemence with which he did so in 1965, in the company of Asoka Mehta and L. K. Jha, the fact that his writ has not run this time indicates how far this nation and its Government have travelled along the road of self-respect in these five years. Of interest should be Lyndon Johnson's bouquets to Subramaniam for holding similar ideas, as quoted in the former US President's memoirs.

Another significant development is the current debate that has been going on the question of US aid. The Nixon embargo on economic aid as a pressure move against this country over the Bangladesh question has boomeranged. There are, of course, pundits in the Finance Ministry and the Planning Commission—once again Subramaniam is in their company—who cannot think of any development programme without a generous dose of US aid. But the growing volume of opinion in the Government against getting any more US aid—reflected in the Prime Minister's talk to the Planning Commission this week—is the reflection of the same spirit of independence which refuses kowtow to the Almighty Dollar. One has only to recall the day when S. K. Patil congratulated himself ten years ago for having secured from Washington the largest quantum of PL 480 bounty. One more indicator to show how far this nation and its Government have travelled along the road to economic independence.

At the same time, New Delhi is not unaware of the magnitude of the tasks to be faced. Bangladesh poses a formidable challenge; it is multidimensional, embracing all manner of very sensitive problems from the role of the Indian Army to the long-range question of development programme, the building of the new state's administrative infrastructure to the evolution of a mutually beneficial trade policy. In all this, Indian expertise and guidance cannot be withheld since it is asked for by a Government which regards New Delhi as its friend in need.

From the Marwari businessmen in Calcutta to the Big Business interests assembled in the Federation of Indian Chambers of Commerce and Industry in New Delhi—they are all calculating their investment prospects in Bangladesh. It will be necessary for the Government of India to take a firm stand against the private sector spoiling national assets in terms of political goodwill in Bangladesh.

In the national sphere, New Delhi has to chalk out concrete measures for the country's economic development. The mid-term appraisal of the Fourth Plan, due to be released shortly, brings into sharp relief the tasks ahead if the objective of growth with social justice is to be realised. The minimum programme chalked out at Bangalore in 1969—which marked the parting of ways between the Syndicate and the present leadership of the Congress—is yet to be realised.

The excitement of the coming elections to the State Assemblies by next March can no longer be used as an alibi for urgently required concrete steps to put the economy into the right gear.

The experience of Bangladesh has also been a tremendous education in the handling of foreign policy on New Delhi's part. Here too a sense of realism pervades which is a sign of self-confidence as also of maturity in understanding. The massive vote in the UN General Assembly on the Bangladesh crisis has neither unnerved nor angered this country's policy-planners. It is realised that much more of spadework has to be done to bring home to the Afro-Asian nations about the significance of Bangladesh. It is this realisation that has led the Foreign Minister himself to spend a long period in the UN, and he has taken along with him two of the most distinguished intellectuals in this country from among the Muslim community—no doubt to effectively counteract Pakistan's propaganda in the Arab countries which do not seem to have registered the fact that Bangladesh has the largest Muslim population in the world, next to Indonesia.

A conspicuous development is the manifestation of Anglo-American contradictions over Bangladesh, which New Delhi is not only aware of but is capable of using in a positive direction.

An important region with potentialities of closer understanding and economic ties for this country is Latin America. It is worth noting that two countries with the most significant developments to their credit in recent times—Cuba and Chile—have demonstrated their positive understanding with regard to the Bangladesh developments.

Few will deny the strengthening of India's relations with the Socialist world as a result of the Bangladesh crisis. Even the most conservative elements in Parliament have come out with unequivocal appreciation of the Soviet Union's support for India, and equally widespread is the praise for other members of the Socialist world which have stood by India.

Apart from Peking's aberration, what is intriguing, however, is the stand of Romania and Yugoslavia; both, it is to be noted, have recently taken up a pro-Peking posture in contrast to their cooling off towards Moscow. Belgrade's position has no doubt annoyed New Delhi, particularly after Marshal Tito's recent visit to this country when he expressed his support for India's stand with regard to Bangladesh. The subsequent Yugoslav explanation that its stand in the UN is largely guided by its own difficulties with regard to Croatia has carried little conviction in New Delhi; rather, the fact that Belgrade is under the double pressure of Washington and Peking explains its strange posture with regard to Bangladesh.

As for Bucharest, there was hardly any illusion in New Delhi about its attitude towards Bangladesh after President Giri's encounter with the Romanian President during the Persepolis celebrations in October. The impression has strengthened since then that in its present acrobatics as the go-between for Washington and Peking, Bucharest can hardly be expected to annoy either over any issue affecting Pakistan.

On the whole, there is no feeling of pessimism in New Delhi with regard to its foreign policy, nor is there any isolationist trend, just because many countries in the Afro-Asian world have yet to understand the significance of Bangladesh. Rather, New Delhi has taken this up as a challenge, and there is little doubt that in the months to come, this inadequacy will be overcome as Bangladesh herself proclaims her will to live and grow in friendship with India.

The sense of pride and glory is invested with a new sense of responsibility as the nation comes to the end of a momentous year which opened with the excitement of a massive election victory for Indira Gandhi, and is about to close with the elation over the liberation of Bangladesh.

(December 25, 1971)

18

Murree and Beyond

What the Murree talks have achieved has an important positive bearing for breaking the intense cold-war estrangement in Indo-Pak relations.

This is borne out by the experience of D.P. Dhar's team which, when it reached the heights of Murree, was received with severely chilly protocol politeness with nobody trying to conceal the bitter stare reserved for the delegation from New Delhi. By the time the four-day deliberations were over, the thaw set in and the Joint Statement could at least note: "This was the first occasion on which representatives of India and Pakistan were able to meet and communicate directly with each other on behalf of their Governments since the tragic developments of last year." More important was the recognition of the fact that the sessions were "marked with cordiality and a readiness on both sides to appreciate each other's point of view".

The fact that the Pak President himself had to intervene in the middle of the talks is indicative of the pronounced rigidities shown at Murree at the beginning. This was neither unexpected nor is it inexplicaple since one has to take into account the fact that the Pak officialdom has for years been conditioned by intense anti-Indianism, and on top of it, has come the psychological complex of a military defeat.

On the other hand, Bhutto is in a hurry to pull off a settlement with India, because the debacle to which he has succeeded has left him with very little options in foreign affairs; while, on his part, he aims at making use of any accretion of popularity as a result of a deal with India to stabilise his precarious position inside Pakistan. Immediately, he is anxious to get his ninety thousand POWs back home, but he has also realised that the return of the POWs is linked with two other inescapable issues—the de-escalation of the war-time alert on the frontier, and the recognition of Bangladesh which is a party to the acceptance of the surrender of the overwhelming bulk of the POWs on the eastern front.

Dhar seemed to have spared no pains in making clear New Delhi's stand on these points. The reference in the Joint Statement to the discussions "bearing on the establishment of durable peace in the subcontinent" is significant. This is no mere rhetoric nor pious wish; concretely, it implies that the readiness to settle issues in dispute between the two countries without resort to arms, even if Bhutto is not immediately in a position to settle all disputes, particularly over Kashmir. The absence of any reference to the question of the release of the POWs in the Joint Statement leaves room for the assumption that New Delhi's position that the POWs' release is linked with steps towards durable peace, has been substantially conceded by Rawalpindi.

There has obviously been no mincing of words on the part of the Indian delegation with regard to the imperative of the Bangladesh recognition by Pakistan. Realism has to dawn upon Bhutto on this score if he has to get his boys back home. On this point, one cannot help noting the specific formulation in the Joint Statement about "durable peace in the subcontinent"—instead of just between India and Pakistan—which can hardly be achieved without Bangladesh participating in all formality as the third member-state of this subcontinent.

The overall assessment of the Murree talks, therefore, warrants the assumption that solid ground has been prepared for not only the convening of the Indo-Pak summit early in June but its tangible success towards the settlement of outstanding disputes between the two countries. Bhutto should have reasons to feel assured that New Delhi, dictated by its own enlightened self-interest, is interested neither in the break-up of Pakistan as it stands today, nor in the overthrow of Bhutto with all his mercurial manoeuvres and acrobatics.

The fragmentation of Pakistan into petty principalities can be the happy hunting ground of international power-politics, while the uncertainty that may come over Pakistan in the event of Bhutto being toppled will bring no peace for India but may force her to heighten her vigilance—unless, of course, such a development ushers in a stable democratic order in Pakistan, ready to live in peace and friendship with India, as Bangladesh has been doing to the mutual benefit of both.

The crux of the entire problem of normalising Indo-Pak relations—and for the matter of that, achieving durable peace in the relations between the three countries, India, Bangladesh and Pakistan—depends on one crucial decision that Bhutto and the people of Pakistan have to take if any endeavour at settlement of disputes whether at the Summit or any other level has to succeed.

This is the question of third-party intervention or active

interest in the disputes relating to the countries in this subcontinent. This is not an isolationist outlook. This compulsion is born out of the tragic history of Indo-Pak relations in the last twenty five years.

Apart from the fact that Pakistan was born largely as a British-inspired counterblast to the militant anti-imperialist nationalism of the Indian people, the scourge that has never left Pakistan has been the domination of the Western Powers, first the British and then the USA. While internally this domination has undermined the democratic urges of the people as also the quest for economic independence by installing a military elite propped up with US aid, in the sphere of external relations it has clearly helped to intensify Indo-Pak intransigence.

The British backing of the Pak raiders into Kashmir in 1947 was followed by the intensification of Pakistan's drive towards militarism in the late fifties and throughout the sixties.

It is important to note that the first full-scale armed conflict between India and Pakistan, in 1965, took place at a time when the US influence was at its high water-mark in both the countries. By then, Pakistan under Ayub had become, in the words of President Kennedy, "a friend of immediacy and constancy". On the other side, the US influence over India registered a phenomenal rise after Nehru's death. Under Shastri, the pro-West elements got entrenched in the establishment.

The significance of all this comes out from the fact that the dominance of US influence over either or both Pakistan and India can never bring peace and amity between the two countries. Instead, it has led to the path of war and mutual ruin. Indo-Pak relations in the last twentyfive years provide a sophisticated variant of the traditional Washington policy of making Asians fight Asians.

With US imperialism in retreat after the spectacular beating that American prestige has been getting at the hands of the heroic Vietnamese people, Washington has been forced to establish its rapport with Peking. In the case of Pakistan, this is an additional source of encouragement for provocation, since China in her present mood would not like India to get stronger, particularly in the context of closer Indo-Soviet ties.

While the US and her Afro-Asian allies like Saudi Arabia, Libya, Jordan and Iran are engaged in offering arms and aid to Pakistan in a bid to keep up the confrontation against India, the Chinese approach, so far as it can be known, is that Pakistan need make no attempt to settle with India on a give-and-take basis since in Peking's view, India can be made to eat the humble pie even on the POW issue by a massive denunciation through the UN machinery. The newly acquired vantage point in the UN is being utilised by Peking to the maximum for playing the game of power-politics in this region as well.

The Asian policy of both the USA and China today does not permit either of these two powers to sustain a durable peace in this subcontinent. The strategy of both Washington and Peking at the moment—though for different reasons—strongly favours the continuation of a state of hostility, if not actual conflict, among the countries in this region, particularly between India and Pakistan. It is not without reason that the Chou-Nixon communique made specific reference to the dispute over Kashmir and encouraged a posture of provocation over the issue.

It is in this background that New Delhi has consistently been insisting on direct, bilateral talks between the two countries. Even in the matter of arranging the preliminaries of the Indo-Pak talks, Indira Gandhi chose to write direct to Z. A. Bhutto instead of seeking third-party good offices. On the question of selecting the venue of talks, both at the envoys' level and for the Summit, she has declined all suggestions for any place in a third country.

Similarly, in the substantive negotiations, New Delhi's stand has been that both the countries should agree not only not to resort to arms but also not seek outside mediation in any form, through the UN or otherwise. The Joint Statement makes no mention of this important element in New Delhi's stand as having been accepted by Rawalpindi, nor is there any other sign of Bhutto being willing to give up the UN crutches now that his Peking physicians have been enthusiastically prescribing it.

Bereft of this important support, any readiness on Pakistan's part to renounce the use of arms in settling mutual disputes loses much of its strength in the specific conditions of power-politics postures towards this subcontinent. This is a point which New Delhi will have to emphasise over and over again in the coming crucial weeks, and finally Indira Gandhi herself will have to take it up with Bhutto at the Summit.

This will involve a major operation in Pakistan's foreign policy; but if Bhutto goes in for it, the gangrene that has set in Pakistan's politics, both at home and abroad, will definitely be removed. And this alone will ensure not only peace among the three countries of this subcontinent but also open up the prospect of well-being for their peoples.

The journey beyond Murree is no doubt hazardous but the risk is well worth taking.

(May 6, 1972)

19

Miles to go for Pakistan

It is usetui to look upon the Indo-Pak Summit against the wider background of social and political awakening in Asia. What do the two states stand for? What has been their respective record in the last twenty five years since they attained Independence? To a large measure, the answers to these questions provide the clue to the ultimate outcome of the Simla Summit which is yet to be known as these lines are being written.

By the yardstick of accepted ideological categories, India and Pakistan belong to the same type of social system, namely, they are what is called in the language of the Marxist, bourgeois states. And yet between the two, there is a world of difference and it is this difference that accounts for the divergence in the course of developments that the two countries have traversed in the last two decades-and-a-half.

From the outset, Pakistan started as a political set-up more inclined to depend on Western imperialist support, at that time mainly the British. The very origin of Pakistan was, to a large measure, facilitated by the British strategy of dividing the powerful national upsurge for freedom in India, and the founding fathers of Pakistan, even the best of them, did not object to it, because of their misgivings-turned-into-obsession about the danger of domination by the majority community in an independent India. This obsession was exploited to the hilt by those in the leadership of the Pakistan movement, who really acted as the camp followers of the British.

It may sound irrelevant to recapitulate this history, but if one goes deeper, one finds its importance for the contemporary developments. The very first months after independence saw the outbreak of a conflict between the two new-born states which has continued like a festering sore even today, and provides the biggest hurdle to cross at Simla.

This is the problem of Kashmir. And subsequent disclosures have made it clear how the British engineered to make it an issue of bitter acrimony between the two states. On the side of Pakistan, the British hand in inciting the armed attack on Kashmir is now undeniable, for even British officers were found to have masterminded the offensive. On the Indian side, Mountbatten tried his best to delay the defence of Srinagar and when, overruling his objections, the newly-formed Government in New Delhi rushed reinforcements and the Indian troops were about to clear the entire Valley of the invaders, Mountbatten persuaded it to agree to a Cease Fire, thereby letting Pakistani forces have a foothold on a portion of the Valley. Again, it was Mountbatten who initiated the idea of taking the case to the UN and, almost on his own, put forward the proposal for a plebiscite despite the fact that the State's ruler had already signed the Instrument of Accession to India, and the accredited leadership of Kashmir's national movement, with Sheikh Abdullah at its head, had taken the lead in Kashmir remaining a part of India.

After the British came the Americans. It is no secret that the US strategists could succeed in enmeshing Pakistan into its military alliances because the democratic resistance to it was weak inside Pakistan. In the power set-up in the newly-carved state, it was the western wing which dominated, and in the western wing, it was the military-feudal complex that held sway, and it is this clique which was strengthened by Western support to suppress democracy at home and make Pakistan a client state of the US in the international sphere.

The culmination of this politics came in the mid-fifties when Pakistan's military alliances with the USA were not only formalised but the hand of the CIA and the Pentagon could be discerned in the political convulsions that rocked the state, leading it through a succession of unstable regimes until by the end of the decade, a military dictatorship was put on the saddle at the behest of Washington. The entire economy of the state became dependent on dollar aid, while its defence, foreign policy and foreign trade were mortgaged to the USA. Neo-colonialism ceased to be a mere Left jargon in Pakistan; it became the stark reality.

The vassal state became almost a plaything of the global politics of the USA. The setting up of the U-2 spy flight base near Peshwar was only one example—though the most dramatic—of this great conspiracy. Constantly, the hate-campaign against India was worked up and the constant infiltration and almost non-stop efforts at subversion inside Kashmir culminated in the war of 1965. As part of the same strategy of consolidating a military junta to act as the watchdog of US imperialism, the politically awakened eastern wing of Pakistan was sought to be stifled.

This grand strategy met its first rebuff in 1965 when with all the myth of Pakistan's first-class war machine—in contrast to the then discredited Indian military standing after the 1962 debacle of the Chinese attack—was broken, since Kashmir could not be captured, and for the time being, Washington lost face so badly that it could not even take the initiative for a truce, as it could in the first round of clashes over Kashmir in 1947-48. Hence came the Soviet initiative for peace at Tashkent—the first time Pakistan had to move out of the US orbit in international diplomacy.

Then came the new stage in US diplomacy. The Sino-Soviet rift provided it with a god-send and so the first overtures were made to Peking, and Pakistan, as the client state, was used for the job. President Ayub himself claimed to be acting as the broker between Washington and Peking, a role which was confirmed when Dr Kissinger chose Islamabad as the safest point of departure for his secret flight to Peking last year. This new role of Pakistan as an ally of Peking helped to mislead a large section of the world into the false hope that Islamabad's ties with Washington were being weakened. And Ayub played this false role with consummate skill, and even undertook the mission to Moscow.

However, the basic loyalty of Pakistan's military junta to the USA remained steadfast. This could be seen not only in the rapid replenishment of arms by the USA and its allies and stooges, but by the blatant stand that the USA took during last year's struggle for the liberation of Bangladesh. With all the publicity in the world press about the Pak military genocide in Bangladesh, Washington remained unmoved and determined in its support for Yahya Khan's regime, to the point of even despatching its formidable Seventh Fleet to the Bay of Bengal. Washington's bitterness against New Delhi was heightened with the Indo-Soviet Treaty and the subsequent intervention by India on the side of the freedom-fighters in Bangladesh.

But the Bourbons do not die easily. And even today, the Generals, though humbled, are not totally dislodged in Pakistan's politics. Today Pakistan finds herself in a strange twilight—the glittering days of the military regime, giving a false sense of security to the country, are over, and yet the democratic forces, long suppressed, are not still in a state of health that can enable them to take over power. Hence, a quick-change artiste of the type of Bhutto can dominate the stage. His contradictory statements, hysterical postures and unbalanced political moves reflect the state of instability in which Pakistan finds itself today.

Which way should she go? The path followed during the last twentyfive years has led her to humiliation, disaster and disintegration of the state-structure itself. If this path is pursued further, then Pakistan's viability as a state is in danger. The different nationalities inside can no longer be suppressed by the jackboot of the military junta. And even as a military power, she has lost face both with India and Bangladesh.

The alternative path not only ensures her much-needed peace but guarantees her security in a system of neighbourly amity and mutual pledge of non-aggression. The economy can be reorganised on the principle of self-reliance, without the cramping crutches of the dollar. But to take this line, it has to delink itself from Washington's military-bloc politics. Bhutto's recent move to activise Pakistan's membership of the CENTO is a step in the wrong direction.

It is only out of the suffocating grip of the military alliances that Pakistan can breathe the air of freedom.

Non-alignment has given strength to India both politically and militarily for she did not have to move by the puppet-strings from Washington.

Hence, the two key points in India's stand at Simla are, firstly, that all disputes between the two neighbours have to be settled through peaceful means and not through resort to arms. This will on the one hand dispel all fears generated by interested propaganda that India's superior might poses a threat for Pakistan, and on the other hand neutralise the grip of the military clique which will be bereft of the bogey of India.

Secondly, India's insistence against third-party intervention will not only help to strengthen the natural relations between two neighbouring states, organically bound together, but will undermine the grip of Western imperialism over Pakistan.

The road ahead from Simla offers for Pakistan a new vista, not only of peace with honour but of reassertion of real independence, both political and economic. It is for the people of Pakistan to decide how they should mandate their leadership to make the right choice.

(July 1, 1972)

20

Prospect from Simla

If cautious optimism marked the approach of New Delhi to the Indo-Pak Summit before it took place, it persists, more or less in the same measure, even after the Simla Agreement. At the same time, there is no question of belittling the positive achievements of the accord reached between Indira Gandhi and Z. A. Bhutto.

It is difficult to draw up the balance-sheet of the Simla Summit at this moment because one is not clear how Bhutto will not only be tackling his critics at home but how he himself would be viewing the problems involved in the establishment of a durable peace between the two countries, of which the Simla Agreement marks but the first, though a very important, step.

The two basic points in the Indian stand have throughout been that there must be no resort to arms in the settlement of all disputes between the two countries, and secondly, that there should be no third-party intervention in any of the Indo-Pak disputes, the two countries to adhere to the principle of bilateral approach. The very first chapter of the Simla Agreement elaborates both these basic points in great detail.

It is an open secret now that the Pakistan delegation at the Simla Conference, particularly the seasoned officials in it, fought hard to retain the option of calling in the UN intervention in the Indo-Pak disputes; but at the end, they subscribed to the Indian position as laid down in the opening chapter of the Agreement.

On this aspect, the Simla Agreement marks a definite advance over the 1966 Tashkent Declaration. At Tashkent, the two sides stated: "They reaffirm their obligation under the Charter not to have recourse to force and to settle their disputes through peaceful means." But nowhere was there any commitment to settle differences not only by peaceful means but "through bilateral negotiations or by any other peaceful means mutually agreed upon between them".

On the substantive question of Kashmir also, the advance made at Simla over Tashkent is noteworthy. The Tashkent Declaration only mentioned that "Jammu and Kashmir was discussed, and each of the sides set forth its respective positions". In contrast, the Smile Agreement committed both the sides to meet "to discuss further the modalities and arrangements for the establishment of durable peace and normalisation of relations" and these were specifically to include "a final settlement of Jammu and Kashmir".

This is indeed the first time that India and Pakistan agreed to explore the ways and means for a final settlement of the vexed issue of Jammu and Kashmir, and that too, through the wisdom and statesmanship of their own leaders without outside help. This way, Simla marks a new stage in the maturity of Indo-Pak leadership in the field of diplomacy.

This is partly the result of the bitter experience of the last twentyfive years which has shown that neither periodic resort to arms nor protracted debates, negotiations and behind-the-scene talks at the UN could bring the two countries nearer to a solution of the problem of Kashmir. An equally important contribution towards the evolution of this new bilateral approach has been provided—at last for Pakistan—by the fiasco of the military-bloc policy under the aegis of the USA. When Pakistan joined the US-sponsored military blocs in the mid-fifties, its military leadership was supremely confident that the superiority in arms that this policy would fetch for them would help them to overpower Indian defence, and so Kashmir could be seized without difficulty. It was not without significance that the first major attempt to do so was made in 1965 at the height of the prestige and glory of President Ayub, who was the best product of the US-Pak military-bloc politics. And the second attempt to seize Kashmir was made last year when President Yahya Khan was sure of getting the arms backing of not only Washington but of Peking as well.

The failure of both these attempts made it clear that the military prowess generated by the politics of armed blocs can be no match for a democratic country whose basic strength lies in the support of the masses—an element which was totally lacking in the Pak leadership until Bhutto came to the scene. It is therefore a testimony not only to the fiasco of the military-bloc politics that Pakistan has so long followed but to the sense of realism born out of an awareness of the mass urges that could enable Bhutto to agree to the need for a final settlement of Jammu and Kashmir.

At the same time, his inability to undertake the job of settling the Kashmir issue at Simla, is proof of the yet fragile structure of the democratic process in Pakistan itself. On the one hand, the hawks represented by the unrepentant section of the Generals and the die-hard civil servants—whose weight could not but be felt at Simla—and on the other, the disunity and mutual squabbling of the popular forces, stood in the way of a bold policy over Kashmir being followed by the Pakistani delegation at Simla. It was rather surprising that the political elements that came in Bhutto's entourage chose to play no role at all in the evolution of the Agreement; rather they gave one the impression of being waiting and watching to catch Bhutto where and when he would trip. The maturity of India's democratic order, with the unassailable mandate that Indira Gandhi enjoys today, has come out in bold relief when put side by side with the incipient democratic urges represented in the Pak delegation at Simla.

Bhutto did represent the consensus inside Pakistan when in his press conference a few hours before the Agreement was signed, he said that over the issue of Kashmir, Pakistan was sticking to the "principle" while India to its "position". On the face of it, this sounds rather patronising as if the Indian position in Kashmir is bereft of principle—particularly when it was India that had originally lodged the complaint against the Pak invasion of Kashmir, which had legally and constitutionally opted to join the Indian Union. However, Bhutto's phraseology was the politician's way of putting across the suggestion that Pakistan was only propagating the principle of self-determination while the Indian position was born out of the reality of the Kashmir situation.

It was obvious that at Simla this question could hardly be thrashed out: since Bhutto by his own admission during the talks was scared of the attack he would have to face at home if he had explicitly abandoned the political position that the Pak rulers had so long been preaching about Kashmir. While he publicly reiterated Pakistan's adherence to Kashmir's right of self-determination, he left it in no doubt, during the talks at the highest level, that he did not believe in the theory of exporting self-determination.

In the Agreement itself, Bhutto had to concede that "in Jammu and Kashmir the line of control resulting from the ceasefire of December 17, 1971 shall be respected by both sides without prejudice to the recognised position of either side. Neither side shall seek to alter it unilaterally irrespective of mutual differences and legal interpretations. Both sides further undertake to refrain from the threat or the use of force in violation of this line."

Moreover, in the very first chapter, the commitment was jointly made that "pending the final settlement of any of the problems between the two countries, neither side shall unilaterally alter the situation and both shall prevent the organisation, assistance or encouragement of any acts detrimental to the maintenance of peaceful and harmonious relations".

This puts the stamp of a commitment not to encourage saboteurs, infiltrators and the raising of the so-called Azad Kashmir forces on the part of Pakistan. Incidentally, the Tashkent Declaration did not, on this score, go beyond declaring that the relations between the two countries "shall be based on the principle of non-interference in the internal affairs of each other".

Another indication of the recognition, by implication, of the need for a final settlement on Kashmir is provided by the stipulation in the Simla Agreement that the Cease Fire Line in Jammu and Kashmir would be the one of actual control as it stood at the end of the December conflict. This is an admission by the Pakistani authorities that the UN fiat would no longer hold good in Jammu and Kashmir, for the UN had always insisted on the 1949 Cease Fire Line, a point which was conceded by both sides at Tashkent. An obvious by-product of this stand should be that the UN Observers still clinging on to the Jammu and Kashmir border should be asked to withdraw, since they no longer can claim to have any *locus standi*.

Regarding the other aspects of the Simla Agreement, India has vindicated her stand that there could be no settlement behind the back of Bangladesh on the question of repatriation of the POWs. Although this was made clear at Murree, the Pak delegation in the initial round of the Simla talks gave the impression that they could persuade India to treat Sheikh Mujibur Rahman much in the same way as they were used to treating the so-called Azad Kashmir leaders. When Bhutto and his team found that Indira Gandhi not only regarded Bangladesh as an independent and sovereign state but that Sheikh Mujibur Rahman as entrenched in the confidence of the people in Bangladesh as much as she herself in India or Bhutto in Pakistan, the sense of realism led him not to press for the release of the POWs until he had sorted out the question of the recognition of Bangladesh which, according to informed sources, he is expected to do by the middle of August, if not earlier.

The entire question has brought out a significant dimension in India's foreign policy. If New Delhi is keen on burying the dead past in its relations with Islamabad, it is equally eager on strengthening the edifice of friendship and solidarity that has already been consolidated in the ordeal of struggle in its relations with Dacca. There can be no question of placating the one at the expense of the other, however difficult and complex this new responsibility may be.

The Simla talks have also brought out the correctness of India's sense of priorities. It started by laying down the general principles that should guide the relations between the two countries. Once that framework of durable peace was conceded, India had no hesitation in accommodating Pakistan's demand for a step-by-step approach. Hence, the resilience on India's part not to try to force a settlement of the Kashmir issue at Simla and the commitment was readily made in the Agreement itself that the Heads of the two Governments "will meet again at a mutually convenient time in the future" and in the meanwhile, the representatives of the two sides would be sorting out all the details towards normalisation of relations, which include, besides Kashmir, the question of not only of POWs but civilian internees as well, and also the question of resumption of diplomatic relations.

From Tashkent and the experience that followed from it, there is reason for India to activate its approach to Pakistan in the coming months. Once Bhutto succeeds in getting the Simla Agreement ratified by the Pak National Assembly, it will be the responsibility of India as the more powerful of the two parties to initiate, in a sustained manner, the drive towards detente in all spheres—from political to cultural, from the exchange of scientific delegations to working out the norms of what the Simla Agreement lays down as "the dissemination of such information as would promote the development of friendly relations between them".

There were sufficient indications, available even during the hectic days at Simla, that the response to such an initiative will be definitely positive and fruitful as could be made out from the brief but significant statement made by one of the leading progressive figures in Pakistan today,

Mazhar Ali Khan, who, when taking off on his return journey, hailed the Simla Agreement as "the first step" and held out the hope that the last war would be "the last in every sense". It would be the urgent task as well as the final responsibility for the forward looking forces in this country to act in such a way that such forces are strengthened and the wall of hate between the two countries built over the years is finally pulled down.

For that, the progressives in both countries will have to pledge themselves never to allow the forces of imperialism to gain a foothold and sow the seeds of discord, and in this noble endeavour they have to welcome with open arms the brothers in Bangladesh to form a new fraternity of friendship and mutual help, providing a model for the rest of Asia.

(July 8, 1972)

21

Mobilising Mass Sanction

It would have been naive to have expected that the ratification of the Simla Summit Agreement by the Pak National Assembly would have been marked by a temper of peaceful friendliness towards this country. The forces which persist to be hostile, egged on by powers that are definitely sore at India's success in helping in the liberation of Bangladesh, are still entrenched in Pakistan's bedlam of politics although they have lost the whip-hand with the military debacle in the December conflict.

It was indeed a strange spectacle to find the patently contradictory picture in the Pak National Assembly: on the one hand, it ratified the Simla Agreement by an overwhelming majority, and on the other hand, the debate was made into an occasion for anti-India diatribes by a fairly large number of speakers. The voice of sanity was feeble despite the collective wisdom displayed in ratifying the Simla Agreement.

Bhutto himself by his startlingly contradictory postures represented the dilemma in which Pak politics has been placed today. On the one hand, it has perforce to agree to a policy of non-confrontation with India, at least for the time being, while the logic of a policy of peace and good neighbourliness with India is yet unacceptable with all its implications. To borrow a cliché, Pakistan indeed has reached the crossroads: the very compulsions of the objective situation demands the establishment of a durable peace with India, while the powerful vested interests, political, economic and military, forged during the last twentyfive years, militate against the acceptance of such a relationship with this country.

It is immaterial what Bhutto's personal predilections are, because if any political leader in the wide world today is a creature of circumstances, no doubt it is Bhutto. However, he has learnt the hard way that his own survival in power demands, in the ultimate analysis, the staving off of another military showdown; hence his final plea for the ratification of the Simla Agreement. At the same time, he has yet to gather the political stature to overpower his thunder-jet critics or the wisdom to conduct politics with the least amount of self-contradictory antics and utterances.

Under the circumstances, it is but natural for New Delhi to follow a line of cautious optimism. As the Prime Minister made it clear at her press conference on July 12, the Government has taken the Simla Agreement as "a very important beginning". Already, the preparations for the next stage of this policy of dialogue are being made, as revealed this week by her Principal Secretary during his mission to Dacca and the Foreign Secretary during his mission to Kathmandu.

While at the Governmental level the necessary steps are being taken towards laying the foundations for a durable peace—the high-level talks in Dacca are part of the same endeavour—what is rather striking is the conspicuous absence of any political campaign inside the country to educate public opinion about the significance of the Simla settlement and the perspective that follows from it.

In a functioning democracy, such as ours, it is not sufficient to face Parliament with a massive majority behind the ruling party. There are elements in the ruling party itself which are either ignorant about or indifferent to the implications of the Simla stand by the Prime Minister and her colleagues. It is rather extraordinary that no campaign has been launched by the Congress nor by the parties that agree with the Government about the necessity and the positive potentialities of the Simla Agreement, to politicalise public opinion on this crucial issue of national urgency.

The result has been that the Jan Sangh has taken the opportunity to start an uninhibited campaign against the Simla Agreement as a sell-out. The Jan Sangh, which was practically sent out into the wilderness after the terrible mauling it received in the State Assembly elections three months ago, has been trying many palliatives to keep together its disillusioned and frustrated ranks. Fissures appeared in even the leadership as was evident from the revolt by M.L. Sondhi. It tried the gimmick of launching a crusade against the AIR which turned out to be a fiasco. It has now announced a new campaign against price rise, perhaps a revised version of another misfired agitation a few months ago.

However, Vajpayee seems to have taken a lot in his campaign against the Simla Agreement, though it is interesting to note that he can also make overtures to the new Swatantra chief, Piloo Mody, who claims to be a personal friend of Bhutto.

The Jan Sangh campaign against Simla is indeed a measure of the political lethargy into which the Congress and other progressive parties have lapsed back since the strain and stress of the March electoral battle. Neither on the issue of the Simla Agreement, nor on the question of the drive towards self-reliance from US aid nor on the subject of land reforms, there is as yet a wide-awake awareness of the need to gear the masses into action. Unless this is done, the field is left free for the discredited and the undesirable to carry on with their campaign of misinformation and confusion, on which parties like the Jan Sangh ultimately thrive.

It is not enough to climb the heights of Simla but to open the floodgates of mass support that alone can ensure a rich harvest in the days to come.

(July 22, 1972)

22

Tripartite and Beyond

The Indo-Pak-Bangla Agreement signed this week in New Delhi is no doubt a significant landmark on the political scene in this part of the world. Its immediate implication is that the crisis that had been brought about by the brutal military crackdown by the Pak Government upon the people of Bangladesh three years ago, has at last been solved—at least on the formal plane—with the vindications of the stand taken by Bangladesh and upheld by the Government and people of this country.

There are hack writers in this country with pronounced pro-US leanings who have been taking great pains to sow seeds of discord between India and Bangladesh, just as there are scribes, both known and anonymous, in Dacca who have been trying to belittle the stature of Sheikh Mujibur Rahman and desperately trying to spread misunderstanding between the two countries. Not accidentally, it is the tribe which has been frowning upon New Delhi's criticism against the setting up of the American naval and air base at Diego Garcia. What is strange is that this species get the liberal hospitality of the Government's mass media perhaps to demonstrate how freedom of opinion operates in this country.

But these pompous pundits, are they really free? Have

they been expressing their own opinions as good Indian patriots? Would it not be more correct to say that they have been serving the interests for which Ambassador Moynihan is accredited to this country? Washington's game is to drive a wedge between India and Bangladesh, and nothing could be better than to get this done by the natives masquerading as moulders of public opinion. Obviously all this costs the US Administration less than sending the Seventh Fleet into these waters, and the dividends are expected to be higher, for it seeks to unleash confusion. Another variant of the infamous US strategy: Make Asians fight Asians.

How much harm these toadies can do is questionable. Since the common people, whether in this country or in Bangladesh, are imbued with robust anti-imperialism. It was largely this which led the people of Bangladesh to get out of the US-dominated Pak regime and it is the same anti-imperialist consciousness which has enabled the Indian people not only to actively help in the liberation of Bangladesh but also to refuse to give in to Dr Moynihan's blandishments on the economic front despite the back-breaking economic privations they have been facing today.

The long-range perspective opened up by this week's New Delhi Agreement imposes certain responsibilities which demand statesmanship in the conduct of our foreign affairs. No doubt the three years of painstaking diplomacy has borne fruit. In 1971, New Delhi had to strain its nerves and resources to the maximum to convince both friends and adversaries about the justness of the cause of Bangladesh.

In 1972, it applied itself to the building of the structure of durable peace in the subcontinent—a task which demanded not only patience and hard labour but adroitness to bring the mercurial Bhutto round to agree to the Simla Agreement, which had been preceded by the Twentyfive year Treaty of Friendship, Cooperation and Peace between India and Bangladesh.

The year 1973 saw renewed efforts at breaking the deadlock created mainly by Bhutto's failure to keep his assurance to recognise Bangladesh. The initiative came once again from the renewed efforts of New Delhi and Dacca in their Joint Declaration of April 17, 1973. Then came the protracted—sometimes almost agonising—negotiations with Pakistan which finally brought about the New Delhi Agreement of August 1973.

Bhutto's recognition of Bangladesh on February 23 this year was the inevitable corollary of the last year's Indo-Pak Agreement. Strictly speaking, this week's Tripartite Agreement marks the implementation of the last year's New Delhi Agreement between India and Pakistan, while the simultaneous Indo-Pak Agreement provides for the follow-up steps envisaged in the 1972 Simla Agreement.

The normalisation of relations among the three countries of the subcontinent implies something more than the end of a period of hostility. If peace in South Asia has to be made enduring, it is necessary for all the three countries to have a common identity in the direction of their foreign policy. The experience of the Indo-Pak relations in the last twentyseven years since independence has been that the root cause of the tension that persisted throughout has been the widening divergence in the foreign policy approach between the two countries. Pakistan's continued dependence on the West in contrast to India's striving for an independent stand, unshackling herself from the colonial past, was responsible for the attitude of confrontation instead of cooperation in the relations between the two countries.

In the mid-fifties, the logic of this divergence led Pakistan into the American global network of military alliances, and India to assert non-alignment from the politics of military blocs. One led to the path of more and more dependence—military, economic and political—upon Washington; and the other, with all its shortcomings, to the striving for economic independence and political assertion in foreign affairs. The US military-bloc politics has weakened Pakistan even internally, since the Pentagon-propped military junta made it unbearable for Bangladesh to stay within the framework of Pakistan, while India's non-alignment enabled her to garner the resources for building the infrastructure for not only economic self-reliance but a relatively stable democratic order. It is not just an accident that the very forces (whether in Opposition or in the ruling party) which, in the main, have been trying today to cash in on the prevailing economic distress, are the ones that have always scoffed at non-alignment and have sought to undermine the efforts at self-reliance.

Against this background, one has to understand the significance of Indo-Bangladesh friendship. It is based not on mere effusion of sentimentality nor on the sense of jubiliation that Pakistan was dismembered. Essentially, it is based on the solid foundation of an identity of basic outlook in foreign affairs. The leaders and the masses of Sonar Bangla have known from bitter experience what it means to be under the heels of a regime that is caught in the vice grip of US military alliance network: the denial of freedom abroad and democracy at home. Sheikh Mujibur Rahman's adherence to non-alignment is born out of direct experience of life; for, he knows how the grim alternative of the US military bloc politics can emasculate a self-respecting nation.

Nobody need have any illusion that there may be differences in emphasis and presentation of issues between Dacca and New Delhi. For, every country has its own way of expressing and asserting its role in world affairs. However, that does not take one away from the commonness of basic approach between the two countries, and that is, their common abhorrence of the Washington-sponsored military-bloc politics. It is not that Dacca will not be subjected to pressures and pleadings by the Western bloc—and now joined in by the Chinese—to break away from this identity of common foreign-policy strategy with New Delhi. But there is reason to believe that the Bangladesh leadership would be able to see through such a move—as it has already so far—since it is committed to the building of an independent state, refusing to play the vassal to any foreign power.

It is for New Delhi to grasp this significant point and do all in its power to strengthen the ties between Bangladesh and India, unruffled by all the mischievous propaganda in both the countries: such propaganda is to be taken as an index of the despair that has overtaken all those who have been dreaming of establishing Pax Americana in South Asia, muffling the spirit of independence as embodied in the policy of non-alignment. After the ignominious rebuff it has suffered in Vietnam, Washington has been desperately trying to avert the spectre of its exit from this part of the world by combining the demonstration of the Pentagon's mailed fist, as exemplified by Diego Garcia, and the intensification of the CIA's blatantly subversive operations of the Chilean brand, hoping to exploit the acute economic difficulties that face the countries of the region.

In the complex situation such as the present, both India

and Bangladesh will have to firmly deal with domestic Reaction as well as US blackmail—the two synchronising their offensive in the prevailing difficulties. And to do so, neither can afford to deviate from their time-tested policy which in the sphere of foreign affairs means adherence to non-alignment, and in that of economic affairs, the fight for self-reliance.

At the same time, both the countries will have to realise that no peace or amity in this subcontinent can be durable unless Pakistan is also brought within this orbit of independence. The record of the successive regimes in Pakistan naturally raises misgivings about its capacity to break away from the politics of subservience to Washington. Bhutto, with his quick-changing political postures, has yet to prove his bonafides on this score. Sometimes he turns west to establish Pakistan's identity with other client regimes of the US such as that of the Shah of Iran; sometimes he blatantly relies on the feudal set-up in Saudi Arabia, another outpost of the US in the Middle East; sometimes he goes in for bellicosity against Iraq, which has firmly held out against Washington. There is nothing wrong in his playing the host to the Islamic Summit. But all this cannot cover up his continued dependence on the US bounties, whether in the form of military hardware or direct dollar subvention, received direct or through third-party arrangements.

Although the people and the Governments of Pakistan will have to learn primarily from their own experience—as has been done by the leaders of Bangladesh—there should be no missing of any opportunity on the part of Dacca and New Delhi to impress upon Pakistan the positive advantages of rallying by the side of Bangladesh and India in a common endeavour for the defence of the independence of the subcontinent against the inroads of colonial powers. If Islamabad draws the correct lessons from the reverse it suffered in 1971, it should not be difficult for it to comprehend the folly of reliance on the Pentagon. But it has yet to display that wisdom has dawned upon it from the setback: it is one of the few countries of the Indian Ocean littoral that has not objected to the US plan of the Diego Garcia base.

To build the edifice of durable peace in the subcontinent is not going to be an easy job. Nevertheless, its prospects have definitely brightened with the enhanced political standing that India and Bangladesh today command—both individually and jointly—in the affairs of Asia. It is this, together with the projection of a policy of friendly overtures on the part of New Delhi and Dacca, that may help Islamabad to retrace its steps from disastrous dependence on the US and its cronies, and join its two subcontinental neighbours in evolving a common strategy of independence based on non-alignment.

This alone can ensure the building of the structure of durable peace in this subcontinent, once lacerated by colonial domination and now refusing to be a prey to any neo-colonial offensive.

(April 13, 1974)

23

Kashmir: Journey to Settlement

There is persistent optimism in Srinagar that an agreement on the broad framework of constitutional arrangement between the Government of India and Sheikh Abdullah has been already arrived at, and that the current dialogue between G. Parthasarathy and Mirza Afzal Beg is aimed at detailed discussion of concrete issues—an exercise meant to prepare public opinion all over the country for an eventual settlement.

The priorities held earlier for such a settlement are being changed to fit in with fresh thinking on the subject. With a shift in the correlation of forces marked by Pakistan's hostility towards Sheikh Abdullah, enabling the latter to increasingly demarcate himself from the extremist fringe in Kashmir, there is confidence both within the pro-Abdullah camp and New Delhi that time has come for a Kashmir settlement.

Informed sources say that a formula has been hammered out under which issues of substance raised by the Sheikh have already been dealt with and the stage has been set for a change over in the State. According to these sources, the present Government headed by Syed Mir

Qasim will step down—around October-November—to pave the way for a mid-term poll either in March 1975 or in 1976, coinciding with the scheduled election for Parliament.

The remaining constitutional issues which need a threadbare discussion and participation of representatives of two other regions of the State, namely, Jammu and Ladakh, are expected to be entrusted for solution to an experts' committee headed by a person of high judicial experience. It is to prepare the ground for such a step and also to win back the confidence of the public in Jammu and Kashmir that Sheikh Abdullah took the initiative for the recent convention at Srinagar.

One of the major factors enforcing a change in the priorities is the situation created by Pakistan which has been concentrating forces on the State's borders in a bid to make its claim on Kashmir known to the world, at a time when settlement is in the offing. These troop concentrations are of considerable magnitude, as if these are preparations for a first-class military offensive.

Coinciding with this fresh spurt of armed activity in the border regions is the report of increased espionage inside the State by Pakistan. Eleven Pakistanis, who had managed to recruit themselves in the State Militia, have been arrested. These include two officers of the Pakistan Army. There are also reports about some of the leading members of the Pakistani underground mission being busy, and these include the reported trip of one Bashir Kitchlu having gone to China for brain-washing and guerilla training. Kitchlu was active also during the 1965 war.

Another straw in the ill-wind is the increased anti-Abdullah activity by Mirwaiz Farooq's party which is currently heading the forces opposed to the dialogue with New Delhi.

The Sheikh has welcomed this shift in the situation marked by open hostility of Pakistan towards him. This enables him to demarcate himself from the pro-Pakistani elements in Kashmir and take the battle to the streets to mobilise his followers firmly on his side for a settlement with New Delhi.

In the recent clashes between pro-Abdullah groups and those of the Awami Action Committee, the Sheikh's men raised slogans like "Raj Karegi, Raj Karegi—Indira Karegi, Indira Karegi" and "Azad Hindustan Zindabad". These and other changes in the totality of the situation in Kashmir indicate that the situation is ripe for effecting major changes in the existing set-up in Kashmir.

This should not, however, be construed to mean that success is round the corner without any impediments in the way. Both Indira Gandhi and Sheikh Abdullah have been moving in the direction of an agreement, overcoming a complex situation in which advance towards success is inhibited by their respective commitments—the Sheikh wanting a solution which can approximate to the pre-1953 situation in the State and Indira Gandhi under pressure not to give in to reversing the clock of "integration". It is an open secret that within the Union Government there is an in-built resistance to granting any major concessions to the Sheikh's viewpoint.

Likewise, there are strong misgivings in the Sheikh's camp that a settlement which does not fully meet the major demand of restoring the pre-1953 position would leave the Sheikh and his supporters powerless against the onslaught of those in the State who have been accusing him of betrayal. What the Sheikh wants is a solution which "I can sell to the people here". But such a solution, while it gives the Sheikh an unassailable position might at once open Indira Gandhi's Government to the charge that she has "surrendered" to the old secessionists and reversed the order of integration of Kashmir with the rest of the country. Already the Jan Sangh and its Rightist allies have been accusing Indira Gandhi of attempting a settlement with the Sheikh which they malign as part of the alleged secret deal with Bhuttoo at Simla.

It is, therefore, very vital for Indira Gandhi to seek such a solution which, while substantially salvaging the position of the Sheikh, also leaves her less vulnerable to the Opposition charge that she has given in on the issue of Kashmir at a time when the trend at the national level is to work for closer integration right up to Nagaland.

It is thus clear that only a solution which neither tilts in favour of the so-called "localists" working for Pakistan and other reactionary forces, nor for the so-called integrationists, accords well with the objectives held by the national democratic movement in the country. The major factor in ensuring the success of such a solution inside the State is the ruling Congress which has been of considerable importance in warding off the onslaughts of Reaction and its foreign imperialist backers, notably the Americans.

It is also obvious that the Sheikh's agreement with the Centre would put the seal of people's approval on the controversial question of the State's accession to India and thus bring about the real emotional integration of Jammu and Kashmir with the rest of the country. More important, such a transformation in the Kashmiri political scene would bring secular democratic forces in the State out from their isolation and generally strengthen these forces at the national level.

But, if Sheikh Abdullah does not get a substantial concession from New Delhi and signs on the dotted line to merely step into the seat of power after years of sacrifices, would he be able to consolidate his position? It is the Sheikh's assessment that without securing such a position he would render himself open to the accusation by the localists and pro-Pakistani elements that he has gone in for a sell-out to India and has thus frittered away his sacrifices and those of hundreds of others who believed that he was working for "freedom and a place of honour for the Kashmiris".

It is also Sheikh Abdullah's contention that without a substantial concession from Indira Gandhi he would not be able to tell the world that from now onwards the dispute over accession was buried forever and all that remained to be done was to strengthen the bonds that bound Kashmir with India.

While there is considerable logic in the Sheikh's argument, one cannot lose sight of the fact that his approach emanates from the fact of his having been the main votary of anti-India sentiments in the State over the past two decades and more. It was the Sheikh who had presented himself as the central figure of the anti-India movement fostering sentiments which only strengthened the secessionist positions and overshadowed his own role as a robust secularist and democrat opposed to Reaction, whether of the Pakistani or the Jan Sanghi variety. Today the position is that the very arguments which he had used to defend his mistaken position against the issue of accession are being hurled at him by Reaction to show him up as a wavering and unstable politician who changes the course of his ship to suit the winds.

At the other end are his critics, not excluding some

from the Congress, who say that in the changed circumstances, there is no validity for the Sheikh adhering to a stand which reverses the present integration to the pre-1953 position to appease the sections who would reconcile to nothing less than de-accession even if full autonomy was granted to Kashmir.

While the Sheikh has in recent months shifted his stand in a positive direction on a number of vital issues affecting the relations of the State with the Centre, such as the issues of plebiscite and Pakistan, his present position still leaves much scope for interpreting his definition of autonomy as a stepping stone towards independence. A review of the course of negotiations between the Centre and the Sheikh would make it clear that the Sheikh has been "inching towards an agreement" by shifting from one position to another to come close to what New Delhi can consider reasonable to grant.

The Sheikh started with the 1949 position saying that the accession was conditional to New Delhi's acceptance of the 1949 position when the Instrument of Accession secured for the State residuary sovereignty. He began by saying that that formed the only basis of the State's relations with the Centre. This position—called a quantum of accession as distinct from a quantum of autonomy—was later modified in 1952 when the principles of the State-Centre relations were defined under an Agreement with New Delhi. The 1952 Agreement which only took into consideration the Kashmir Valley had the seeds of inter-regional conflict in it and gave rise to controversies which were utilised by Reaction and the imperialists to drive a final wedge between New Delhi and Srinagar, resulting in the Sheikh's defection.

In recapitulating, the Sheikh has justified his slide-back

to the 1953 status on the ground that such a position alone would satisfy the urges of Kashmiris who have been robbed of their rights by India. In defining these rights the Sheikh has again, taken his stand on the constitutional position that obtained before 1953 saying that everything done after his ouster from power—whether in terms of constitutional changes or on the political plane—lacked the people's sanction.

In the list of the "impositions" from 1953 onwards are not only constitutional amendments to the State Constitution and but also political extensions like the Congress which, he says, should go from the Kashmir Valley as the price for his winding up the Plebiscite Front—also a post-1953 phenomenon.

As the negotiations proceeded, the Sheikh and his representatives have generally sought New Delhi's consent mainly on constitutional points, which may be summarised as follows:

Restoration of the Fundamental Rights Chapter of the State Constitution under which the State's law had secured itself firmly against any encroachment from the Centre. The State Constitution in its early stages also limited the operation of the Fundamental Laws as defined in the Indian Constitution: This was necessitated by two considerations, one to safeguard the land reforms and another to prevent the Supreme Court of India from acting in a manner as would hinder the State Government's operation against the enemy agents.

But this position gradually changed with the change in the correlation of forces in the rest of the country especially after Pakistan got entangled in the American aggressive bloc and Jawaharlal Nehru took the position that there could be no plebiscite in Kashmir. This led to the ratification of the accession and the promulgation of the State Constitution in 1956 which concretised the 1952 Agreement defining the principles of the State's relations with the Centre.

Accordingly, the jurisdiction of the Supreme Court was applied to the State but limited only to Fundamental Rights. The State's right to have elections under State Laws was recognised with Members to the Parliament being nominated after being elected from the State legislature. The 1954 Presidential Order also did not approve of a change in the nomenclature of the Sadar-i-Riyasat and the Prime Minister of the State was meant to uphold the separate identity of the Jammu and Kashmir.

As regards the extension of the emergency powers of the President, the Agreement specified that Parliament had no jurisdiction on the State unless the State legislature by a two-third majority empowered the President to intervene in case of breakdown of law and order.

Similarly, the jurisdiction of the Auditor General of India was accepted as limited and it was made clear that he would not audit the State accounts.

The notable feature of the Agreement was that it retained the concept of residuary powers for the State in the sense that it limited the operation of the powers of Parliament and that of the Union Government only to a limited extent. For instance, Article 248 and Clause 97 of the Constitution was not applied to the Jammu and Kashmir State. Article 254 concerning the Concurrent List of subjects was so applied as to make it clear that the State Laws would prevail where laws under the Concurrent List were not applied with the consent of the State Government or the legislature. Another article not applied to the State was 249.

The Presidential Order of 1954, while it upheld the special position enjoyed by the State under the Constitution, was more specific on the crucial issue of protecting the State subjects against the operation of the Fundamental Rights under which a citizen of India could purchase and sell property in any part of India. While Chapters Two and Three of the Constitution were applied to the State giving the same rights of citizenship to the subjects of the State, as are available to other citizens of India under the Constitution, it was made clear that nobody except the State legislature would have the right to change or modify the existing boundaries of the State (which include those under Pakistani occupation).

In the exercise of the Fundamental Rights by the citizens of the State and other Indian citizens inside the State, the position was reiterated that while the State subjects could seek the protection of the rights in the same manner as those in the rest of the country, non-State subjects residing or not residing inside the State would have no right to purchase or sell property in Jammu and Kashmir, nor acquire the rights of State subjects without going through the process prescribed under law.

But the operation of the 1954 Agreement, instead of being a weapon in the hands of the progressive democratic sections in the State, actually became a hindrance in the way and led to such processes as lent strength to almost a form of dictatorship under Bakhshi Ghulam Mohammad. Strangely enough, it was the then Democratic National Conference under G.M. Sadiq that became the main instrument for demanding modifications of the clauses under the Agreement, especially in relation to extending full jurisdiction of the Supreme Court, the Auditor General of India and the Election Commission of India.

As Sadiq took over in 1964 in the wake of the upheaval that rocked the State on the theft of the holy relic of the Prophet, the process of integration received a new spurt with the change of nomenclature of the Prime Minister to that of the Chief Minister and the Sadar-i-Riyasat to that of the Governor, application of the full jurisdiction of the Supreme Court, the Election Commission of India, control of the Auditor General of India over the accounts of the State Government, and the application of the President's emergency powers to the State under which the Governor could suspend the Constitution in case of internal disorder or breakdown of the law and order machinery.

The immediate backdrop for introducing these emergency powers was the upheaval of 1964 and the Pak infiltration during the 1965 war which had shown that lack of supervisory control by the Central institutions could mean easy contamination of the State organs by enemy agents who had wormed their way at practically every level of the administration and people.

In the administrative field also, Sadiq made far-reaching decisions in that he went ahead with the acceptance of the extension of all-India services like the Indian Police Service, the Indian Forest Service and the Indian Administrative Service to the State. And as the demand for the development tempo increased, the State Government also modified the State subject law to the extent of making the banks State subjects and allowing lost leases of land to outsiders for industrial purposes. Permission was also granted to the Government of India to purchase property in the State for cantonments and other developmental purposes through the agency of the State Government as representing the President of India.

Such being the pattern of integration of the State,

acceptance of the Sheikh's demand for a return to the pre-1953 position would mean considerable roll back, leading primarily to consolidation of separatist sentiments inside the State even though there would be a superficial alignment of secular democratic forces as a result of the agreement on the issue of accession.

A cursory review of the list of steps that the Sheikh intends taking as a price for his return to the mainstream would make it clear that the Kashmir leader would have to pander to localist sentiments while implementing his programme of action.

To begin with, the Sheikh assures that he will ask the people to account for everything including how they got their worldly goods during the last twentyseven years, that is, since the day he was ousted from power. This includes all the Congressmen, National Conference people and top bureaucrats who have taken firm anti-Sheikh positions since 1953, even though for gains which had nothing in common with patriotism.

Second, the Sheikh wants to do away with the Indian administrative personnel to replace them by local talents, replacement of outside police forces from the CRP to BSF to Central Intelligence Bureau personnel. While these steps would normally evoke welcome response from the democratic elements, in the context of Kashmir their wholesale ouster would practically amount to creating a vacuum on the security front which can only be filled in the present shape of things by forces and elements whose ideological motivations are not entirely beyond question.

Moreover, it has to be realised that by confining the attack against the intelligence set-up to the CBI, the Sheikh is forgetting and unwittingly trying to put a screen on the activities of other intelligence networks operating in the

State, not excluding those of Pakistan.

Added to the Sheikh's demands are other steps which need to be taken to enable him to sell the deal to his own people in Kashmir. These are return to old positions including the nomenclature of Sadar-i-Riyasat and the Prime Minister. This, coupled with the posture of no-truck with the Congress, would mean that in the eyes of the rural masses and the bulk of uncommitted following, the Sheikh would appear as a man who has finally humbled India and got back his pre-eminent position. Even though innocuous to look at, the concession on the nomenclature would amount to deepening the roots of the forces represented by the Sheikh, tolling almost a death-knell to the Congress in the rural areas.

There are many who argue that it would not be a heavy price to pay for the Sheikh's return if in the bargain the Congress organisation in the State has to be sacrificed; for, in any case the Sheikh's come-back would be victory of the Congress ideology. What is more important, according to this school of opinion, is the victory of ideals rather than insistence on the maintenance of the identity of the parties.

The role of the Congress in the peculiar context of Jammu and Kashmir is not similar to that in any other part of the country, say, in a place like Amritsar or Ludhiana. First as the National Conference when it spearheaded the upsurge against the Pakistani onslaught on the State in 1947, right through the crisis of 1965 and 1972, the Congress served as the only political instrument which withstood the attacks on the sovereignty of India in Kashmir. Because of its existence, it was possible to mobilise the patriotic sections of the people in the State against pressures being brought to bear by Right Reaction and its foreign imperialist backers.

In the absence of a Left alternative, with all its weaknesses, the Congress, which is the only all-State political vehicle through which progressive ideas permeate to all parts of the State, is also a weapon to counter the regionalists in each of the three regions of the State aligned to different reactionary fronts from the Jan Sangh in Jammu to Pakistanis in the Kashmir Valley and the votaries of the Central take-over in Ladakh.

It has also to be pointed out that the process through which Right Reaction inside the Congress gets differentiated from the Left democratic elements at the national level cannot be mechanically applied to Kashmir. While the demarcation lines between the secular and anti-secular forces is clearly discernible in the State, the forces representing the two are not so easily differentiated on the economic level because of the low level of economic development and the lack of industrialisation in the State. To say, therefore, that all those opposed to the Sheikh inside the Congress do so because of inspiration of the Right reactionary ideas is wrong.

In the complex situation and in the absence of a wide social base as elsewhere in the country, the Centre has evolved a policy of "not putting all the eggs in one basket" to effectively manipulate and manoeuvre in its contest with the forces opposed to it. Yet the fact shows that there are elements within the Congress Party who fear the outcome of the present Sheikh-New Delhi dialogue.

By themselves, these elements, however, would not count for much in the context of the new correlation of forces emerging around the dialogue. But the fact that a new constellation of forces opposed to the dialogue is emerging around Mirwaiz Farooq of the Awami Action

Committee imparts to their hostile posture a qualitatively new meaning insofar as their aims coincide at one point to prevent the Sheikh's return to power.

Prominent among those in this constellation are Maulana Mohammad Sayed Masoodi who acts as the mentor of Mirwaiz and has a stable following of about twenty to thirty thousand families confined to downtown Srinagar. It is this hard core of popular backing behind the Mirwaiz that provides the pro-Pakistanis, including those separating from the Sheikh's camp, a sanctuary for anti-Indian activities. Others aligned with the Mirwaiz in their anti-Sheikh crusade are large sections of the Shia community led by two Maulvis, Abbas Ansari and others.

However, the hard core of the student and youth activists who are the spearhead of anti-Indian agitations, does not wholly depend on the Mirwaiz. Some of them are still clinging on to the hope that the current dialogue with the Centre would yield no positive results.

But the more important and effective instrument of the anti-Sheikh opposition in the Valley and some parts of Doda and the Muslim belt of Jammu is the Jamaat-i-Islami which is also aligned with the Mirwaiz trying to frustrate the Sheikh's effort for settlement with New Delhi. The Jamaat with its wide network of dedicated activists has spread its tentacles wider, especially after the last General Elections.

The Sheikh's camp, on the other hand, is now more united behind Mirza Afzal Beg. Except for a tiny opposition led by the Vice-President of the Plebiscite Front, the entire party led by Beg is united behind the Sheikh in his bid for a compromise with New Delhi. In fact, the possibility is that if the talks fail, a large chunk of the organisation, including some senior workers especially those from Anantnag district, would abandon the Sheikh's fold to join the Congress.

Yet the Sheikh faces a formidable opposition in the combination brought together under the leadership of Mirwaiz Farooq. Left alone, and with the Congress out of gear, it would be difficult to prevent the Sheikh from relying on the very forces which are today arrayed against him for his adopting a pro-India posture. The logic of the events, therefore, demands that he should extend a hand of cooperation towards the Congress and utilise its strength in the big task of consolidating the secular democratic forces.

But the objective situation today is vastly different from what it ever was in the past. Not only is there a strong possibility of the Congress and the Sheikh's forces pulling together in one direction, the imperatives of the two forces coming together at the State level are sharper today than ever before. It should be clear even to the most obstinate in the Sheikh's camp that the success of the new set-up largely depends on the Sheikh's capacity to muster support for it from Jammu and Ladakh.

The Sheikh's real strength lies in his ability to make a direct appeal to the masses over and above the heads of organised parties in the State. He is the tallest of the State leaders whose secular bonafides have never been in doubt. But Right Reaction in Jammu, in the form of the Jan Sangh, is raising the bogey of regional discrimination. It finds a sympathetic hearing inside the Congress there, especially from those who have been working for Jammu's separation from Kashmir. Similar is the situation in Ladakh where Kushak Bakula's group has been demanding Central take-over of the region.

Inside the Sheikh's own camp, notably the Plebiscite

Front, there is no open challenge to his policy of reconciliation, but a small minority led by the Vice-President, Safi Mohammad Akbar from Sopore, along with some younger elements from the city with almost no backing anywhere among the people, are reportedly disagreeing with any concession to the Centre on the question of autonomy. Safi is said to have, however, assured that he will not take his differences to the open to challenge the leadership of Sheikh Abdullah.

Similarly, a small minority of leadership from the Doda district is also opposed to watering down the demand for full autonomy. But to construe from this that the Sheikh would find it difficult to carry the Plebiscite Front with him for acceptance of a solution, is incorrect.

But the real problem may arise when it comes to ascertaining the wishes of Jammu and Ladakh. The popular feeling in the two regions is that it is the Kashmir Valley which needs the concession of autonomy as price for being retained inside India. On the contrary, the opinion in Jammu is in favour of merger to escape the imaginary fear of Kashmiri domination which is being drilled into the ears of the population there by reactionary parties, notably the Jan Sangh.

An argument which easily cuts across party lines in Jammu is why should the Jammuwala have to pay any price in terms of his bondage to the Kashmiris and go all the way with the Valley for autonomy to sacrifice his own interests which do not lie in greater autonomy for the State but rather with more closer relations with India? It is, therefore, natural that any step towards reconciliation with the Sheikh on the basis of autonomy for the State might bring together diverse elements to oppose the move.

Yet it is surprising that there is no strong hostility to the

Sheikh from the region despite the efforts of the Jan Sangh, whose stalwarts have been coming too often to Jammu to prepare for an agitation and satyagraha scheduled for September and October, the time when the new agreement is expected to take shape.

In these circumstances, how does the Sheikh and the Congress plan to counter the threats coming from Jammu? It is obvious that the Plebiscite Front and the Sheikh do not command any significant mass following in the Jammu region. Except for a small following in the Muslim belt of Doda and the border regions of Rajouri and Mehnder, the Jammu region is distributed mainly between the Jan Sangh and the Congress which is definitely stronger both in terms of mass appeal and cadre than the former. But inside the Jammu Congress, there are trends which are not firm insofar as the question of extending support to the Sheikh is concerned.

The right course under the circumstances for the Sheikh would have been to bring together the secular elements in Jammu and avoid extremes like the Jan Sangh and the unreconciled elements in the Congress. It is yet to be seen if he takes this wise line.

Similar, through qualitatively different, is the situation in the Ladakh region were the Sheikh has yet to make his scheduled visit.

While the foregoing would make it clear that it is imperative for the Sheikh to seek the cooperation of the Congress if he is serious in the implementation of the agreement with New Delhi, it is clear that the way for such a get-together would, to a large extent, be paved by the type of agreement that emerges out of the talks between the Sheikh and New Delhi.

In the talks with New Delhi, the Sheikh and Beg have

been insisting on the creation of an atmosphere of mutual trust and dependence. This, the Sheikh says, is more important than securing guarantees, constitutional or otherwise, from each other about the implementation of the agreement.

Given such an atmosphere, the Sheikh believes, it should be possible for Indira Gandhi to concede his demand for autonomy as it obtained during the pre-1953 period. Beginning from this maximum demand, the Sheikh has steadily come down to a set of demands which, in his opinion, are the minimum for an equitable solution of the problem. These mainly emanate from his fear of Hindu domination and desire to maintain the distinct personality of Kashmir with the assurance to the Muslims that they would not be submerged in a Hindu-dominated India. The central theme of these demands relates to greater weightage for the Kashmiri-speaking people with its nearly ninetynine per cent Musl'm population.

The first pertains to the exercise of Fundamental Rights as defined in the Indian Constitution under which while every citizen has the right to purchase property and own or purchase it in any part of India he also enjoy the rights of free speech, assembly and conscience. It also forbids discrimination on account of religion, a clause which will militate against the interests of the Muslim educated in the Kashmir Valley, as against those who have been relatively more advanced, say, for instance, Kashmirl Pandits.

The second issue closely related with the question of maintaining unhindered the weighty position of Kashmir is that of delimitation. It has been noticed that the Jammu population has been increasing during the last decade or more at a more rapid pace than that of the Kashmir Valley.

The net increase of the Jammu population is three lakhs more than the rate of population increase in the Kashmir Valley. This would mean that in the event of any new delimitation, Jammu would have three more seats in the Assembly while those of Kashmir would remain at the present level. Added to this is the fear of the State subject law being watered down in the event of the non-Kashmiri majority gaining the upper hand in the State legislature, which alone has the right to modify or amend the State subject law.

As a guarantee against the reversal of the State subject law, Beg wants that the rights of amendment should be taken away from the legislature and made conditional on a reference through a referendum on the subject by two-thirds majority of the people of the State. Since this would mean leaving scope for regional divisions and separation, the Centre seems to be inclined to give guarantees on the subject by making the law more fool-proof through the action of the State legislature.

Even as the law figures today, there are two categories of State subjects, the agricultural and non-agricultural subjects. The latter, even though being State subjects, cannot purchase or sell agricultural land.

As regards the fear of increased population in the two non-Kashmiri regions of the State submerging the weigh-tage of the Kashmiris, the Centre seems to be ready to provide only one guarantee which is essentially political, that of providing checks and balances through appropriate political representation in the legislature. The Sheikh is being asked to enter into a deal with the Congress majority from Jammu to offset the strength of those who want the complete merger of the State and the annulment of its separate Constitution.

As regards the jurisdiction of the Auditor General and that of the Supreme Court and the Election Commission, the differences between the two sides only relate to details and not on the substance—the Sheikh having agreed to accept these institutions as necessary for the orderly development of the State.

However, on the nomenclature of the Sadar-i-Riyasat and the Prime Minister of the State, and on the question of the President's emergency powers, the differences continue to persist between the two sides, though it is expected that these items will be settled since there is no rigidity on either side.

Compromise suggestions are already being mooted such as one that the State legislature may submit to the President a panel of names from among whom one may be nominated by him to be the Governor, or Sadar-i-Riyasat. The Government of India has, of course, to take into account the likely chain-reaction of such an arrangement in other parts of the Indian Union.

There is no doubt that the present round of discussions has roused unprecedented expectations, and neither of the two sides negotiating for an amicable settlement can afford to blight the hopes of the common people in this beautiful vale of Kashmir.

(August 17, 1974)

24

From Bhutto's Fall

Zulfikar Ali Bhutto has fallen, but his impetuous innings in power has lessons to teach for many.

After Pakistan found itself disintegrated in December 1971, a leader emerged out of the shambles left behind by the Army junta. The nation's morale was low but the new leader lifted it. Instead of the blanket slogan of *Garibi Hatao*, Bhutto spelt out his promise to the people—*Roti, Kapra, Makan*. An air of great expectations stirred the dispirited people. They thought the long night was over. Men and women of perception and enlightenment—the forward-looking elements on the political fringe like Mazhar Ali Khan—thought Bhutto was their only hope for revival of democracy: after a long time, the windows were thrown open, conversations became free, the press began to recover its self-respect and political activities surfaced. And they all prayed the process be irrepressible.

Bhutto's Pakistan People's Party itself brought within its fold a large number of democratic and progressive elements. It took a stand against the powerful feudal *sirdars* of Sind and Baluchistan, and there were loud talks of fighting the feudal diehards and the bigoted *mullahs*. Without pressing the analogy too far but making it comprehensive for Indian experience, one may venture to say that the promise of 1969-70 in India came to Pakistan in 1971-72.

Thereafter the same inexorable logic followed in different scenarios.

Many politicians who manage to stand out have a way of rationalising their conduct. They first convince they are the only instruments for bringing about decisive changes in the life of their people, and nothing more is wanted but their personal eminence in leadership. And, then, when difficulties crop up, they strive desperately to somehow remain in power, forgetting the hopes they have roused in their people and the promises betrayed.

This is the way Bhutto has gone as others in his neighbourhood, though under different circumstances. He got preoccupied not in restructuring Pakistan's polity on a genuinely federal basis and giving it a new social content, but in indiscriminately wielding power divorced from purpose.

Gradually, the progressives faded out or were eliminated from his People's Party. And so the *mullahs* became stronger and aggressive, and a conglomerate of atavistic forces—from the remnants of the Muslim League to the revivalists of the Jamaat-e-Islami—overnight became the vociferous champions of democracy.

Inevitably, in such a situation, foreign interference, covert and overt, played its part. And as in India so in Pakistan, one could hear about the omnipresence of the CIA and its omnipotence too. Bhutto thought he might be able to excite the imagination of the populace, deceived and embittered, by a contrived confrontation with the USA on the issue of the plutonium processing plant. He thought he could enlist the support of his Islamic brethren as a countervailing force to the Islamic revolt within his own country.

But once you lose your links with the masses at home, the foreigners can at best prop you up for a while but you cease to be a leader on your own right; and when your roots are so severed in your own country, there is nothing surprising that the Army as an organised force inevitably appears as the saviour of the people. This has happened before in Pakistan when a succession of squabbling politicians and civil servants discredited themselves and corroded the fibre of the nation's polity; and it has happened again this time when Bhutto wrangled with his opponents making a mockery of the elective political structure.

Contemplating the present scene in Pakistan, one is reminded of the tragedy that overtook Sheikh Mujibur Rahman less than .two years ago in Bangladesh. Riding on the euphoric popularity as the father of the liberated Bangladesh, the Sheikh also systematically severed his connections with the genuine forces of national liberation, isolated himself from the normal political processes; and thus the way was paved for the Army to take over, unhesitatingly indulging in bloody massacres.

Case-hardened politicians never seem to learn, but looking at the fateful developments in these two neighbouring countries, it is time to tender in all humility, a warning to our political leaders not to play with promises to the people. Once the effect of the promises wear out and the leader thinks only of how to cling on to power without bothering about the pledges that go with it, then there is little room for escape. Sheikh Mujib lost his life, Indira Gandhi lost her power and Zulfikar Ali Bhutto was pushed out of it unceremoniously.

Those who are enthroned today should look back to what happened yesterday and the day before.

(July 9, 1977)

25

Kashmir's Majestic Chinar

The sweeping victory of the National Conference in this week's election for the Jammu and Kashmir Assembly is a measure of the sturdy secularism with which Sheikh Mohammad Abdullah has reared his political movement for over four decades.

It was a folly on the part of the Pradesh Congress to have fallen out with the Sheikh, forgetting that the Accord that the Kashmiri leader had arrived at with New Delhi was the most unequivocal assertion of Kashmir being part of the Indian Union since his return to politics. Petty considerations grew into a major blunder which led to the rift between the National Conference and the Congress after the installation of the Janata Government at the Centre.

More serious, however, was the disastrous policy pursued by the Janata leadership. Forgetting that Sheikh Abdullah has been a life-long friend of Jayaprakash Narayan—trying his best to be of help to JP even when he was in detention under the Emergency—the Janata leaders, instead of coming to an understanding with the National Conference, threw the gauntlet at him.

Frankly speaking, there was no such thing as the Janata Party in Jammu and Kashmir. Mechanically projecting their experience in India, the Jan Sangh (which was the old Praja Parishad) was inducted in Jammu under the banner of the Janata to fight the National Conference. But in the Kashmir Valley, there was neither the Jan Sangh, nor Congress-O, nor Socialist, nor BLD, nor CFD. So, the Janata leaders recruited the rank communal elements, the Jamaat-e-Islami followers and the rump of the Plebiscite Front which had refused to subscribe to Sheikh Abdullah's Accord with Delhi—and the virtual leader of this Janata motley was Mirwaiz Maulvi Farooq, who for long has been known for his pro-Pak leanings. So, Hindu communalism in Jammu and Muslim communalism in the Kashmir Valley became the monstrous base of the Janata in this strategically sensitive State.

What was amazing was that the top Janata leaders made it a prestige contest. Charan Singh and Jagjivan Ram went on a whirlwind election campaign, not sparing personal attacks on the Sheikh. Then Morarji Desai himself undertook a tiring campaign, rounding it off with a much-publicised dinner with the Mirwaiz—an open provocation to all secular Kashmiris. To cap it all, all the three top Central Ministers made an extraordinary display of discourtesy by not calling on Sheikh Abdullah as he lay bed-ridden with a severe heart attack.

The electorate of Jammu and Kashmir has given a fitting rebuff to this opportunism. As in the rest of India, it has demonstrated a remarkably high level of political consciousness in totally rejecting this Janata strategy and giving a powerful mandate to Sheikh Abdullah's National Conference.

It is necessary to recall here that thirty years ago, it was under Sheikh Abdullah's leadership that the people of Jammu and Kashmir warded off the attack of the Pakistani raiders with their communal ideology that a Muslim majority State should *ipso facto* be part of Pakistan. With this allegiance to secularism, the Muslims in Kashmir have always stood against all forms of communalism. In 1971, when an insidious propaganda was launched that India was helping in the dismemberment of Pakistan, the leaders of Kashmir came out in support of the liberation struggle of the people of Bangladesh.

Today, forty years later, Sheikh Mohammad Abdullah, defying age, has once again reiterated his unswerving commitment to secularism by leading the people of Jammu and Kashmir in this crucial electoral crusade against the disruptive communalist forces. The shining example of Kashmir under Sheikh Abdullah will be a warning to communal forces all over India, and an inspiration for all those who stand for a secularist society in this great land of ours. Today new challenges face Sheikh Abdullah. Armed with the renewed mandate of his people, he has to see to it that the programme of New Kashmir, which was formulated forty years ago, is realised. And in this he will have the support of every democrat from all parts of India.

The majestic Chinar has braved one more storm, undaunted.

(July 9, 1977)

26

Pakistan : On the Brink

One more military ruler has taken the mad initiative to destroy Pakistan. Yahya Khan by his ghastly persecution of the Bangladeshis brought about the disintegration of Pakistan leading to the loss of its eastern wing. Eight years later, Zia-ul-Haq has today virtually signed not only his own death warrant but also that of the country over which he rules to oppress its people, by hanging the person from whom he had usurped power two years ago.

Zulfikar Ali Bhutto was no angel and he, himself least of all, never claimed to be one. It was however preposterous even by the standards of Pakistani politics that he should have been executed while an accredited assassin like Yahya Khan is allowed to live. During his turbulent political career, Bhutto might have been responsible for many a sin: his crimes, in the eyes of his adversaries, might have led to the loss of many lives. The Kasuri murder case, for which he was sent to the gallows, was not an ordinary one: the charge-sheet itself makes it out to be a political case. In such a case, with the Supreme Court Bench divided and the death sentence verdict delivered by a four-to-three majority, and that too recommending reprieve, Zia-ul-Haq has had no alibi whatsoever for hanging Bhutto except the fear of Bhutto being alive.

This was the same fear that gripped the military junta in Bangladesh in 1975 that not only killed Sheikh Mujibur Rahman but massacred all his leading political associates in cold blood. A military regime, prowling for power, cannot afford to keep its adversaries in prison, because it is always anxious to ensure the impossibility of any return to civilian rule. The Bangladesh Zia, another Army boss, might have tried to legitimise his coup by a neat election stunt, but the scars do not heal, nor can democracy be sustained at gun-point, however much it may be clothed in Dacca muslin.

There was no doubt a lingering expectation upto the eleventh hour before Bhutto was taken out of the Death Cell in the Rawalpindi prison that the appeal of world opinion, embracing both the Governments and the people, might sway Pakistan's military ruler into granting clemency to Bhutto. But the quality of mercy is not an attribute of a tin-god dictator unsure of his position as Zia obviously is. His sceptered sway is deceptive since it has no legitimacy whatsoever in the eyes of the people over whom it is held.

Military coupists are rarely invested with political wisdom. The self-appointed President of Pakistan does not seem to have the perspicacity to realise that Bhutto dead may be more dangerous for him and his regime than Bhutto alive. In neighbouring Iran, the much-vaunted Shahen-shah, with all the deadly arms stacked for him by the Pentagon, had to flee the country. The rumblings within Pakistan, with unconcealed regional antagonisms reaching the bursting point, can be muffled for some time by bayonet, but only for some time. No military mafia can keep the people down, despite all the pep-talk by the CIA that Bhutto's liquidation would lead to no upheaval in Pakistan.

Like an army commander in panic, Zia-ul-Haq has opened a new front. The entire political spectrum of the country—much larger than Bhutto's Pakistan People's Party, no small force by itself—will now be convinced that there is no other option but to fight to overthrow the regime. And there is no guarantee for Zia that the armed forces will remain loyal to him. Even if one is reluctant to set much store by the report that the Pak Air Force, by and large, was pro-Bhutto, there can come up at any moment another ambitious General to make short shrift of Zia-ul-Haq and his regime. The wise warning by a distinguished Irishman that green grass grows over battle-fields but not over gallows, seems to have had no impact on Zia's cerebrum. The point of no return has been reached.

In India, Zulfikar Ali Bhutto will be remembered not by his extravagant rhetoric about Pakistan waging a thousand-year war with India, but by his statesmanship in signing the Simla Agreement in 1972, which promised to open a new chapter of Indo-Pak amity after Pakistan's traumatic loss of its eastern half and the birth of Bangladesh. It is true that the perspective opened up at Simla was not consistently pursued by Bhutto, mainly due to the pressures at home and allurements from abroad, but it would be naive to expect that those who overthrew him are at all capable of building enduring friendship with India. A regime, generating by its folly hatred within the country and incapable of standing up to pressures from abroad, can never be strong enough to establish a foreign policy of peace with a neighbour. The record of Pakistan shows that every regime, whenever it was beset by threats at home, whipped up frenzy against India. Zia-ul-Haq cannot be an exception, whatever our wishful policy-makers in South Block may think, or are made to believe by more powerful elements from outside.

The execution of Zulfikar Ali Bhutto may very well turn out to be the flash-point in the highly explosive situation that Pakistan represents both at home and abroad. More than at any time before, India has to be alert and vigilant about the fast-changing developments that are bound to overpower those clinging on to power in Pakistan.

The ghost of Zulfikar Ali Bhutto shall finally overtake Zia-ul-Haq.

(April 7, 1979)

27

Passage through Pakistan–I

Getting acquainted with a neighbour next door but long estranged can hardly be an easy job, and one cannot presume to have done it in just a single trip.

I have just returned after a 25-day tour of Pakistan. This is my first visit to that country and as I belong to the eastern part of India, I never had any links, pre-partition, with it, nor do I know its national language. With such a background, it has been a rewarding experience, this visit, whose itinerary extended from Karachi to the Karakoram Highway, from Lahore to the Khyber pass, from Islamabad to Quetta. And as a student of history, I could not afford to miss Mohenjodaro and Taxila.

My interviews covering a wide spectrum of public opinion—from the President, Ministers and Secretaries, to political party leaders, educationists, defence specialists, lawyers, youth and student leaders, bussinessmen, and, of course, the journalists—were all off-the-record, since I felt it would be invidious for a reporter to take on-record interviews from the Government and off-the-record from the Opposition which is debarred under the Martial Law regulation from giving interviews to the press.

The overpowering impression, which will abide with me is the abundance of friendly feeling towards India in all sections of the people in Pakistan: I emphasise, *all sections,* because this goodwill transcends all barriers. From the embittered Opposition leaders, gagged and immobilised, to different layers of the establishment, high and low, young and old, from academics to professionals, the youth and the cultural elite—among them all there is an irrepressible desire to remain in friendship with India.

To be candid, I did not expect this when I landed at the rather provincial airport at Lahore on a December afternoon. From the very same evening as I went out for a walk alone in the city, a total stranger, to the morning when I came to the same Lahore airport twentyfive days later, it was one unending progress in friendly warmth. There was no artificiality about it, no diplomatic stance or contrived *Bhai Bhai.* It was like brothers, after having fallen apart, feeling the urge to come closer.

The old generation is nostalgic about India, while the young is keen to know the neighbour, to get acquainted, to become familiar. In the train from Lahore to Karachi, the elderly middle-class gentleman, now living in retirement from Government service, talked on and on about his early years when he used to cycle from Lodi Colony to the Central Secretariat, reminiscing about Delhi's landmarks on the way—like Lodi Gardens and Sunehri Bagh: I could go to sleep only when he got down at Multan after a warm embrace.

In the biting cold of Quetta, it was warm inside the local office of the APP, almost turned into a press club, with free, uninhibited talks common among pressmen all the world over—all over cups of *kawa:* the next evening one of the elderly correspondents knocked at my door in the hotel and spent nearly two hours sentimentally recalling his days in Delhi as a young boy, his school days at Ranikhet and imploring me to locate a class-friend of forty years ago.

The weather-beaten face of the old man with the Hunza cap, selling sun-dried apricot along the Karakoram Highway, lit up when he heard that the stranger was from Delhi: "You are not a *mehman,* you are a brother" as he gave me an extra helping of the dry fruit as a spontaneous gesture.

The ex-serviceman, selling entry tickets at the museum at Mohenjodaro, went out of his way to show me round the place: when I thanked him at the end, he took me in both hands and pointing to the five-thousand-year old ruins, said: "These treasures belong to you and me, both."

The smart young lady at the hotel reception counter in Karachi, looking at my passport, came out with a smile: 'Oh you are from Delhi!' and then the whole lot of them put so many eager questions about our country.

The senior officer in the Information Ministry at Islamabad spoke with the softness of a scholar and told me that he was from Rampur, a descendent of Maulana Mohammad Ali, about whom and his times he is doing research and was keen on getting material for his subject from India.

It is not a question of anybody wanting to undo the Partition of 1947: it is a question of forging bonds of friendship between two neighbours with common heritage and organic cultural links.

In the midst of this warmth all round, one of course has to encounter many questions and dispel many a misunderstanding. Despite a democratic order, why are there communal riots in India? Don't Muslims in India face disabilities? As a very perceptive Lahore lawyer, critical of the Martial Law regime, put it: "There is a lot with which I am unhappy in Pakistan, but I feel perhaps I am better off here than I would have been in India." Many friends, mostly from the establishment and its periphery, wondered how Indira Gandhi as Prime Minister looked at Pakistan: is she going to repeat 1971? When it is pointed out that Bangladesh was born, in the main, because of Pakistan's inner malady, there is general concurrence though there are diehards, some of whom I came across, who blame Indira Gandhi for breaking up Pakistan.

There are, of course, others who think differently. A Sindhi militant asked me in all seriousness why the Indian Army withdrew in 1971, why it did not move in deeper into his part of the country at a time when the Pak Army was in a shambles. Many in the Government commended the Janata as being friendly to Pakistan, though they could not explain to themselves how the RSS got respectability and strength under the very same Janata. There is the other recurring question: India is so strong, economically, politically and militarily: why should it object to Pakistan modernising her defence? The discussions were frank and there was no rancour.

And yet one could not overlook expressions and incidents which could not but sow bitterness. *Nawa-i-Waqt* is not the only newspaper that spreads poison about India: Pakistan's controlled press, just granted self-censorship, which makes it more loyal than the king, picks up all that is negative in the Indian scene and plays up items that could only help to keep the two countries apart. The wonder is that despite this role of the media, there is such an effusion of friendly feelings in the populace towards India. One more instance showing that the media, when controlled, are not really effective.

1971 has a significance for the people of Pakistan very different from the perception we in India have about it. It no doubt brought about a tremendous heart-searching—more in the common people than among those in authority. What struck me about it is that there is absolutely no nostalgia about it, not the remotest urge to undo what happened in 1971. Rather, a perceptible adjustment to the existing realities. One does come across an occasional shop in Karachi with a Bengali signboard, and the tomb of Liaqat Ali Khan with his name inscribed in Bengali as well as Urdu. And in the brand-new capital of Pakistan at Islamabad, one of the poshest localities is called Ramna after the name of the elite sector of Dacca.

From this, it would perhaps be rash to conclude that Pakistan's national identity is as cohesive as that of Bangladesh, or for that matter, India. A 30-year-old PIA officer, highly intelligent, asking me about my impressions of his country, himself volunteered: "We do not have an all-Pakistan national consciousness: we think more in terms of our regional nationalism. When *we* go abroad, we try to think as Pakistanis, but at home, we are Punjabis or Sindhis, or Baluchis or Pathans."

The delinking of Bangladesh from Pakistan led many to expect that the rest of the country would become more cohesive. Instead, regional animosities have sharpened rather than subsided in post-1971 Pakistan. Today even with a relatively small population of eight and a half crores, Pakistan has not graduated into a homogeneous national entity—each of its five distinct regions has a consciousness of its own: Punjab, Sind, Baluchistan, North-West Frontier and the Northern Region (consisting of Gilgit, Hunza and Swat) apart from Azad Kashmir have hardly been brought nearer to each other.

The overall economic development of Pakistan has not so far been marked by any major stride towards the building of industrial infrastructure which could promote the consciousness of interdependence among these disparate regions. Rather, whatever economic growth has been registered has widened the disparities between these regions. By far the bulk of Pakistan's industrial and agricultural development has been confined to Punjab and Sind, with very blatant neglect of the rest of the country. The consequence has been the intensification of regional consciousness and also regional animosity.

The cultural unevenness within Pakistan can be measured from the prevailing disparity in the status of women in different parts of the country. Travelling by a deluxe bus from Rawalpindi to Lahore, I found three very modern ladies smoking cigars at a wayside restaurant without attracting any notice: in Islamabad, Karachi or Lahore, one comes across no visible discrimination against women in this Islamic Republic. But go beyond Peshawar in the Frontier Province or in Baluchistan, you find yourself in a primitive tribal society in which the woman is kept behind the *killa,* the high mudwalled enclosure round a cluster of houses. At the new hotel in Quetta I found no window opening outward because that might defile the *purdah* of the neighbours. But in the picturesque valleys enclosed by the Hindu Kush, Karakoram and the High Himalayas, the woman's lot is hard but there is more freedom of movement for her than in the strictly tribal society.

Talking to different sections of the intelligentsia in different parts of the country, I could realise the fallacy of the impression that the armed forces have provided a unifying element in Pakistan's national life. Unlike the situation in India, the character and the composition of Pakistan's armed forces have weakened, instead of strengthening national unity.

Traditionally, the Pakistan Army has largely been from a compact zone comprising four districts of Punjab (Rawalpindi, Jhelum, Campbellpur and Mianwali) and three of NWFP (Hazara, Kohat and Bannu). Added to it are the refugees from East Punjab (General Zia himself comes from Jullundur, while among his closest colleagues are General Arif from Batala and Rao Farman Ali from Rohtak). Such an Army is looked upon by the rest of the country as largely a Punjabi Army dominating over the entire country. It is no accident that political dissent, reaching today the boiling point repudiating the very concept of Pakistan, is concentrated in the very regions which are left virtually unrepresented in the armed forces—namely, Baluchistan, Sind and the Pathan belt.

More than four and a half years after his overthrow in 1977, Zulfikar Ali Bhutto appeared to me to be a formidable political force wherever I went round Pakistan. Despite an obviously one-sided campaign from the official side painting his six and a half years in office in the blackest colour, Bhutto remains a spectre for the present regime. His execution two and a half years ago made a martyr out of a leader who played the most magnificent populist in this part of the world. In fact, it was under Bhutto that politics reached the masses. His election campaign in 1970 certainly gave a mass base to his Pakistan People's Party, but all his campaigns on coming to power after the military disaster of 1971 could sway mass emotions in a manner never seen before. If Indira Gandhi's *Garibi Hatao* was deadly in trouncing her opponents in 1971, Bhutto's *Roti-Kapra-Makan* has become the emblem of hope for the millions in Pakistan.

The jawans and younger officers remember Bhutto as the man who through his astute diplomacy got thousands of them back from the prisoners-of-war camp after the defeat in Bangladesh: and the slogan of *Roti-Kapra-Makan* could not but sway the ordinary Punjabi villager finding his way into the armed forces as much as the PPP follower in the countryside. From more than one dependable source I heard that many Army units did not take their meals when the news came of Bhutto's execution. Two young officers in one of the Ministries themselves volunteered that for a couple of days they could not eat their food when Bhutto was executed; and these are quiet, law-abiding elements.

The Pakistani working in West Asia and sending remittances home remember Bhutto as the man who initiated the process which gave him this opening; the exodus abroad was started and encouraged by Bhutto.

One can understand the anxiety of the Martial Law authorities in keeping both Begum Bhutto and Benazir away from Punjab. These two ladies by their active participation in mass campaign in the last four years, facing persecution, have graduated to political leadership on their own count. With the banner of the martyred Bhutto in their hands, there is no political force which can stop the PPP from sweeping the polls particularly in Punjab.

Here lies the most acute contradiction in Pakistan politics today: the Army which is ruling today is based mainly on a pocket covering four districts of Punjab and three adjoining areas of NWFP while the biggest political force ranged against the Army rule is concentrated in that very same Punjab.

An indication of this could be available in the local bodies election that took place late in 1979. The Martial Law Administration decreed that a member of any political party (all being banned) would be disqualified in this election. Despite this ban and the total embargo on all political campaigning, the PPP supporters swept the local bodies poll: in Lahore city, in a house of over one hundred, about fifty of the elected members were disqualified on the plea of being PPP members, and the mayoral election took place only when the nominee of the Government supporters numbering a paltry 26 could claim to have the majority.

This force brings out the dilemma of the present regime: it cannot afford to hold any form of elections, not even a referendum—despite General Zia's now forgotten broadcast on July 5, 1977 in which he claimed to have set up "an interim Government" and gave "a solemn assurance" that he would hold elections in three months. It was the fiftyfourth month since that solemn pledge when I visited Pakistan in December.

During my hour long talk with him, General Zia took half the time in trying to impress upon me that he was not interested in holding on to power, but he was candid enough not to tell me that he would soon be holding elections.

The recurring theme of most of the talks with high-ups in Islamabad, including some of the Ministers and Secretaries, was that any election campaign would create new tensions and destabilise the country. An air of unreality prevails in all this as the present regime has evolved no indicator by which to gauge the public mood towards it: I was told that the very fact that large numbers participated in the August 14 celebrations this year could be taken as the indication that "we are moving in the right direction", as General Zia himself put it at the flag-hoisting celebration on that day. To me it sounded rather risky on the part of any regime to take the mass turn-out on a national day (which August 14 is for Pakistan) as the only indicator of its own popularity.

It would, of course, be incorrect to say that the present Martial Law Administration has made it clear to the people of Pakistan that it would never hold any election. People in authority in Islamabad told me about the setting up of an election cell by the Martial Law Administration as earnest of its intention to hold elections. The chairman of this election cell is Major General Rao Farman Ali of Bangladesh fame. After his retirement from the Army on return from Bangladesh with a rather dubious reputation for all his pro-Al Badr record there, Bhutto appointed him the Managing Director of the Fauji Foundation, a charitable trust for the welfare of the ex-servicemen and their families: the budget of its annual welfare activities exceeds Rs 6 crores, while its industrial projects (from textile, sugar and tobacco to fertiliser, synthetic fibre and construction) have assets totalling nearly Rs 120 crores.

Soon after Bhutto's overthrow in July 1977, Rao Farman Ali wrote that it was a fatal mistake on General Yahya Khan's part to have had agreed to hand over power through elections which were held in December 1970. Two other mistakes of the past, according to Rao Farman Ali, were Ayub's decision to give up the post of the Army Chief when he took over power and his decision after stabilising his regime to having appointed civilians as Governors and other key posts in the administration.

This was followed by Rao Farman Ali's rapport with General Zia, and he has since become the Minister of Energy and Natural Resources, apart from heading the

Fauji Foundation. Today he may be regarded as the ideologue of the present regime. It is worth noting that General Zia has continued to be the Chief of the Army Staff—he continues to live in the Army House in Rawalpindi and not in the President's House in Islamabad—while all the Governors are Lieutenant-Generals and not civilians.

Among the persons I met in Pakistan, including quite a few supporting the present Government, many felt it rather odd, if not ironical, that the retired Major General, Rao Farman Ali, with his known views, should be heading the election cell of General Zia's regime.

A civil servant with a perceptive mind made a pertinent point about the Army regime in Pakistan. The two previous Martial Law regimes brought no stability in Pakistan, although that was the promise with which they had been clamped down: in fact, under one of these, Pakistan got dismembered in 1971. If Bhutto was brought to power when the military regime was in a state of thorough discredit in December 1971, it was the military regime which brought about the erosion of Bhutto's power and ultimate ouster.

In 1973, pressed by the Shah of Iran to put down the Baluch unrest, Bhutto let loose the Army in a full-scale operation in Baluchistan where as many as 16 cantonments were set up, military roads, air-strips and helipads were built at record speed. The fall-out of this military operation was the bitter antagonism generated among the Baluch political leadership against Bhutto. From this point onward Bhutto became more and more dependent on the armed forces but in his supreme arrogance he was cocksure that the Army could never strike at him. In 1976, he appointed as the Chief of the Army Staff the junior most of his Lieutenant-Generals, namely, Mohammad Zia-ul-Haq.

28

Passage through Pakistan–II

If General Zia is unable to take the risk of handing over power via a general election, the Opposition in Pakistan faces difficulties of their own in forcing the lifting of the Martial Law.

From my fairly long and extensive talks with leaders of practically all the Opposition parties, I have come back with the impression that the present regime is continuing largely because of the lack of cohesion among the forces ranged against it. While it is obvious that the Martial Law authorities would never on their own countenance any mass action aimed at ending their *raj*—all political parties are banned, not to speak of their functioning—there is as yet hardly any sign of any mass activity in the offing.

The extent of repression under the Martial Law against its political opposition also acts as a deterrent on any form of mass activity. It was difficult to find out how many political opponents are in prison. While some Opposition leaders put the number at six or seven thousand, the more conservative ones put it at between two and three thousand. The Government figures put it at less than a hundred: it is to be noted that the Martial Law regime does not treat as political prisoners anybody involved in violence. For instance, all Al-Zulfikar suspects—numbering well over a thousand—are treated as criminals. There are reports of torture on women in the dreaded Lahore Fort but the Government agencies deny it. Public lashing of student militants of the PPP and even some journalists is well known.

The biggest political force in Pakistan today is Bhutto's PPP, but it is riddled with serious problems. For one thing, Bhutto did not build any party organisation nor did he rear up any leadership. He depended almost wholly on his personal dynamism which was undoubtedly tremendous, as was his capacity to strike deals with other parties which, however, declined with years as arrogance of power overtook him.

Although many of Bhutto's lieutenants dispute the charge of his having antagonised a large body of opinion by reckless action against his political opposition, I found them conceding that no well-knit party organisation was built up in the heydays of the PPP's glory. They, however, claim allegiance from a large body of following which responds whenever called.

This is particularly true of Punjab. In Sind, however, the PPP, while having a number of sophisticated leaders from the upper set of the rural aristocracy, can hardly claim the active support of the mass of the rural poor. I came to learn that the 'Jiye Sind' movement, with which is associated the old veteran, G.M. Syed, is fairly active and the Army has not been finding it easy to put it down. In fact, the second Indo-Pak rail link between Sind and Gujarat (next to the one through Punjab), planned as a follow-up of the Simla Agreement, could not be opened because of the disturbed condition in this region.

At the beginning of his rule, Bhutto could be persuaded by the wiser among his advisers to come to an understanding with the leaders of the regions where his PPP could make little dent. That was how he could make peace with Khan Abdul Wali Khan in NWFP and Ghaus Baksh Bizenjo and Ataullah Mengel in Baluchistan. But this was a very short-lived honeymoon. Wali Khan was put in prison by Bhutto and later, after Bhutto's ouster, General Zia released him, and while leading the Pakistan National Alliance (PNA), Wali joined hands with the Jamaat-i-Islami to cooperate with General Zia. But this too was short-lived. Today Wall Khan with his National-Democratic Party (NDP) is in a state of forced hibernation. During my visit, he returned to limelight by a controversial interview to a political weekly in which he held the view that the Partition was the brainchild of Zafrullah Khan, passed on to the Muslim League leaders in 1940 by the British authorities. The Government confiscated the weekly, sealed the press, though I understand this was later revoked. Zafrullah Khan protested and there was a first-class furore, but Wali Khan seems to be unruffled.

The main reason for the prevailing inaction on the part of Wali Khan's NDP seemed to me to be the Afghan developments. While he is known to have a fairly friendly rapport with the present regime in Afghanistan, Pakhtoon politics can surface only when conditions settle down in this zone stretching across the Pak-Afghan frontier. As for the inner politics of Pakistan, Wali Khan suffers from the handicap of having alienated himself from the PPP by joining hands with General Zia and the Jamaat against Bhutto, although he has abandoned his short-lived entente with the Martial Law.

In Baluchistan, I could sense a totally different climate. If Wali Khan has talked of the British-backed 'conspiracy' to foist partition, in Baluchistan I found political elements of various shades asserting that the accession of Baluchistan to Pakistan was managed by the British authorities under false pretence: in fact, this is common talk in Quetta today.

Of the four important political leaders of Baluchistan, two are out of the country—Mengel and Khair Bux Marri. While Mengel is in London, Marri has recently shifted with his family to Kabul. Originally the outlawed Baluchistan Liberation Front, operating from across the Afghan border, wielded minor influence in Baluchistan politics, but today with Marri setting up his headquarters in Kabul, a very different prospect stares the Pakistan authorities: From more than one source I got the report that quite a considerable number of militant youth—the Baluchistan Student Organisation is a highly active body wedded to militancy—have trekked across the frontier to prepare for armed action for Baluch liberation. For them, there is no hesitation in trying to secure Afghan help.

A two-hour session with the veteran Bizenjo and a longer one with Akbar Bugti with his impressive presence, provided me with an understanding of the present temper of the Baluch people. It reminded me of Netaji Subhas Bose in the weeks before his disappearance in 1940: my enemy's enemy is my friend. Bizenjo's political maturity enabled him to say that even at this late hour the grant of autonomy to Baluchistan can save it for Pakistan, but he was thoroughly pessimistic about such wisdom dawning on Islamabad. The theory that Pakistan has emerged as a buffer in super-power confrontation is dismissed by the Baluch leaders on the ground that the present Pak regime has openly thrown in its lot with the USA; rather Baluchistan placed between the USSR in Afghanistan and the USA in the Gulf can act as a real buffer, they claim.

In Quetta, Bhutto is remembered for his military

operation trying to suppress Baluch militancy. Although Bugti had cooperated with Bhutto even after the ouster of Bizenjo as Governor, I could see in Baluchistan, no sign of any rapport with the PPP. For the Baluch, independence is on the agenda today—at least that is how its more significant leaders view the critical international environment around it.

Judging by our conventional yardstick of Opposition unity, one may argue there is no threat to the present Martial Law regime. The PPP with its unchallenged primacy in Punjab can only hope to reap a moderate harvest in Sind, very little in NWFP and nothing at all in Baluchistan.

But a military regime in Pakistan can hardly ignore the political challenge coming to it from its own base in Punjab. Hence the prevailing obsession with the PPP. At Islamabad and even in Lahore, pro-establishment friends were at pains to assure me that there could be no resurgence of the PPP since it has no leader after Bhutto. There is certainly no leader as mercurial or charismatic like him, but Begum Nusrat Bhutto does command the allegiance of the PPP activists and a large section of middle leadership.

There are differences over tactics inside the PPP, some sections are not convinced that the Movement for Restoration of Democracy (MRD) was worth forming along with elements opposed to Bhutto. But, one PPP leader explained to me that the MRD is meant to demonstrate the political isolation of the present regime and is not an electoral alliance or platform.

While the normal political process in Pakistan is plugged by the continuation of the Martial Law, it is not surprising that there should be signs of impatience and despair. The Al-Zulfikar terrorist programme, whose author is supposed to be Bhutto's son Murtaza, now stationed in Kabul, is officially not approved of by the PPP, but nowhere in the Opposition did I find any outright hatred or disgust at the Al-Zulfikar claim of having drawn up a list of kill target. I was reminded of my college days in Bengal in the late twenties and early thirties when political establishments used to disapprove of the method of terrorist revolutionaries while pleading for an understanding of the conditions that could lead to such desperate action.

At some places, I found one or the other young member of a family having disappeared to join the Al-Zulfikar, while the living room is dominated by a garlanded portrait of Bhutto. There is no sign of condemnation of Al-Zulfikar, but concern about the fate of these young militants.

Discontent in recent months has been more pronounced in the world of the youth. The campus is no longer peaceful. I read long sermons by Generals-turned-Governors addressing colleges and schools, with long exhortation on moral values.

At the same time, even the controlled press has to carry reports of student disturbances. During my stay in Karachi, I came to learn about the armed exchange between the Jamaat followers and the united student movement led by the PPP over the Students Union election. PPP students complained that the police persecuted them and that the authorities falsely declared the Jammat candidates as elected. Cachés of arms were seized in the campus, and I was told that in one case guns with Israeli markings were found, suspected to have come from the black-marketing of arms meant for the Afghan guerillas.

The talk of student unrest invariably brings in Pakistan

the memories of the fall of the Ayub regime. The parallel may not be correct: behind the anti-Ayub stir there was the hand of Bhutto, while today there is no such outstanding personality directing the student militants. On the other hand, the anti-Ayub student unrest was spontaneous, while today's student unrest in Pakistan is the extended arm of the overt political parties opposed to the Martial Law. Small beginnings can be deceptive and it would be risky to ignore them particularly when such sectoral unrest has been persisting in one form or the other. More than one observer told me that in the last three months there has been a marked increase in clashes—not confined to students, but affecting other sections as well, including the tribal population in NWFP.

There was no time for me to go to the so-called Azad Kashmir area: but I met some of the militants from there. Mirpur, I am told, has been passing through a tense time. Early in December, six political leaders of the area met at Muzaffarabad and these included two former Presidents of Azad Kashmir; they raised the demands for election in Azad Kashmir in 90 days; all acts of the Martial Law regime to be declared null and void in Azad Kashmir; and the independence of the judiciary to be restored. Interestingly there was a reference in these demands to the fact that in the Indian part of Kashmir, there is an elected Government functioning. Followed repression and arrests. The situation, a Minister claimed, is calm in Azad Kashmir, but in official semantics, calm does not mean peaceful.

Listening to all the different and often conflicting assessments, I could not help sensing an uneasy twilight in Pakistan politics. There may not be a charismatic leader, but one cannot vouch for the viability of the present

Martial Law regime. At least it is not a safe bet.

The drive for Islamisation that General Zia has undertaken has had far less impact on the life of the people in Pakistan than the Islamic Revolution has had on that of Iran.

No doubt new mosques have come up, some of them having strikingly modern architecture. A massive mosque is under construction in the capital, at Islamabad. There is a special pavilion with a replica of the Holy Book set up recently in Lahore next to the Islamic Summit Minar, which Bhutto had built. Alcohol is banned but the rigidity of this ban is not as severe as it is in Iran. A friendly Major offered me a glass of rum while taking it himself in biting cold.

One sees many of the Muslim divines, high and low, flocking to five-star hotels where seminars and conferences on some aspects of Islam or Islamic life have become a common site. The television carries plenty of exhortations from the Holy Book interspersed with quotations from Iqbal or the Qaid-e-Azam.

To go back to the root of this drive for Islamisation, Bhutto at a critical moment, faced with the onslaught of the clerics, banned alcohol and disqualified Quadianis from holding principal offices in the state. While these were tactical moves, there has been more substantive grounds for Islamisation under General Zia. Apart from the fact that General Zia himself is the son of a maulvi, his political alliance with the Jamaat-i-Islami brought about the downfall of Bhutto. The more conservative wing of the Jamaat which has remained steadfast in its support for the Martial Law regime has insisted on the Islamisation, and it is conceivable that the Martial Law authorities have looked upon the entente with the clergy as providing some amount of mass support for the regime.

But Islamisation today is inextricably linked with Pakistan's growing Arab orientation, particularly the Saudi connection.

The amount of remittances from Pakistanis abroad—that is, mainly from West Asia—comes to two billion dollars a year. I am told that every fourth family in Pakistan benefits from such remittances from abroad.

I learnt in the Ministry of Planning that the rate of savings in Pakistan is low, roughly at 13 per cent, though the economy is better off with three good harvests, and the country has become self-sufficient in wheat. However, agricultural productivity is lower than in India.

Apart from remittances from Pakistanis working in these countries, the West Asian assistance comes in the form of credit support for balance of payment, loans for development projects and also for general purposes. Obviously, the Saudi share in all these is the largest. While it is difficult to get details on this score, I was told by a foreign specialist that upto June 1980, economic assistance for Pakistan from Muslim countries totalled about 8000 million dollars. There is also the *zakat* fund for internal charity: in that the Saudi contribution, according to some sources, comes to 200 million dollars.

The extent of West Asian connection is not confined to financial assistance or economic cooperation. Pakistan has the finest fighting force in the entire Muslim world and its standing Army is the second largest in this world.

It is, therefore, natural for Pakistan to have sent out military instructors, pilots, engineers and also training material for the armed forces of these countries, while it has thrown open its military training centres for trainees from the Muslim countries. Since the days of Bhutto,

Pakistan has concluded protocols for military cooperation with more than twenty countries.

The most important of such collaborations in the field of military training and exchange of defence personnel are with the United Arab Emirates, Jordan, Oman, Bahrain, Somalia. Saudi Arabia is a class by itself: it has from Pakistan a large number of Army, Navy and Air Force personnel on deputation, which will number about a thousand, seven task forces of Pak engineers and about 5000 ex-servicemen. Besides, there is the stationing of two divisions of the Pakistan Army (that is, about 40 thousand soldiers) by agreement with the Saudi Government.

The picture that emerges is that Pakistan today has definitely set its face towards West Asia. Its economy and its development prospects depend on cooperation and assistance with the Islamic countries of West Asia; militarily Pakistan is emerging as the kingpin of Arab strategic framework, particularly as visualised by Saudi Arabia. It is not without reason that Pakistan could get Saudi credit for buying F-16s. According to one Asian diplomat specialising in Pak-watching from his vantage point in Islamabad, General Zia has made fifteen visits to Saudi Arabia since his assumption of power.

While the Saudi connection has brought rich dividends for Pakistan, it has thrown up certain internal problems. I came to know that within the armed forces, tension rises in the matter of selection for postings abroad, since the salaries and perquisites are higher in Saudi Arabia and the Gulf: the unlucky ones feel frustrated. There are reports of corruption in the armed forces as kickbacks come along with large-scale arms deals.

One Opposition personality was blunt: "Our armed

forces are getting corrupt, and I don't think they will be able to defend our borders because they are involved in big money and have got used to air-conditioned comforts. There are three categories of people in our armed forces today; those who are running the country and have become administrators: those who are sent to Saudi Arabia; and those who are just in the Army. The first two are satisfied moneywise, but the third is grumbling and getting cynical.

I was waiting for the delayed flight from Quetta: looking out of the airport lounge with its magnificent vista of the airfield. I watched an Air-Force helicopter landing and out came two Arab dignitaries putting on their traditional toga; a few minutes later, an Air-Force plane taxied upto them and they flew out. A middle-aged Pakistani gentleman with double-breasted three-piece, looking like the scion of the upper set, murmured almost to himself: "There goes our new rulers in their dressing gown." A slight touch of disdain on the handsome face.

General Zia in his talk told me that Pakistan wants to remain in friendship with all its neighbours and dismissed the question if any one of them, in his perception, is the main enemy to be isolated. He talked of the Soviet Union and said he was trying to evolve a method of coexistence with it.

From the Foreign Office in Islamabad, I got the feeling that the Afghan question is now left, in its perception, as an item due for super-power negotiation. On its part, the Pakistan Government is not supplying arms to Afghan rebel groups, claimed Foreign Minister Agha Shahi. But Wali Khan's NDDP circles rebut this and offer even to show the arms deposits and the routes by which these reach the Afghan guerillas.

Visiting an Afghan refugee camp near Peshawar, I came away with the impression that these refugees have begun to create social tension in the area. The tribal refugees led by their respective *maliks* began to cross over the Sulaiman Range since 1978, but very large numbers came from early 1980. *Maliks*, in their lovely pashminas, looked very different from the type of dispossessed refugees we were familiar with from Bangladesh.

Coming from inhospitable terrain, most of them are unlikely to go back even if conditions change inside Afghanistan. Hard-working, many of them have set up shops—from butcher's to tailors—and are becoming an eyesore for the local people. In Quetta, a junior Government officer told me about house rents having shot up due to the influx of well-to-do refugees from Afghanistan: he said he could vouch for the refugee *maliks* actively involved in smuggling across the troubled frontiers.

At Torkhaim, at the Afghan end of the Khyber Pass, the atmosphere was surprisingly relaxed, a bustling bazaar where many cross the barrier from both sides without visa: the village elders sitting there can spot a stranger. The solitary Afghan sentry and his Pakistani counterpart did not at all look forbidding. At the shops, I noticed good stock of smuggled goods—from Wilkinson blades to Channel perfume. I bought a torch and found it is made in the People's Republic of China.

The Chinese presence is conspicuously minimal considering General Zia's assurance of excellent Sino-Pak relations.

Talking to people from different walks of life, I found that while China is considered a friendly nation, the average Pakistani feels that nothing very much could be expected from China. "They thundered over the radio in 1971, but did nothing to help us when our Army got defeated in Bangladesh," said a retired officer.

Inside Qaid-e-Azam's beautiful mausoleum in Karachi, there hangs a magnificent chandelier, a gift from the People's Republic of China. I wondered how Jinnah would have personally felt at such a gift from a Communist country hanging over his tomb.

In my 70-mile drive along the Karakoram Highway from Gilgit to Hunza, I could spot no Chinese, not even a military truck. The highway itself is a marvel of engineering, literally hewn out of the rock wall of the Karakoram range, while on the other side of the Hunza river, I could see the old Silk Road by which Marco Polo had travelled. Winter was yet to cover it with its blanket of snow; the orchards along the river were bare, waiting for the snows.

In the narrow picturesque valleys of Gilgit and Hunza, one comes face to face with majestic mountains—Hindukush in the west, Karakoram in the east stand like two sentinels, with the Rakaposhi crest in all its beauty glistening in the sun. To the north of this enclosure is the Pamir and in the south is High Himalaya with Nanga Parbat as its crown at this end—and down below the mighty Indus wending its way. No doubt a strategic location; what is its destiny tomorrow? Travellers and traders have ceased to trek; will the armoured cars and gunships disturb this heavenly peace?

Stark, bare mountains of a totally different genre I saw in Baluchistan—another area which is threatened to be engulfed in armed clashes of international dimension. The convulsions in Iran may be nearing the point of explosion as life ebbs out of the aging Ayatollah Khomeini. What happens to Iran after that? Although nobody in

Pakistan's establishment would talk about it—understandably everybody is tightlipped on this sensitive subject—a newsman's nose has a strong sense of smell. Pakistan may officially claim that it is not in Reagan's strategic consensus, but that does not rule out its involvement in the event of a struggle between contending forces in Iran tomorrow. The Saudi strategic framework, which Pakistan can hardly ignore as it is already part of it, would not remain idle in such a battle for the oil-rich Iran. Perhaps here one can find the answer why Pakistan is keen on having F-16s and why the Saudi regime lends it money for the purpose. The scenario is getting clear, as the air bases at Quetta and Peshawar are being expanded, and a new one set up at Bannu, cantonments spruced up, and the Iranian frontier heavily guarded. And in this scenario, the Baluch politics assumes a new dimension.

(January 23, 1982)

29

Passage through Pakistan–III

My twentyfive-day journey through Pakistan has convinced me that the time has come for an in-depth re-appreciation on our part of the prevailing mood of the people of Pakistan towards India. I could not escape the conclusion that although there is vested interest in certain sections in Pakistan—as there is in India—to fan the embers of mutual animosity, there is a very perceptible desire on the part of the overwhelming majority of the people to establish close rapport with the people of our country—provided they get an opportunity to express themselves through the ballot box.

"Bridges must be built even if barriers take time to be pulled down," said an elderly lady from a very political family. The lifting of restrictions on travels is a universal desire and non-official exchange of men and women in the intellectual and cultural world would go a long way towards better understanding at all levels.

From Mohenjodaro to Fatehpur Sikri, from Taxila to Hyderabad, there are a number of reference points in the common cultural heritage of the two countries that need to be kept alive for the generations that have come up after Partition. From Lahore to Lucknow via Delhi, from Karachi to Calcutta via Bombay, the crossroads of culture and commerce need to be repaired and broadened. It is not just a question of a no-war pledge, we have to build the structure of durable peace.

General Zia's offer of a no-war pact makes sense so far as he is concerned: if he has to be alert on the western front, he would naturally like to keep his rear in peace, sanctified by an official Indian commitment to it. Secondly: rapprochement with India pays good dividend inside the country, as one takes into account the present mood for friendship with India in Pakistan's populace.

But the Martial Law regime is, by General Zia's repeated commitments, a stop-gap regime: it makes no claim to having the sanction of Pakistan's electorate. Would not acknowledged political leaders in Pakistan resent if a solemn no-war pact is signed by India with a regime which is admittedly tentative?

An Opposition leader reminded me that when Bhutto went to Simla, he had taken all the Opposition bigwigs with him, as he was at that moment not a plenipotentiary elected by the people of Pakistan. A veteran Pakistani journalist explained that MRD had questioned the US giving aid to one person, and similarly there could possibly be no tangible political sanction behind any no-war offer coming from the present Martial Law bosses, who can only claim to be running a caretaker establishment.

I looked out of the plane window and watched the Lahore landscape disappearing. Our brothers and sisters down there are eager to live in peace and friendship with us, but would they not misunderstand if we sign a pact with a regime that they intensely dislike and want to replace by an elected one?

In the struggle for democracy in Pakistan lies the future of friendship between the two countries of the same subcontinent.

(February 6, 1982)

30

Behind Pak Bomb

The excitement over Pakistan having a nuclear bomb has naturally touched off widespread reaction in the country. Hardly anybody has taken seriously the Pakistani nuclear specialist Dr Khan's subsequent recantation of what he had told two journalists—one Indian and the other Pakistani—towards the end of January last. Any case, the Government of India's assessment based on its own reports is that Pakistan is ready, for all practical purposes, with a nuclear weapon.

The Rajiv Government has so far reacted with dignified restraint. Beyond saying that in the event of Pakistan acquiring the nuclear weapon, India would have to seriously reconsider its options, it has displayed neither hysteria nor indifference to this major development. The Government has to take into account the serious implications that any change in its nuclear policy—from peaceful to strategic—may involve. Not only in terms of its foreign-policy stand but also in terms of the heavy, backbreaking Defence burden that it would amount to, have to be carefully weighed by the Prime Minister and his colleagues. At the same time, the Government has to think seriously about the impact of Pakistan having a nuclear bomb on the morale of the Indian armed forces:

the psychological impact on a soldier about the knowledge that his adversary has got a deadly weapon, which can negate the outcome of any conventional clash of arms—a weapon that his own side does not possess—can be a very serious impediment towards building up effective defence. Besides, one has to take into account the reaction of such an Indian decision on the mind and morale of the people of Pakistan, for after all, they, the public of Pakistan, constitute potentially a friendly bastion for this country and not the military junta that today rules over them.

All this enjoins upon Rajiv Gandhi's Government a very serious in-depth appraisal of the entire problem thrown up by the Pakistan bomb before a considered decision is arrived at. It can afford to be neither impervious to the serious development nor be hustled into an irretrievable decision.

What is important to take into account by not only the Government but the public as well is the role of the US Administration in the entire Pakistani move. With all the hysterics and histrionics about Washington's commitment to non-proliferation—supposed to have been reinforced by the much-publicised Symington Amendment in the US Congress—it appears almost certain now that there would be no stoppage of American arms aid to Pakistan: on the contrary, the US military assistance budget for Pakistan is expected to be continuously enhanced as part of the US global strategy. This is in line with the latest Reagan move to increase arms supplies to the Afghan rebels just at the time when there is a major exercise by Moscow and Kabul to withdraw Soviet troops from Afghanistan and bring about national reconciliation there. In other words, the Reagan Administration is dead set on pouring in and amassing large arms depots in this region covering the Gulf and Afghanistan, with Pakistan as its main base, much in the same way as it over-arms Israel, despite its possession of nuclear weapons. In fact, one has the suspicion that a cluster of nuclear weapons in the hands of Pakistan fits in beautifully with the Pentagon's strategic view of this part of the world.

At a time when the standing of the Reagan Administration has touched the all-time low with the disclosures in the Tower Report and the possibility of many more stinking White House linen being washed in Washington, it is important for our Government to realise that there is no chance whatsoever for it to get a fair deal from the US when it comes to our national needs, not to speak of security requirements. From the discrimination perpetrated against India on the question of contracted fuel for the Tarapur nuclear reactor right up to the endless dragging of feet over permitting the sale of a single supercomputer—one gets an object lesson on the meaning of the much talked about Indo-US "shared perception" that intellectual innocents of our country are often led to believe. It is strange, if not embarrassing for the Government, when our Ambassador in Washington is known to be disconsolate at the strong Indian objection to the US supply of AWACS and other arms to Pakistan. We thank the Lord that we do not have many such specimens in our diplomatic service, who reflect the views of the Governments they are accredited to more faithfully than those of our own.

The Pakistan bomb is thus not a matter of concern for Indo-Pak relations alone. It brings out the rather serious dimensions of Indo-US relations. Rajiv Gandhi and his team of foreign-policy and defence experts have thus to take a total view of the situation, not just the acquisition of a nuclear device, that the Generals next door may have managed to assemble with materials mostly pilfered from abroad.

(March 14, 1987)

31

Measuring the Colossus

The Republic of India is now thirtyeight years old. It has weathered many a storm and has come to be recognised as a functioning democracy. The tremendous interest of the voter to exercise his right to vote is taken as proof of the enduring quality of our democracy. From this phenomenon, our Prime Minister seems to have drawn the conclusion that an unlettered electorate has a wider vision, a broader outlook. According to him, literacy "does more to narrow the vision than it does to widen it", as he told a Harvard audience last fall.

The prime ministerial profundities apart, the heightened political consciousness of the Indian voter is not because of his being denied the opportunity to be literate, but the gift of political awakening that Gandhi and Nehru left behind as their legacy to this nation. The key point in Gandhiji's leadership of the freedom struggle was his confidence and ability to infuse into the common humanity of this far-flung country the sense of fearlessness, the realisation of the massive strength that lay in the unity of this great nation, a unity that could overthrow the foreign rule. Let it not be forgotten that our Independence did not come through engineering a revolt of the armed forces, but by awakening the consciousness of our people.

Gandhi was the great communicator.

As his successor, Nehru carried forward the same tradition of his master, tirelessly communicating to the people of India on all issues, national and international, that faced this country. His constant peregrinations throughout the length and breadth of the country were not for mere collecting of votes at the hustings. He communicated to them to awaken them to the need of building a strong, self-reliant nation, to instill into them a scientific outlook, to abjure obscurantism and enrich our old civilisation with the benefits of a modern, rational perspective.

Those great communicators are gone and today there is hardly any communication worth the name between the rulers and the ruled. Hence, the democracy that was set up by the labours of the Constituent Assembly four decades ago, has become debilitated. Our democracy is under siege today assailed from all sides. The monster of communalism is again raising its head. The propagation of communal divide strikes at the very root of our democratic tradition and the edifice of democratic functioning. The direct offensive of secessionists has turned a corner of our country into a battle-ground of terrorism and police violence and this is spreading to other areas as well. Caste divisions instead of being obliterated have been sharpened in these forty years. The mass awakening in different regions instead of adhering to the principle of brotherly coexistence is manifesting itself in a distorted form in which rancour and acrimony take precedence over fostering of shared experience and shared benefits. The development process of these forty years has brought about a dehumanising disparity between the impoverished and the affluent. The rich have become richer without the poor getting their share of the national wealth. Politics, as a result, has been polluted with corruption, corroding public life at all levels. The nation is facing today a crisis in its value system.

In this context, one finds significant indicators of the mood of the nation. The overflowing homage spontaneously paid by this nation to the memory of Badshah Khan on his passing away this week is the measure of its unshakable attachment to the legacy of Gandhi. Badshah Khan's life is one long saga of indomitable courage, which he acquired as the true follower of Gandhi. Like a rock he stood. Independence did not bring him freedom. Thrown to the wolves, as he himself said with bitter sorrow at the partitioning of our great country, Badshah Khan continued his struggle relentlessly against the military dictators of Pakistan, who defiled his fair land of noble Pakhtoons. His life itself bears testimony to the might and grandeur of Gandhiji's teaching.

One perceives today all over the country, men and women in different walks of life seriously thinking about the state of the nation, about the collapse of values, about the degeneration of politics—"a fen of stagnant waters". Even wider questions about the future of humanity and our responsibility as the legatee of a rich and continuing civilisation are finding their way into the thought process of the serious sections of our intelligentsia. The signs of an impending intellectual ferment are discernible. And, History enjoins that every great revolutionary upheaval has been preceded by tremendous intellectual upsurge.

It is in this context that one senses an urge for rethinking on Gandhi and his teachings. The radical Left in our national spectrum, while acknowledging Gandhi's undisputed political leadership, did not pay in the past any serious attention to his totality of thinking, his moral exhortation; in a sense, they ignored Gandhi's ideological baggage, which was picked up by the pious do-gooders who, abjuring the dynamics of Gandhi's thought and action, his basic commitment to arouse the unlettered, underprivileged millions, reduced Gandhism into one more sect with its dogmas, *mantras* and commandments. Today, one notices refreshingly in the Left a groping towards Gandhi, an earnest revaluation of the essence of his work.

As the Republic faces the future with trepidation, as turbulence besieges it from all sides, it has to throw up new leaders, new pathfinders, who can take it to that haven of freedom and prosperity which indeed it deserves in full measure. Not a copycat Gandhi, not just the surname, but men and women of the heroic mould of Gandhi—that is what this great nation needs today at this critical juncture.

(January 26, 1988)

32

Pentagon's Loss

With the passing away of President Zia-ul-Haq, Pakistan enters a new phase in its chequered political career. His death is also bound to bring about a significant shift in the mosaic of regional politics in South Asia.

For eleven long years, General Zia ruled over Pakistan—the longest that any personality, civil or military, has held power in that country. As a military dictator, General Zia lacked legitimacy in the eyes of an overwhelming segment of public opinion in his own country but he displayed consummate craftsmanship as an astute political figure in the sphere of international diplomacy.

Playing on the so-called strategic imperatives of the US foreign policy, General Zia could skilfully extract maximum aid, both economic and military, from Washington. If Pakistan became the main base of operation for the Afghan *mujahideen,* it exploited this role to become the major beneficiary of the US arms bounty in consequence.

Son of a *maulvi* attached to the Army, General Zia throughout kept up his links with the Jamaat-e-Islami, which provided the mainstay of his political support when he engineered in 1977 the coup against Bhutto, who had chosen him as his trusted commander-in-chief superseding the claims of several Generals senior to him.

Unlike Field Marshal Ayub Khan, who on becoming President had divested himself of the post of the Army chief, General Zia never gave up his position as the supremo of the Army. Throughout he maintained his iron grip over the armed forces operating through a coterie of trusted men among whom the only civilian was Ghulam Ishaq Khan, who has now taken over the reins on the sudden demise of President Zia.

In his death the US has lost one of its most trusted stooges in this part of the world. After the fall of Shahenshah of Iran, it is Pakistan under President Zia which has provided the political and strategic foothold for Washington in South and South-West Asia. In the formation of the US Central Command, in working out its strategic thrust in the Persian Gulf area, in coordinating the US naval presence in the region with ground support for any eventuality, General Zia emerged as an indispensable factor in the Pentagon's scheme of things. Under President Zia, Pakistan provided military advisers to a large number of Arab countries. Two divisions of troops were until recently engaged in the service of the Saudi Arabian regime. Of all the key figures in Pakistan it was General Zia who held out till the end against the signing of the Geneva accords on Afghanistan, and even after Pakistan was compelled to sign the accords, it was General Zia who was in the forefront in violating its provisions with impunity. The *mujahideen* caucus has lost one of its protectors with the death of Zia-ul-Haq.

Because of the key position that General Zia held in the Pentagon's list of priorities, there was never a hold-up of US arms aid to Pakistan during his regime despite the clamour in the US Congress for a democratic order in that country. Even his policy for the acquisition of nuclear weapons did not come in the way of Pakistan getting abundance of US aid. It is an amazing case of poetic justice that the US Ambassador should lose his life alongwith General Zia in an aircraft gifted by the US.

President Zia played striking histrionics in his relations with India. His education at the Doon and St Stephens, his hi-fi passion for watching cricket, his generous hospitality to mediamen and Sikh pilgrims from India—all these bear testimony to his superb public relations exercise. One of his last stunts was to bestow special honours on Morarji Desai while backing Khalistani terrorists in Punjab. At the same time, General Zia fought shy of signing a friendship treaty that India offered and he never hesitated to provide hospitality to promoters of Khalistan and asylum for extremist terrorists carrying on their dastardly acts in Punjab.

General Zia-ul-Haq could never countenance a democratic set-up in Pakistan. Even the truncated one he set up with Junejo as the Prime Minister was snuffed out earlier this year. His campaign for Islamisation was meant as an antidote to democratic urges in different parts of Pakistan.

There is no question that the removal from the scene of this hatchet-man of democracy will open up new possibilities which no military junta will find it easy to muzzle. The coming weeks and months will be the testing time for the Generals as well as the democratic forces in Pakistan.

(August 17, 1988)

33

Dawn over Pakistan

After a long, dark night, there are signs of a new dawn over Pakistan. The overpowering interest and excitement over the recently-held General Elections in that country—at many places taking the form of a veritable mass upsurge—demonstrated the clearest repudiation of the eleven-year old military dictatorship which had actually come to power through a coup in the wake of the last general elections.

There have been many impediments in the process of the elections and there are undoubtedly pitfalls ahead on the road to a stable democratically-elected Government in Pakistan. These are only to be expected, because no military junta consents smoothly to abdicate power, particularly when it has so long enjoyed the generous patronage of the Pentagon.

Besides, the imbalance that has been fostered for four decades to sharpen the disparities among different well-marked regions of Pakistan—with the Punjabi domination of the armed forces and to a large measure of the civil service—is likely to be exploited by the entrenched vested interests, scared at the prospect of having to face a democratic Government. There are no doubt other constraints and contradictions in the complex situation prevailing in Pakistan politics today. The journey ahead can by no means be smooth and easy.

But the *central* point in the reality of Pakistan today is that the most powerful military dictatorship in Asia, if not the world, has been overthrown. And with all its pulls and pressures, bullying and blandishment, it cannot return to power. Benazir Bhutto, who has emerged as the symbol of the democratic assertion in Pakistan, is certainly not going to have an easy time. Many problems and harassments will beset her. But there can be no going back to the days of Zia's ruthless dictatorship clothed with the trappings of fundamentalist bigotry.

The historic significance of the democratic elections in Pakistan lies precisely in this that in South Asia today, the days of military dictatorships are over. What has happened in Pakistan, coming in the wake of Burma, is bound to have its wholesome repercussions on Bangladesh, where the political base of the democratic forces has been traditionally stronger. General Ershad's has been a tinpot outfit compared to General Zia's iron rule. The reactionary forces in Bangladesh, which have so long been seeking inspiration from Pakistan and patronage from the oil-soaked Arab world, will be put to difficulty by this remarkable leap-forward towards democracy in Pakistan.

More directly a matter of interest and concern for India is that these momentous developments in Pakistan will have their impact on its relations with this country. The democratic forces in this country shall always share in the jubilation at the victory of democracy in our immediate neighbourhood. Many of the outstanding problems that come in the way of improving relations between the two countries will no doubt require patient and painstaking handling before solutions could be reached. At the same time, let us not forget that the war-cry of the Generals in Pakistan has always been against India, and that the most important Indo-Pak Agreement signed in Simla sixteen years ago was between the elected representatives of the two countries. The prospect for reconciliation has certainly been enhanced with the present democratic upsurge in Pakistan.

To facilitate this significant development it is for India to take the initiative. Not only is India the bigger neighbour, it has a long and sustained career as a viable practising democracy, and it is, therefore, its privilege and responsibility to stand by the democratic forces in Pakistan.

(November 26, 1988)

34

Road Ahead for Benazir

Benazir Bhutto's accession to Prime Ministership is undoubtedly a watershed in Pakistan politics. Apart from the fact that a woman has been voted to power in a country which has so long been sought to be kept under the tutelage of reactionary forces, the exit of the military dictatorship that her triumph symbolises, is of historic significance not only for Pakistan but for the entire South Asian region as well.

Benazir's road to power has predictably not been strewn with roses, roses all the way. The alignment of forces in Pakistan on the morrow of General Zia's death was such that one could hardly predict with confidence that her PPP would win an easy majority. Rather, the calculation of the ruling clique in Pakistan was that her path to power could be thwarted by the Islamic Democratic Alliance round the then ruling Muslim League, to be backed by the Army and also the Americans. The coordinator of these three elements could be located in the Presidency of mild-mannered Ghulam Ishaq, who personally enjoys the confidence of Washington and who was a party to the overthrow and liquidation of Zulfikar Ali Bhutto. The calculation of this trio was that Benazir's PPP would not be able to muster more than 70 or 75 seats in the National

Assembly while the powerful Inter-Services Intelligence put it at below 70.

However, those calculations went wrong as the Islamic Democratic Alliance fared badly at the poll—much worse than what its patrons expected with all the lavish spending of resources and demonstration of official backing.

As Benazir emerged from the election as the most important figure with a clear claim to Prime Ministership, the game of blocking her passage to power was started in full swing. Protracted talks with her were undertaken by President Ishaq, the Army Chief and even by the American Ambassador, an extraordinary manner of respecting Pakistan's sovereignty. While Benazir Bhutto kept her cool with them all, listening to them more than giving away, she at the same time kept up a running dialogue with the public through the press, recalling that the flouting of the electoral verdict of 1970 had led to the disintegration of Pakistan and the creation of Bangladesh; and warning that if this were repeated this time, the integrity of the present Pakistan would also be jeopardised. She had a strong case on this count as her PPP had done exceedingly well even in the Assembly election in Sind. In this exercise Benazir has shown a degree of political maturity which many others in such a station may not have mastered.

The forces opposed to untrammelled democratic functioning in Pakistan have had to acquiesce in Benazir Bhutto's coming to power, but it has indeed been rather painful for them to be reconciled to the new realities. The Army lobby wants the continuation of the policy of interference in Afghanistan. Though the Americans have not been able to block her coming to power, they are pressing for the retention in the Cabinet of two of their favourites, Shahibzada Yakub Khan and Mahbub-ul-Haq.

The Army cannot come back to power, but at the same time it refuses to quit.

Benazir Bhutto's coming to power is undoubtedly a magnificent triumph. However, she faces the prospect of very difficult days ahead when the forces that could not block her way to power would be active in continuously nibbling at her regime and thereby disrupting it. The road ahead seems to be strewn with minefields, both indigenous and imported. It is only the strength of mass support within the country that can sustain her, and it is for her and the leaders of the PPP to sharpen the vigilance of the people against any attempt at subverting democracy in Pakistan.

(December 3, 1988)

35

Walls Must Come Down

In all the big news that pour in nowadays, the element of surprise is almost overpowering. And this is not confined to the Soviet Union and Europe. The infection is spreading over Asia and Africa as well. Mandela talking to the aparthied chief without being nabbed, Americans talking to the Vietnamese Government, reversing the hostility of decades.

If we look around, we find that all the partitions brought about at the close of World War II are being dismantled. Germany, divided by the might of four victorious powers of that war, is getting unified. And the compelling force behind this unification is not the decree of Governments but the determined power of the people. The barbed wires have been pulled down, the Berlin Wall—that ugly symbol of angry confrontation—has been dismantled not by the armies of any power but by the sheer force of popular will. The unification of Germany, which now awaits only protocol formalities, symbolises the triumph of popular will. What the rulers design, the people can undo.

This is the order of the day as we have stepped into the nineties. Frontiers are being redrawn by the might of the awakened humanity, which the chanceries of big powers can no longer withstand.

And is this upheaval confined to the communist world or its periphery, because of Gorbachev's mischief, as some of the orthodox Brahmins of the Marxist fraternity are deceiving themselves into believing? Look at Korea. Here was fought the first full-scale war of the post-World War epoch in course of which General McArthur wanted to drop the atom bomb. In bringing about an uneasy truce, Nehru played a role—becoming the first leader of a newly-liberated country to intervene in world diplomacy. Some of our diplomats and Army personnel, who were sent for peace-keeping under what was then called the Neutral Nations Commission, still remember how bitter was the animosity between the two parts of partitioned Korea, how truculent was the mood of hatred that prevailed. Those days, in the early fifties, it used to be said that mutual hatred between two parts of a partitioned country seemed to be stronger than that between traditional enemies.

But today that is being falsified. For quite some time, there have been moves for getting over the barriers that divide Korea. The Government in the North made some noise about the two parts coming nearer to each other, but they did not touch off a movement. In the South, there was ferment, particularly among the youth. The Government tried to suppress it, but the persistence of this new urge to break barriers has finally had its way. And now it is the South Korean Government leader—no cousin of Gorbachev—who has announced his readiness to open the frontier. The first step towards reconciliation. Today this looks like a long process, but in the new temper, developments get telescoped and what might look as a long-drawn-out prospect suddenly appears on the agenda for tomorrow, if not today.

This tidal wave of human restlessness breaking down barriers, doesn't it touch our shores? Shouldn't we too start thinking afresh and join the process of readjustment and reconciliation? The Partition of our country was effected about the same time as the Partition of Germany and Korea, and it brought with it rivers of blood and unredeemed sorrow. If the German people can force reunification and the Korean people reconciliation, why should we lag behind? The people of India and Pakistan, the common humanity who live in penury and privation, what have they gained by this wall of anger and hate, of bloody conflicts that the two countries have suffered? We pile up deadly arms, stacks of them, to kill each other to the delectation of all those who have made a virtue out of animosity. The leaders of both the countries realise that thousands of crores of rupees that are being spent on Defence could have been invested in the well-being of the people.

To talk of undoing the Partition itself may frighten many people in both the countries, conditioned as we all have been to accepting the dividing line as something permanent and sacrosanct. And if some of us in India talk about it, there are elements in Pakistan who will see in it some sinister conspiracy to undo that country.

But surely we can think of something short of reunification. My friend Madhav Kamath has been tirelessly pleading in his writings for an India-Pakistan confederation. And he has eminent referees to back his views. Rammanohar Lohia and Deen Dayal Upadhyay too, at some point of time, talked openly about the need for such a confederation. No doubt the context was different, but the idea of a confederation was by itself no anathema. Much later Sheikh Abdullah felt that amity between the two countries alone could bring peace and stability in Kashmir, and he too talked about the prospect of a confederation. He tried to convince both Pandit Nehru and Field Marshal Ayub. But Panditji passed away before Sheikh Sahib's long-cherished summit could take place.

The time has come now for us to think and think hard about new ways of settling old problems. Political leaders are hamstrung by their traditional postures and it will be unfair and unrealistic to expect them to initiate such thinking, as whatever they may say on either side of the frontier will be suspect in the eyes of their respective counterparts. For, make no mistake, many of our leaders have made a virtue out of such captive mentality, captive to the pride and prejudices of the past. But yesterday's postures cannot be sustained today and they are certain to be rejected tomorrow. It is for the intellectual community to take the initiative for new thinking.

It is time we ourselves forced our Governments to let us cross over to each other's homes and establish a bond of unbroken amity. Why should we be scared of restrictions? If we come forward in hundreds and thousands, the Governments of our two countries are bound to respond. Why can't we take a pledge, the intelligentsia of our two countries, that we shall never permit our Governments to use the nuclear bomb to destroy our people, no matter what the provocation? And then there is the question of trade and market. If countries engaged in fierce competition, like those in Europe, can form a common market, which in turn is leading to political integration, why can't India and Pakistan take the lead together to establish a South Asian common market? No, we must not lose time. The tidal wave of human turbulence is not going to spare us. We can hardly live in isolation from the world trends.

Time to think, and not only to think, but to act.

(August 4, 1990)

36

We Shall Overcome!

A refreshing breeze indeed. In the midst of all the dirt and squalor, hatred and violence, tensions and clashes that pervade between the two neighbours, the spontaneous euphoria that welled up in our country the moment it was known that Pakistan had lifted the World Cup trouncing England, was heart-warming by all counts.

I am no cricket addict and I can tell you nothing about the mysteries of the game or about the respective merits of rival teams and the players. Naturally, I am overjoyed when I see Sachin Tendulkar wielding the bat as I used to when Sunil Gavaskar was in action. Kapil Dev I look forward to. In my school days, I remember watching Dilwar Hussain fighting back an English team led by Gilligan. Ranji and Duleepsinghji were legends whom I had not seen. The favourite in Calcutta was Mushtaq Ali. We used to see Bradman's face in the newspaper—there was no live radio commentary in those ancient days, and the television was beyond our imagination.

As I watched people in different parts of the vast city of Calcutta celebrating Pakistan's victory, I thought to myself why and how this came about. I have seen in the past how tension mounts and the people get divided when Indian and Pakistani teams face each other in any game.

This is not confined to Srinagar, but could be seen in Surat and Moradabad, Delhi and Hyderabad. Only last year communal vandalism spoilt the pitch in a Bombay stadium to bar Pakistan playing in India. How then is this transformation today?

Surely, Imran Khan emerged as a great leader who could invoke the best out of every member of his team—like an Alexander or a Napoleon in the battlefield. And his team also played magnificently which even an unversed like me could get excited about. But does the superb performance of the Pakistani team account for the instant exultation among all sections in Calcutta, or for that matter, in most of the cities in our country?

No, there is something more to it. Imran himself said his team's victory is a victory for the entire subcontinent. He said this in so many words:

> "This cup that we have brought today with us is for the entire subcontinent—for Pakistan, India and Bangladesh. I know people in India and Bangladesh have great love for us. They appreciated our performance, prayed for us. That's what really matters."

One may say Pakistan's victory was a victory for the continent of Asia itself. The game which our White masters of yester-years used to claim as their heavenly gift to civilisation, is now mastered by the people who are not White, and who had been kept down in subjugation by the Whites for a century-and-a-half.

But I would go further. The meaning of this unbounded enthusiasm cannot be measured as having a mere geographical dimension. It is the upsurge of the heart of the millions upon millions of our two countries. As a young airline officer on duty at the Calcutta airport thought aloud to me: "If we had not had the Partition what an invincible team we would have had which nobody could have ever dared to trounce!" Here is the sentiment of the common humanity in our two countries, pristine and transparent, that is latent all over.

My ancestral home was in Barisal, the waterlogged district of south Bangladesh. I was brought up in Calcutta, and now for the last forty years, I have been living in and working from Delhi. When I was eight years old, I went to Lahore with my grandmother—faint memory of a clean and beautiful city. I am a bit of a nomad and my wanderlust has taken me to many parts of the world. In 1983, when I got a chance, I spent a fortnight in Pakistan, travelling by train, air and bus—Lahore, Karachi, Mohenjodaro, Islamabad, Peshawar, Khyber Pass, Gilgit and Hunza, Quetta and Ziarat. What was my impression of that opening into my neighbour's land? Without knowing a word of Urdu, I met them, hundreds of them, as if they were my own—I could feel the old generation is nostalgic about India and the young are curious. Incidentally, although I have never met Imran Khan, I have recently got acquainted with him through his book on the land and the people that live by the great Indus as it flows from the High Himalayas to the Arabian Sea—an unforgettable experience that takes you to the roots.

As a young reporter, I had covered the ghastly nightmare of the Partition in which brother slaughtered brother in a fury of political insanity—from the Great Calcutta Killing to the heart-rending trek of refugees. And I was also a witness to the heart-lifting glimmer of hope that Gandhiji sought to bring through his crusade for communal brotherhood in Beliaghata and Bihar. He would have taken it to the heart of Pakistan as he had done in Noakhali if he had not been slain by one of his own countrymen. Fortyfive years later, it is the same glimmer of hope that I felt as I sensed the feelings of elation at Pakistan's victory in the streets of Calcutta.

Hardheaded politicians will dismiss all this as just a passing sentimental effusion which has no place in the stern realities of confrontational politics in which two neighbours are involved—armed alert on the Line of Control, the JKLF, the Khalistani infiltrator in Punjab and the Hizbul secessionist in Kashmir, the *Hindutva* and the Islamic assertion, and then the nuclear bomb. We have built forbidding walls of hatred between ourselves, and our Governments to not hesitate to make an exhibition of this antipathy before the world. We have by mutual consent introduced a visa system by which our citizens have to report to the police every few days as if we are suspected criminals. The visa-holders from distant lands are allowed to move about freely in our two countries, but not the nationals of the two neighbours. We pile up huge arsenals of deadly weapons and frankly declare that our threat perception comes from each other more than from anybody else. We make a complaint to distant powers about each other conspiring to have the nuclear bomb, but we do not sit down and talk it over beween ourselves.

The Partition that divided India was the product of fear and folly, arrogance and insensitivity, for which we can blame our leaders, but that is not going to undo an act of history. To think in terms of undoing that Partition is today not only unrealistic but may turn out to be dangerous. What as realists we can do and must do is to boldly bring our two peoples together without hurting the sovereignty of either country. When the entire world is in a state of ferment and convulsion, when mighty totalitarian structures are collapsing without a whimper, and millions upon millions are on the move in search of new moorings, new identities, we, the two largest peoples in this region, the proud inheritors of the same history, have also to think hard and bestir ourselves to bury our arms and abjure our fears, prejudices and misgivings, and respond faithfully and abundantly to the irrepressible urge of our peoples to live in peace and harmony—share our moments of joy and help to mitigate our pangs of sorrow and deprivation.

It is said that when a people wills it, it can move mountains. On every issue that divides our two countries, have we not reached a blind alley? The torments that beset us, haven't we had enough of them? If Kashmir is the stumbling block, isn't it time to think of new ways of looking at it? The mess that we have both made in our respective parts of this paradise on earth, should make us hang our heads in shame. We have spilled blood in plenty, we have squandered crores and we both have lost the trust of the people of that picturseque Valley. Isn't it time that we acknowledged our bankruptcy and sought new ways of bringing peace, and listened to the people right there? Can India's sovereignty be asserted only by the gun? And can Pakistan's glory be enhanced by ceaselessly stoking a low-intensity war which can never be won?

There is abundant fund of goodwill and far-seeing wisdom in our two peoples to work out new designs of enduring amity. And out of that shall emerge the true confederation of heart and head of the two independent countries, the neighbours that bear the stamp of a great heritage of History's richest civilisations.

(April 4, 1992)

37

Kashmir Crisis

For long it has been fashionable to talk about the Kashmir crisis as the most intractable challenge before the country and yet do pretty little to deal with it and thereby let the blood-letting go on. Recently, however, one notices some stir in diverse circles both at home and abroad to tackle the Kashmir problem. A feeling appears to have crept in both within the Government and the Opposition that Kashmir can no longer be kept on the back-burner. This sense of urgency has to a large measure been accelerated by Pakistan's mounting pressure in both the diplomatic and political fronts.

The Prime Minister himself publicly mentioned in his August 15 address from the Red Fort about his "keenness to hold free and fair elections within the framework of the Indian Constitution and to instal a popular Government" in the trouble-tossed State. The Union Home Minister on his part too has been talking about the possibility of holding elections in Jammu and Kashmir within the next six months. It needs to be noted that the President's Rule in Kashmir cannot be continued indefinitely: it has to end by September next year.

Of late there has been quite a lot of activity in the Opposition camp too about what's to be done in Kashmir.

Recently the National Conference leader, Dr Farooq Abdullah, and the Janata Dal leader, Mufti Mohammad Sayeed, spent sometime in Srinagar, and on their return, a meeting was held at Mufti's place to discuss the critical situation of the Kashmir Valley which was attended by most of the top leaders who included V.P. Singh and S.R. Bommai, Surjeet and Indrajit Gupta, and Murasoli Maran from the DMK. Also present was Iftikar Ansari, the Congress leader in the now-defunct Assembly, who is an influential Shia leader of the Valley. The assessment at the meeting was that the militants practically run the show in the Valley while the Army and the para-military forces are only holding on to the terrain but have practically lost the populace. The consensus among these Opposition leaders was that no election would be possible in the Kashmir Valley unless it is preceded by some thaw in the situation, some opening of political activity which, in its turn, could be possible only if the Government could indicate about the extent of autonomy it would be prepared to grant to the State. The Opposition leaders are reported to have apprised the Prime Minister about their assessment and have left the matter in his court.

It is generally conceded in the official circles that while the Army and the para-military forces can indefinitely hold on to the Valley, no matter how much it costs in terms of resources and manpower, it is not possible to dislodge the armed militants except by means of the political process.

It needs to be acknowledged that the Kashmir crisis has four facets each of which has a distinct angle, and it is only through the management of these four can there be a viable solution of the Kashmir problem. These are: the situation in the Kashmir Valley itself; the international facet, particularly with relation to the US and the UK; the Pakistanii facet and its impact on Indo-Pak relations; and lastly, its bearing on the home front, that is, on the Indian politics as a whole.

The actual situation in the Kashmir Valley is that all civic activities are controlled by militants—in some area by one militant group, in another area by another militant group. The Indian Army guards the frontier along Pakistan, but the terrain is mostly mountainous and it becomes almost impossible to prevent continuous infiltration of militants from the Pakistani side. Inside the Valley, the Indian police and para-military forces have to clash most of the time with the militants, and the administration is practically at a standstill. There are reports of the local administration having been infiltrated by the militant agents. Many people sympathise with the militants, giving them shelter. Even those in the villages and towns who do not want any armed clashes, do not condemn the militants. Propaganda among the public in the Valley is mostly hostile to the Indian Government.

The clashes between militant groups and Indian forces were a little lower in the period of May and June this year. But they have grown more in August, and it was difficult for the Indian authorities to hold any function to mark the Indian Independence Day on August 15. Only a flag hoisting could be managed under tight military security.

The militants in the Kashmir Valley are broadly of three groups:

The Hizb-e-Islami which is the most fanatic group and is affiliated to the Jamaat-e-Islami of Pakistan. They want that the Kashmir Valley must be merged into Pakistan. They get direct support in arms and training from Pakistan.

The second group is the Al-Jehad which is also obscurantist. However, they are not openly campaigning for annexation to Pakistan, but take an ambivalent position, though fiercely against Delhi.

The third group is the JKLF (Jammu-Kashmir Liberation Front) which wants that the entire State of Jammu and Kashmir (including the portion of Kashmir now occupied by Pakistan) must become an independent State, and be attached to neither India nor Pakistan.

Of these three groups, the JKLF is the most popular among the Muslim population in the Kashmir Valley, and the Hizb-e-Islami is the least popular in the Valley. But the the Hizb-e-Islami has the largest stock of weapons and the JKLF has the smallest stock of weapons. The Pakistan Government gives weapons and training to all the militant groups so that the Indian Government forces are harassed to the maximum possible extent, but actually the Pakistan Government gives the maximum possible support and weapons to Hizb-e-Islami, most of whose militant cadres actually come from Pakistan. The Pakistan Government does not fully trust the JKLF leaders, but because the JKLF is popular in Kashmir, it gives them limited quantity of weapons to combat the Indian forces. It is to be noted that in the area of Kashmir now under Pakistan's occupation, the JKLF faces persecution on many occasions from the Pakistani authorities, because the Pakistan Government, particularly the ISI, does not permit the JKLF to campaign for the independence of Kashmir from both India and Pakistan. It is worth noting that unlike the other two militant formations, the JKLF acknowledges that the Hindu population who had to leave the Valley in large numbers three years ago should be brought back and their houses restored to them.

In the present situation, none of the major parties function in the Valley. All their leaders are out of the Kashmir Valley—either in Jammu or in Delhi. The cadres of these major parties are inactive though they have not left the Valley. They on their own cannot resist the militants. They want their leaders to come and then they may risk holding a mass campaign. At present, it is impossible for any leader to attack or criticise the militants. But it is possible to appeal to the militants that instead of killing people, let there be discussion about the future of Kashmir.

It is in this context that one has to take into account Dr Farooq Abdullah's recent interview to the BBC in which he clearly distanced himself from New Delhi and said that any discussion on the future of Kashmir has to include besides India and Pakistan, the Kashmiri leaders too. Broadly, this is perhaps meant to evoke a positive response from the JKLF and thereby undermine the base of the fanatical Hizb-e-Islami.

While this is roughly the situation on the ground, the international facet of the Kashmir crisis can hardly be ignored. The British public, including the Labour Party, at one stage echoed the viewpoint of the militants, laying particular stress on the violation of human rights in the Valley by the Indian armed forces. This was sought to be countered by the official Indian stand which pointed to the violence indulged in by the militans. This approach by New Delhi had a marginal impact on the Western public.

On the part of the US, Washington has clarified that it disapproved of Pakistan's interference in the affairs of Kashmir. At the same time, it has been pressing for a settlement between India and Pakistan over the Kashmir issue. Though no specific proposals for such a settlement has so far officially emanated from Washington, it appears that the ground is sought to be prepared through non-official overtures. It is in this context that the recent thesis by a Carnegic Fellow, James Clad, has attracted a lot of attention. It wants the present Line of Control to be recognised as the international frontier thereby sanctifying the partition of Kashmir, with some area being ceded by Pakistan on the southern side, while India reciprocating by ceding claim on the north, that is, legitimising the present Sino-Pak deal. One can only say that the James Clad proposal is in the nature of a trial balloon, but it does indicate the likelihood of prodding from the West for a settlement of Kashmir. One more pressure point for New Delhi.

The Pakistan angle was spelt out by its Foreign Secretary during his recent talks with his counterpart in New Delhi, when he said Kashmir is "the core issue" of dissonance between the two countries. By the very tenets of the so-called two-nation theory—which forms the ideological platform for the existence of Pakistan—Kashmir with its Muslim majority population contiguously located must belong to the state of Pakistan. This is precisely the reason why the Pakistan authorities are dead set against the JKLF which wants independence for Kashmir, because any acquiescence to the demand for independence of Kashmir would be a body-blow on the two-nation theory. Further, the right of Kashmiris as a distinct ethnic group to independence, is a matter of utmost threat for the very integrity of Pakistan. Once the Kashmiri people are allowed to be independent because of a distinct ethnic identity, how could the claims of the Baluchis, the Sindhis and the Pakhtoons be denied? And if that is permitted to happen

Pakistan will be reduced to a bloated Punjabi Suba, and nothing more.

Viewed from this angle, BJP leader Dr Murli Manohar Joshi's suggestion for isolating the Muslim majority Kashmir Valley from Jammu and Ladakh—however rational it may appear—unwittingly helps to strength Pakistan's ideological stand behind its Kashmir policy.

Lastly comes the impact of the Kashmir crisis on the Indian political scene. The Congress, the Janata Dal and the Left feel that there should be more autonomy for Kashmir without which militants cannot be controlled. There is, however, no clear view yet as to the degree of autonomy to be given. The Congress feels that if too much autonomy is given to Kashmir, the same demand will come from other parts of India.

The BJP is opposed to granting any autonomy to Kashmir. It wants to cancel even Article 370 of the Indian Constitution which gives a very limited degree of autonomy to Kashmir. The BJP's view in the main is that the Muslim population in Kashmir is unreliable and acts as the agent of Pakistan, and they must not be pampered. It needs to be noted that of all the political parties, the BJP commands preponderant support among the large body of Hindu refugees from the Valley—numbering nearly three lakhs—who have been living in miserable plight, and whose return has become essential for establishing normalcy in the State of Jammu and Kashmir.

Prime Minister Narasimha Rao is, therefore, faced with the dilemma that even if all other parties agree to concede autonomy to Kashmir, the BJP can whip up a campaign against it all over India and say that the Rao Government is surrendering territory to a Muslim population which is anti-Indian. All this may lead to a heightening of communal tension.

It is thus imperative that the building of a national consensus on Kashmir acceptable to all parties in the country becomes the crucial responsibility of all concerned, not only of the Prime Minister but all parties including the BJP. The alternative may be disastrous for the nation as a whole, because the present blood-letting can only end up in the disintegration of not only the picturesque Valley but a blow to India's unity as well. We, all of us, have to bestir ourselves before the grandeur of autumn in the Valley yields to the rigours of a snow-bound winter in three months from now.

(September 5, 1992)

38

Towards Bosnia?

Bombay is burning. Sopore is burning.

Bombay marks the worst of Hindu-Muslim communal violence since the bloody days of the Partition that came with the Independence of India. The civil administration having failed, the Army has been called in to put down killing and looting in the country's commercial capital famous for its cosmopolitan culture.

And Sopore? The Border Security Force under constant attack from the militants fighting for Kashmir's secession, allegedly launched an attack against the civilian population setting fire to their tenements, in which nearly a hundred reportedly perished. Whatever news about this ghastly operation that could trickle in beating the official censor has horrified large sections of the public.

At one place, the Army is called to enforce civil order and at the other place, rampage by the security forces infuriates the civilian population against the Government. In other words, the very forces that the Government summons at one place to maintain its authority, destroys the very same authority at another place. The law of diminishing returns plays havoc upon a Government using the armed forces to establish its authority at home.

The hazards of using the armed forces to deal with internal disorder have long been acknowledged. Only last year, a warning by the Army chief in a press interview created quite a stir but could hardly be denied. He is not the first Army chief to have advised the civil authority on this score. In fact, such internal emergency assignment deflects the armed forces from their primary responsibility of guarding the frontiers of the country from foreign armed attack. Instead, if the Army is used as an internal police, its own morale has the danger of being undermined while it usurps to itself the role that rightly belongs to the civilian authority. All this is known to our national leaders, and yet they are compelled to use the armed forces because of their having allowed to develop a situation which in reality brings out the bankruptcy of their own policies.

If violence in all its hideousness has arrived in Bombay, it is entirely due to the failure of the Government in facing the Ayodhya crisis which itself shook the very foundations of our democratic, secular society. And this failure at Ayodhya has not only damaged our democracy at home but our standing abroad as well. So much so that India has to bear the odium of having to get the SAARC Summit put off because its own Prime Minister could not attend it for the fear of having to face possible demonstrations against him. And if this is the depth to which our prestige has plummeted in South Asia, one may easily imagine how much this in its turn impairs our standing in the world today.

In terms of the durability of our Republic, the Ayodhya crisis has brought to the fore for the first time the serious concern of a large body of opinion in this country whether the embittered polarisation that has been generated between a large section of Hindus and Muslims could be overcome at all, or whether the poison would spread to the five-and-a-half lakh villages where the two communities have been living for ages in harmony and with honour.

One wonders if the perpetrators of the demolition of the Babri Masjid at Ayodhya realised the full impact of their vandalism when they carried out the secretly planned operation on December 6. Because, they have not only hurt the feelings of a minority community which they hate, but they have also in the process despoiled the Supreme Court and defaced the Constitution. To plead that all this is irrelevant in the urge for worshipping Lord Ram does not carry conviction, because behind the whipping of religious frenzy on the part of the political elements involved in the campaign for building the temple by destroying the mosque has been, in the eyes of the discerning observer, the drive to garner votes for accession to power.

Subsequent measures taken to deal with the Ayodhya crisis has not helped to extricate it from the trivial world of petty politics. Neither the ouster of the BJP Governments in four States and the ban on certain parties, nor the ordinance acquiring the disputed area as also the setting up of two Trusts for building a mosque and a temple, has helped to reinvigorate a sense of confidence in the Central Government, just as the much published campaign against communalism by like-minded political parties has hardly made any impact on the mass mood. All over the country, a sense of hopelessness has crept in about the efficiency of and intention behind any action by the accredited political parties. In other words, the public impression is fast gaining ground about the bankruptcy of political parties in dealing with problems facing the country today.

As for the gruesome incident at Sopore, its fall-out will be no less calamitous. Whatever may be the claims of the authorities, it is generally known that the continued presence of the security forces to deal with any militancy leads to the alienation of the local populace, as it has happened at a number of places in the Kashmir Valley in the last three years. The Sopore incident, however, has much more disastrous implications. The clash between the militants and the security forces, by all available accounts, was turned into an all-out attack against the local population of this important town in Kashmir's apple country with the BSF virtually carrying fire and sword against the civilian population.

Apart from this amounting to serious violation of the norms of conduct in any military operation, the horrendous incident indicates that whatever public support the Indian authorities might still be retaining in the Kashmir Valley, even that is being recklessly squandered by the very security forces which are supposed to replenish it. Sopore points to the surest way of losing the Kashmir Valley for good for India. It is true that the Government has understood the significance of the Sopore tragedy, as two Cabinet Ministers were dispatched by the Prime Minister to bring him a first-hand report.

But Sopore is not just an aberration. It is an ominous portent of things to come. The temper in the Valley is turning from alienation to antagonism as the Sopore incident underlines, and with more Sopores to come the militant base will expand and not shrink in the Valley.

At the present moment, our Government is excited over the prospect of the British Foreign Secretary accusing the Pakistani authorities of sending arms to the Kashmir militants. This, however, does not rule out the Western pressure, particularly of the USA and Britain, upon India to talk direct to the militants and settle with them on the basis of conceding the essence of their demand, which of course will means at least autonomy in the real sense. While New Delhi has so long been unable to declare any concessions to win over the militants or their following, it is clear that unless and until the Centre is prepared to concede what may be called the essence of independence—in the shape of extensive autonomy—the Kashmir Valley would be lost to India forever. Here too is a threat to India's integrity unless the challenge is met boldly and politically.

Bombay and Sopore—unless we are prepared to handle with courage and statesmanship, what prevents us from going the way of Bosnia?

(January 16, 1993)

39

Prelude to Brazen Intervention over Kashmir

For nearly a year now, that is, since Bill Clinton's victory in the American Presidential election, New Delhi's policy-makers were deceiving themselves as well as the country that the palpable upturn in Indo-US relations would have its definite impact on Washington's attitude towards Pakistan, particularly in relation to Kashmir.

Many harebrained theories were floated, seminars and lectures arranged to proclaim that the US Administration had been annoyed with Pakistan, particularly over Islamabad's nuclear weapons programme, while the closer ties that Rajiv Gandhi had initiated with Washington had been carried forward under Narasimha Rao vide the generous helping of dollar loans to India for opening up her economy as per the Fund-Bank prescription.

In reality, all such wishful thinking had no basis at all. American pronouncements from authoritative platforms such as well-planned dialogues on strategic thinking and occasional reminders about the Democratic Administration's firm commitment in support of nuclear non-proliferation and human rights, left little doubt about the points of impending conflict in approach between New

Delhi and Washington on these two crucial issues. When the State Department sent in May the warning through John Mallot's rather blunt remarks in New Delhi, one noticed a persistent refusal on the part of the ruling establishment to draw the right lessons. In fact, there has been not a single issue in the last one year in which the Clinton Administration has displayed the slightest hint of a tilt towards India.

Even when the US authorities demonstratively vetoed Russia's contract for the supply of cryogenic rockets and the accompanying technology, our Government pathetically fought shy of blaming Washington. In short, the Government has amply demonstrated in the last one year that its policy-makers and their pronouncements hardly reflected the critical mood of the Indian public towards some of the offensive antics of the Clinton Administration on the international scene. New Delhi's timid reaction to the sneak US bombing of Iraq on the absurd excuse of an alleged plot to kill Bush during his Kuwait visit as also its meek submission to the US pressure to despatch Indian troops to Somalia to essentially serve American geopolitical misadventure there, are two out of a number of recent instances of Indian subservience to the dictates of American policy.

The calculation behind such ignominious display of timidity on the part of New Delhi has so far been that sucking up to Washington would help to avert any pressure on the question of nuclear non-proliferation or Kashmir.

Such calculations have turned out to be utterly mistaken. Thus is now as clear as daylight as one finds President Clinton in his address before the UN General Assembly on September 27 specifically mentions Kashmir alongwith Angola and the Caucasus as one of the theatres where "bloody ethnic, religious and civil wars rage" today. He has been equally hard-hitting when he bluntly warned: "We seek to build a world of increasing pressure for non-proliferation" since, as he announced, he has "made non-proliferation one of our nation's highest priorities".

Over Kashmir, New Delhi has been persistently turning a blind eye to the worsening crisis on the ground particularly in the Valley and to the equally mounting campaign abroad charging Indian security forces of being guilty in violating the human rights of the Kashmiri people. Throughout there has been a wistful expectation on the part of New Delhi to ascribe the armed conflict in the Valley almost exclusively to the supply of weapons and arms-training by Pakistan. This could deceive few as such a plea sought to ignore the failure of New Delhi's own policy with regard to Kashmir. The fact of the matter is that Pakistan has been taking full advantage of a deteriorating situation in Kashmir where for various reasons the measure of the alienation of the overwhelming sections of the people from the authority of New Delhi has reached almost a point of no return. And it is precisely at this moment that one notices utter confusion inside the Government about the policy to be pursued with regard to Kashmir.

It is an open secret that there prevails no convergence of common understanding within the Government on the assessment of the situation on the ground as also about the policy thrust to meet that situation. Between the Minister of State, Rajesh Pilot, the Home Minister, S.B. Chavan, and the Governor, General Krishna Rao, there are sharp differences and this affects even the details of the administration. How disastrous such dissonance could be for any Government to tackle an intractable crisis as the one that Kashmir presents today, is not difficult to gauge. And it is precisely this internal crisis that helps to facilitate Pakistani meddling into the affairs of the Valley.

The Government at the Centre, conscious of its own weak base as shown by its lack of stable majority support in Parliament, has throughout been dithering. In the bargain it indulges in a sort of make-believe regarding the US policy on the issue. For months, the official Indian propaganda was that the US authorities acknowledge that Kashmir forms a part of the Indian Union; hence Pakistan has no *locus standi* in Kashmir. When the American pressure, both official and non-official, mounted against the allegations of Indian security forces violating human rights in Kashmir, then New Delhi made the policy announcement of its decision to set up a Human Rights Commission. By this mere announcement, it hoped to mollify American opinion on that score.

Meanwhile it stepped up its clamour for the US to declare Pakistan a terrorist state and soon, believing in its own propaganda, it sought to pacify critics at home by assuring that Washington was about to accede to the Indian demand for declaring Pakistan a terrorist state. Nothing of the sort happened. Instead Washington's attitude visibly began to stiffen, so much so that one would not be surprised if President Clinton's specific reference of concern about Kashmir in his UN speech was meant to prepare the ground for his Administration seeking to intervene, in the name of UN endeavour, at peace-restoration in the Kashmir Valley.

What is really strange is that throughout this period there has been no serious effort at negotiations with Pakistan for resolving the Kashmir crisis. The series of summit level meetings in the last two years between

Narasimha Rao and Nawaz Sharif were characterised by skirting the responsibility for a definite solution to the Kashmir problem. And the latest in the series of cheap cosmetics has been Foreign Minister Dinesh Singh's bright idea of Oslo type secret talks on Kashmir. Why Oslo type talk at all? There is no impediment at all for New Delhi to pick up the telephone and immediately fix an agenda for talks with Islamabad. The real issue is that New Delhi, above all, has to make up its own mind about such talks for a lasting settlement. Mere drift can hardly help to fetch any tangible results out of any talks, Oslo or no-Oslo.

Side by side one discerns the subtle US move to delink the troubled Valley from Jammu and Ladakh in the name of localising the area of tension and conflict. It needs to be recalled that whenever the Western powers found New Delhi facing difficulties, they came out every time with fresh recipes for partitioning Kashmir. This happened more than once during the protracted UN debates on Kashmir in the late forties and early fifties, and again during the critical aftermath of the Chinese aggression on the Indian border in 1962-63: what the Duncan Sandys mission tried to do by vivisecting Kashmir is being tried today in a different way—exactly thirty years after. More than President Clinton's cryptic reference to Kashmir in his UN speech were the fairly elaborate remarks made by one of the Assistant Secretaries of his Administration, Robin Raphel, before the Asia Foundation in Washington, just a little before, in which she specifically wanted that the people in the Kashmir Valley be consulted before India and Pakistan settled the Kashmir problem. Significantly, she ran down the Simla Accord and hence "new ways have to be found".

There is, therefore, good reason to apprehend that

President Clinton's sharp reference to Kashmir in his UN speech promises to be the prelude to brazen US intervention over Kashmir.

(October 9, 1993)

40

Bijbehara: A Challenge to Nation's Conscience

Autumn has set in—the chinar in its gorgeous robe. But it is an autumn of bitter sorrow for the hapless people of Kashmir. The Valley which was known as the paradise on earth has been turned into a trough of hatred, of blood and tears.

On Friday last week the portals of Hazratbal were barred as the Indian Army had laid siege of the mosque complex in pursuit of the militants. To protest against this siege of the holy of holies for every Kashmiri Muslim, the common folk in the small town of Bijbehara took out a demonstration which was angry in its mood but indulged in no acts of violence. But the defiance of the curfew by the marchers enraged the BSF which went berserk and mowed down to death more than 50 and wounded another hundred or more.

These were no armed secessionists, but unarmed citizens. The authorities promptly barred mediapersons from getting into the town—some were beaten up and their cameras seized—but one intrepid among them who could manage to sneak in, has reported that the dead are young boys, including a Hindu boy. The searing poignancy of this act of barbarism was brought out by his reporting that "not even a single family has remained unaffected by Friday's violence" and when the bodies arrived after the post-mortem, "the wails of womenfolk reached a crescendo" as these were lowered into graves.

This way, mourning turns into anger and unwillingly, the security forces instead of quelling the secessionists seem to unwittingly help to swell the ranks of the adherents, supporters and fellow-travellers of the secessionists in the Kashmir Valley. A thousand cordons along the border shall not help to avert the catastrophe as the mounting anger against the armed might of India antagonises the people of the Kashmir Valley.

Six months ago, a very senior office-holder under the Government with wide experience of administration was explaining to the present writer that while Nagaland in the sixties had lapsed into insurgency, he would not say the same thing about Kashmir, as according to him, the people in the villages were not offering active support to the militants. After the siege of Hazratbal and its fall-out with such a bloody shooting spree at Bijbehara, are not the security forces helping to breed a state of insurgency?

The Government has announced a grant of one lakh rupees for the family of the slain and has instituted a magisterial enquiry into the shooting. Do the Government high-ups feel that such rituals would mollify the people at Bijbehara and the Kashmir Valley? What a world of make-believe are our authorities living in! Even in normal conditions, a police firing in any part of the country raises the demand for judicial enquiry. And here after the massacre—a massacre indeed!—at Bijbehara there would only be a magisterial enquiry. The BSF version was that a mob attack on the police station led to the shooting, but the SHO himself denied any such mob attack. Kashmir's Divisional Commissioner visiting the town next day observed: "There was no witness to confirm firing on the BSF at Bijbehara." And with all this, the Government is fighting shy of commissioning a judicial enquiry into the gory incident.

No, this is not a matter for quibbling over enquiries, magisterial or judicial. Bijbehara has thrown up a challenge to the conscience of the entire nation. It has brought out that in the name of fighting out secessionist militants, those responsible for the governance of this great country are themselves hitting at the very foundations of our democratic republic. Such acts of folly, leading to insensate violence on the part of those entrusted to govern, do not evoke respect and consent but provoke revulsion and angry insubordination. A Republic does not last by enforced submission of its people at gun-point. It has just the reverse effect.

Against this ghastly brutality perpetrated at Bijbehara, it's time for our political leaders to hang down their heads in shame and remorse. For they share, in diverse measure, the guilt for letting things drift into this shocking state of affairs that security forces should be so dehumanised as to run amuck committing such a crime. And is Bijbehara a solitary case of security forces transgressing into barbarity by the strength of the gun? All these four years, the Government told the public that the militants provoked violence and the security forces had to bear the brunt of it. So much so that our Government resorted to an ingenious argument that sought to put the security forces on a par with the aggrieved citizens in the matter of many violations of human rights in Kashmir. It's time that the true state of affairs in Kashmir were brought out in the sun and let the nation judge for itself whether the Republic is reinforced or undermined with the way our Government is dealing with the people of Kashmir.

Every democrat in this great democracy of ours has to stand by the people in Bijbehara at this moment of sorrow and despair. And our leaders from Kashmir, where are they, what are they doing? Mufti Mohammad Sayeed, who became the Home Minister of India, is a native son of Bijbehara. Its lanes and by-lanes, its street-corners and maidans have witnessed Mufti Sahib growing up in the politics of Kashmir. He could not possibly be sleeping in peace, tormented as he must be—at least, should be—by the trauma of his fellow-citizens at Bijbehara. Why don't you go there, Mufti Sahib, at this hour of agony and bring strength to their spirits? And if you stand by them, you will add strength to your own arms and help this Republic of ours. This is the way the sinew of a nation's morale is built, which no amount of politicking from a distance will do.

In our midst, in virtual exile of political isolation, there is Syed Mir Qasim, whose maturity and experience the Prime Minister could have harnessed with profit if he so desired. Isn't it time for Qasim Sahib to go on his own to his native soil, facing all the hazards thereby? When people are in a state of emotional shock, they look upto their leaders to come and stand by them. Such a moment has come for all our Kashmir leaders. If they miss to respond in these testing times, they will become castaways of history. Forgetting petty squabbles and irritations, if they all join hands and put their heads together, there must come a way out of the tragic impasse into which this picturesque corner of our great subcontinent has been forced into. More than at any time in the past, the people of Kashmir today cry for the healing touch and that alone can bring back peace and harmony. And if we succeed in the Valley, it will bring back amity with our neighbour, Pakistan.

Guns on either side do not solve crises. What's needed today is the courage to call for peace—the courage that made Gandhi into the Mahatma.

(October 30, 1993)

41

Arms Salesmanship

The USA has a whole battery of Think Tanks with enormous amount of materials at their disposal. And these Think Tanks are supposed to help in the moulding of public opinion and Government policies.

And yet when it comes to the actual application of policies, the Clinton Administration has been displaying an amazing lack of coherent thinking and mature understanding of the impact of its policies on the world abroad. It has hardly covered itself with glory in Somalia nor has Bosnia added a feather in its cap. The mishandling of North Korea brings it no kudos; one hardly detects a sustainable policy approach towards China. In the ugly trade war with Japan, the honours have certainly not been collected by Washington, and Prime Minister Hosokawa's downfall does not necessarily promise an upturn for President Clinton's Japanese policy, if he has one at all.

In this rather messy background, Deputy Secretary Strobe Talbott's Indo-Pak safari last week has been a rather pedestrian exercise without an indication of any fresh thinking on South Asia. Granted that he was far more cautious and sophisticated than his impulsive Under Secretary, Talbott's visit has been no path-breaking achievement. Strobe Talbott came, saw but hardly conquered.

In New Delhi, he tried bravely to assure that Washington intends "to cultivate good relations with India for the sake of that relationship and to do the same with Pakistan". In other words, New Delhi should not be concerned about what Washington would be doing with Islamabad. Consequently, it is no business of India to bother about what the USA would be giving or denying to Pakistan: that should be treated as a bilateral issue between two countries, just as Pakistan should treat any Indo-US deal as of no consequence for itself. On paper this sounds good logic, but it is really naive indeed. One is reminded of the response from the Indian side when in the fifties the US-Pak military alliance was signed and Jawaharlal Nehru protested to President Eisenhower for having brought the Cold War hazards to this part of the world. The US response was that the military aid to Pakistan at that time was meant to help Pakistan fight the Communist threat that was the Soviet Union, and not its neighbour, India. To which came Krishna Menon's memorable response that he had not come across a gun which fired only in one direction, and that every accretion of arms to Pakistan would be a matter of concern for India. This time even such an alibi is not available to justify the US supply of military hardware to Pakistan.

The strategic importance of Pakistan in the Pentagon's future projections in Central Asia, and the Persian Gulf zone has hardly gone down even after the end of the Cold War. The crescent of potential turbulence that stretches from Sinkiang to Iran calls for an American foothold in this region and that is precisely what Pakistan alone can provide. And within Pakistan, it is the military junta which, in Washington's perception, provides both stability and reliability. The offer to release a fresh fleet of F-16s along with other equipment to upgrade the Pak Air Force serves the double purpose of placating America's most trusted and durable element within Pakistan and also strengthening a very important watchtower for the US strategy in this important region.

During Talbott's talks in New Delhi, there was a feeling that the ingenious formula, offering F-16s in exchange of Islamabad agreeing to cap its nuclear weapons programme, would be a non-starter as no Government in Pakistan would agree to give up its nuclear weapons programme. However, after Talbott's Islamabad talks—which he described as a "total success"—it is becoming clear that what the Clinton Administration is immediately concerned with is the disposal of the F-16 fleet along with other lethal items for the Pak Air Force, for which the one-time waiver of the Pressler Amendment is being pressed in the US Congress. The immediate compulsion of the Clinton Administration is to sell the products of the giant aircraft and missile manufacturers in the USA. Senator Pressler has already exposed this with regard to the F-16 offer to Pakistan. And if Narasimha Rao is willing—as some of his entourage would like to get if they have their way—President Clinton will readily offer to sell another consignment of aircraft, maybe of some other brand to India. Let us not forget the rumpus over our cryogenic rocket deal with Russia which has been bullied by Washington to go back on its contract to make room for the promotion of the American rocket products. And now the pressure is being mounted on New Delhi to abandon its missile programme. "If you need rockets or missiles, we are ready to sell our stuff, why make yours?" seems to be the latest jingle in the American arms bazaar which President Clinton is promoting.

Strobe Talbott tried to be smart, trying to assure the Prime Minister that the supply of the F-16 fleet would not disturb the strategic parity between India and Pakistan. To which came the prompt response that India has many more fronts to guard other than Pakistan which appears to be obsessed with India alone.

The question arises: what about the widely-advertised mission to cap Pakistan's nuclear weapons programme? In New Delhi Talbott elaborated that the deal with Pakistan was "an equation" with "strict unambiguous conditionality"—of which one half is the release of F-16s and the other half is "agreement in advance to a variable cap" of Pakistan's nuclear programme. Two days later, at Islamabad, he threw more light. In carefully-worded comments it was stated that the USA and Pak have agreed to go in for "further consideration" of the American proposal. And this joint effort would be for "developing our approach" to the equation. And for all that only a "preliminary accord" has been reached. And when further consideration was completed and "an approach" was developed, then would they come to produce the goal of capping, then reducing and finally eliminating nuclear weapons. A fairly protracted process which, for all you know, may outlive the Clinton Administration. But the supply of F-16 fighter aircraft would be immediate. Incidentally, the Clinton Administration is likely to run into difficulties in the US Congress over this one-time waiver, as Senator Pressler has threatened filibuster.

In New Delhi, the US Deputy Secretary sought to underplay the issue of F-16s as having only "a potent symbolism" in the South Asian region and urged the need "to look beyond symbolism to reality". However, such pseudo-philosophical profundities can hardly conceal the stark reality. With protocol politeness Prime Minister Narasimha Rao had to gently warn the US Deputy Secretary that the supply of a fleet of F-16 fighter aircraft would be a matter of serious concern for our Defence and this would compel the Government to go in for counter-measures that would be a back-breaking burden on the economy of India. The repeated reiteration of this point in official pronouncements in the last few days since the Talbott visit actually reflects the overwhelming public perception that the American tilt for the military establishment of Pakistan persists despite all the affidavits to the contrary by the US Administration officials.

The non-proliferation drive of the US Administration, particularly after the end of the Cold War, hardly impresses the Third World. Behind the tenacious drive to disarm Iraq and the current threats to North Korea, as also the pressure on India and Pakistan to abandon the nuclear option, there is a clear move to perpetuate the dominance of the nuclear weapons powers over those countries who are denied the nuclear weapons—the very basis of the NPT.

The Western commentators and the policy-makers harp on the anomaly of India preaching to the world of the urgency of nuclear disarmament while refusing to sign the NPT. The fact that the NPT by its very nature discriminates in favour of those powers who have already acquired the nuclear arsenal and are not called upon to dismantle them, but insists on the nuclear have-not powers to pledge not to produce the weapon—this discrimination itself offends the sensitivity of any self-respecting country. This is all the more galling when one takes into account the facts that the big brothers of the nuclear club, particularly the USA and Russia, have a stockpile each which can destroy the entire world, while the maximum that a country like India or Pakistan hopes to produce is a variant of the Hiroshima level which, however hideous, does not threaten the entire humankind.

Secondly, Washington's calculation that if Pakistan could be cajoled to agree to cap its nuclear weapons programme, then it will be possible to persuade India to follow suit, is made invalid by the fact that the nuclear threat to India does not come from Pakistan alone but more seriously from China, and now from other Central Asian countries, particularly Kazakhstan which has a portion of the huge nuclear stockpile of the former Soviet Union. And why should India leave out the danger of nuclear threat from Israel which had once made a sneaking attack on Pakistan's nuclear arsenal at Kahuta? So, if one is really serious about dispelling the Indian threat perception, one has to extend much beyond a two-country arrangement between India and Pakistan, or even its latest version of 5 + 2 + 2 (that is, the five permanent members of the Security Council which includes China, plus Japan and Germany alongwith India and Pakistan—most of whom are heavily weighed against India). Really speaking, there is no earthly reason why India should budge from its original stand of universal approach to the problem, instead of regional.

Thirdly, the Indian perception is that the nuclear powers are not serious about reversing the nuclear arms race towards nuclear disarmament. Had they been genuinely serious about nuclear disarmament, why did they not readily respond to Rajiv Gandhi's initiative when he placed before the UN Special Session in 1988 a realistic and detailed Action Plan—which was updated by Narasimha Rao in his intervention before the Special Session of the UN Security Council in 1992? There has always been a condescendingly polite appreciation of the Indian initiative without any effort at serious follow-up discussions by the big bosses of the nuclear corporate club.

Here is a foretaste of the new form of world overlordship through nuclear monopoly of a select group of powers with the US at the head, and to ensure economic domination through control of world trade as the GATT represents, in which discrimination is sought to be practised even through non-economic means. In this context, the arms sale is first on the priority list for the USA. The message is clear for all VIP visitors to Washington. Don't bother to make your own weapons that is only a fetish. Instead, buy it from us, from our well-stocked arms supermarket.

There is no basic change in the outlook and practice of the world's surviving superpower. Essentially, Washington is a prisoner of the Cold War strategy of domination through areas and trade in the new context. While taking up the crusade to force others to disgorge their nuclear weapons, the USA wants to consolidate its nuclear overlordship. And, by trying to block the hi-tech programme of rockets and missiles of others, it seeks to ensure the market for its own deadly products. A fine vision indeed of a new world order—basically not very different from that of John F. Dulles—only revised and made up to date under Bill Clinton.

(April 16, 1994)

42

Ray of Sunshine

The enthusiasm generated by the two-day India-Pakistan's People's Convention, which was held last week in New Delhi, is certainly not a Government-sponsored outfit.

The organisers on the Indian side are well known for their severely critical stand on many issues pertaining to the handling of the crisis in Punjab and Kashmir. In the understanding of the average newspaper reader in the Capital, many of those who were responsible for arranging the meeting are highly critical of the role of the security forces in the Kashmir Valley and to that extent are not in the good books of the Government and the ruling political establishment.

In this background, the success of the get-together—as reflected in the coverage of the event in the Indian press—brings out the growing public urge in this country for an end to the angry confrontation that marks the official-level relations between the two neighbours in recent years. In short, one may venture to say that while at the official level the Governments of the two countries have been drifting to an eyeball-to-eyeball acrimony, the popular mood is veering round towards a relationship of friendly neighbourhood.

In the deliberations of the meeting, obviously there were divergent perceptions, though these differences were not along the lines of the frontier that divides the two countries. Within the Indian side, there were different perceptions on how to handle the vexed nuclear question and how to go about settling the Kashmir crisis. Similar divergences could be discerned on the Pakistani side as well.

It is, therefore, not surprising at all that there has been a tinge of disappointment when media reports from Pakistan were found to be critical of the deliberations of the New Delhi meet. The burden of the press criticisms in Pakistan has been that the stand of the New Delhi get-together has been such as would weaken the official stand of the Pakistan Government. In other words, the press critics in Pakistan seem to suggest that the friends from Pakistan who attended the New Delhi meeting should have dittoed only the official line of their Government.

This line of approach cuts at the very basis of the people-to-people initiative for bettering relations between the two neighbouring countries. It is precisely because of the bitter deadlock which has beset the relations between the two Governments that this people-to-people initiative has become significant, urging the public in both the countries not to lose hope but to strive harder to explore fresh avenues for mutual understanding. In other words, the message of the New Delhi convention—as was of the previous one at Lahore—has been a message of hope instead of the message of despair that comes out of the official postures of the two Governments.

Further, the message of hope and confidence that the people-to-people diplomacy has generated at the New Delhi meeting is expected to serve as a spur for bold and imaginative Indo-Pak diplomacy by the two Governments. In the democratic set-up through which the Governments of both the countries function today, the manifestation of the will of the public helps to refashion diplomacy to faithfully reflect that will of the people.

This positive trend needs to be nurtured by all forces of democracy and peace in both the countries. Pakistan today is beset with serious problems of sectarian Shia-Sunni violence as has erupted on a large scale at Karachi necessitating the imposition of emergency measures by the Government. Further, the Afghan imbroglio has its inevitable repercussions on the body politic of Pakistan. The emergence of Taliban irredentists asserting armed fanaticism is bound to undermine the foundations of the democratic polity in Pakistan. The recent upsurge of bigotry in the name of Islam, as demonstrated over the case of the Christian youngster charged with blashphemy of Islam, is an ominous signal which the courageous band of human rights activists in Pakistan have boldly sought to thwart. In this case too, the fact that a negative development is being resisted by the positive elements is a sign of democratic assertion.

Much the similar task faces the adherents of democracy in India as well. The fanatic move of the Vishwa Hindu Parishad and the Bajrang Dal to attack the mosque at Varanasi has been thwarted by timely action on the part of the administration backed by the overwhelming public disapproval of the insane move. What is particularly heartening in this episode is the bold and unequivocal condemnation of the VHP stand by BJP leader Atal Behari Vajpayee. Not only as the Leader of the Opposition in Parliament, Vajpayee commands eminence as a national leader by his wise and statesman-like stand. It is worth recalling that Vajpayee was the one BJP leader who unhesitatingly disapproved the demolition of the Babri Masjid by the fanatic fringe of his own party in 1992. It may further be noted that when he was the Foreign Minister in the Janata Party Government in 1977-79, Indo-Pak relations showed definite signs of improvement largely at his initiative.

In the midst of gloom all round, one can detect unmistakable streaks of sunshine in Indo-Pak relations. Here lies hope for the future of South Asia as a whole.

(March 4, 1995)

43

Towards Structuring History

Compared to many of the Western countries, India has a poor harvest of memoirs and reminiscences by those who had held important positions in the wielding of the machinery of power. Many British statesmen, Generals and administrators left behind copious documents from memory which provide the raw material of history. In contrast, we seem to have developed an unhistorical tradition, neglecting this important aspect of recording history.

It is in this context that one has to evaluate the significance of the revival of interest about the Simla Accord of 1972, particularly the understanding between Indira Gandhi and Zulfikar Ali Bhutto. The question revolves round the specific issue: was there any understanding between the two leaders about Kashmir, and what really was the significance of re-christening the old Cease Fire Line into the Line of Control? At one time, particularly when Indira Gandhi was dislodged from power in 1977, there was speculation about a secret deal, a secret clause to the Simla Accord. The rumour was scotched and even the implacable opponents of Indira Gandhi did not pursue the matter, as there is reason to believe that the Foreign Minister of the Janata Party Government, Atal Behari Vajpayee, was aware of the real position with regard to this matter.

Recently the question has come up in a strange fashion. The Foreign Secretary at the time of the Simla talks was T. N. Kaul. He has recently published a book of memoirs, *My Years through Raj to Swaraj,* in which he has sought to dismiss the impression that there was an understanding between Indira and Bhutto. According to Kaul, neither of them "indicated to the other even the rough physical parameters of a possible final settlement". This claim by Kaul has been effectively demolished by Prof P.N. Dhar, who was then the Secretary to Prime Minister Indira Gandhi. Both Kaul and Dhar were privy to the Simla talks. As Dhar has explained in great detail in an article in *Mainstream* (April 15, 1995) there was a last-minute understanding between Indira Gandhi and Zulfikar Ali Bhutto, which led to the midnight signing of the Simla Agreement. Those who were present at Simla during those memorable days would recall that by the afternoon of the final day there was a deadlock and it was taken that the talks had broken down. In fact, Indira's Foreign Secretary, T.N. Kaul, left Simla by car in late afternoon, which led some alert mediapersons to come to the mistaken conclusion that the negotiations had really broken down.

It was precisely from this very point that P.N. Dhar picked up the thread and gave a detailed account as to what really happened. It is this account by P.N. Dhar which provides the clue to the significance of the change in the nomenclature from 'Cease Fire' to 'Line of Control'—with it was linked the perspective of a final solution to the Indo-Pak acrimony over Kashmir. Dhar explains that subsequently Bhutto could not keep to his part of the understanding—probably he was overwhelmed by the pressure of domestic events—and that led to its virtual burial. At the same time, it is important for posterity to note the important development as a significant initiative in the history of Indo-Pak relations.

There were other important participants in the Simla talks whose memoirs or personal papers should be made known to the public for a more informed appraisal of the event. D.P. Dhar, for instance, was sent by Indira Gandhi to talk to Bhutto to prepare the agenda for the Simla meeting. Dhar brought the transcript of his talk with the Pakistan leader which should throw a lot of light on the complexities of Pakistani diplomacy at Simla. In fact, through the greater part of 1971, there were important encounters between Indian and Pakistani leaders whose records should be available.

Earlier, when the Indo-Pak talks were held in the wake of the Chinese aggression on the Indian frontier in October-November 1962, the important participants could have left behind valuable material for the construction of an authentic history of such important developments. Gundevia, then a senior official in the Foreign Office who had accompanied Sardar Swaran Singh in his talks with the then Pakistani Foreign Minister, Bhutto, left behind a very useful account of the talks in his memoirs which came out in two volumes. One does not know if Sardar Swaran Singh himself left behind any notes of the many important events which he covered during his crowded career as a distinguished Minister at the Centre. He was not at all inaccessible but neither the mediapersons nor the scholars bothered to interact with him and get at the root of some of the most intractable events in our foreign affairs.

Sino-Indian relations passed through ups and downs, but very little' has been contributed towards reconstructing them by those directly involved in them. The only exception was Major General Palit whose account of the military debacle in 1962 provides invaluable insights. But all the others have practically kept silent over what they themselves had seen or done. The crisis of 1962 came as a traumatic shock for Nehru who had to swallow his pride in writing to President Kennedy beseeching military assistance to ward off the Chinese aggression. Very few people outside the Government knew about the existence of this letter—though some of the more responsible journalists had knowledge about it—and it was later that Sudhir Ghosh, who was at one time close to Gandhiji, disclosed it in Parliament. The biography of Nehru by Dr S. Gopal makes a very brief reference to it though the letter was important as marking a crisis-point in Nehru's foreign policy.

Earlier still, one would like to have the account of the making of the crisis with China in the 1959-62 period. What really happened when Chou En-lai came to Delhi? Why did Nehru urge him to see ~~his~~ Ministers, instead of he himself discussing the moot points of the border dispute? Important personalities were witnesses to those important events: why have not they written their memoirs?—a very legitimate question for the future generations to raise.

Up and down these fifty years spreading over the onset of Independence up till this day, our politics has throughout been marked by transparency, and our leaders of the early days genuinely believed in open diplomacy. And yet our present generation is kept in the dark about the treatment of many of the important issues, both at home and abroad. Coming nearer, one would like to know how much clout India cared to have in Bangladesh once Sheikh Mujib was in saddle. There are good reasons to believe that New Delhi had warned Sheikh Mujib about the danger of an attack on him a few weeks before his assassination, but Mujib in a state of self-delusion had dismissed such a contingency. It is now twenty years since that event took place. Should not somebody who had known the inside story now give it out after two decades?

Similarly there are many grey areas in our relationship with Lanka. The early discussions on the Tamil question in the island republic led to the Shastri-Sirimavo pact. There are some memoirs written by those who were involved in it. But there is nothing to tell us in this country how Rajiv Gandhi sent the IPKF to Lanka. This was an important issue for discussion in the Indian Parliament. But was it discussed at all even at the official level? There are publications in Lanka which quote verbatim Indian official papers about the handling of the armed militants, who ironically got their first training in arms under Indian official control and direction, and later on, the very same elements were ranged against our forces. The actors who were directly involved in bringing down our relations with Lanka have so far largely avoided telling us the truth, the whole truth and nothing but the truth. Isn't it time for them to speak out? The disastrous nature of the IPKF operations in Lanka is acknowledged by all hands. Why can't this question be thrown open for discussion? The more New Delhi concedes the need for introspection, the more easy will it be for a fair amount of objectivity.

Historical events in retrospect do not as a rule apportion blame, but try to get at the objective reality. It is, therefore, all the more necessary for our civil servants and media specialists to tell the public of this country as also of the world, how a particular development was handled by those who were at the decision-making level, without questioning their authenticity. History is a harsh taskmaster. One does not escape its whiplash by fighting shy of looking it in the eye.

(April 22, 1995)

44

Pakistan : Reporter's Jottings

A week's trip to Pakistan to attend a workshop on South Asian problems—part of the emerging people-to-people movement—may not have been adequate to get a comprehensive view of Pakistan's problems and prospects, but it did provide an insight into many facets of life in Pakistan today which is valuable for a reporter's notebook.

Kashmir is the talking point in almost every circle one meets, much more than what the present writer noted during his last visit there to monitor the general elections as part of a SAARC team nearly two years ago. It is worth recalling that at the general elections, neither India nor Kashmir figured at all as a major item for electioneering by any party. This cannot be said of today when Kashmir has become the headline news all over.

For an average Pakistani, it has come as a surprise that practically all sections in the Kashmir Valley have become estranged from New Delhi. The continued use of the Government's armed forces has created the impression that the urge to break away from the Indian Union has become almost irreversible in the Pakistani eye. Practically nobody in Pakistan believes that India would ever recover even the semblance of authority in the Valley.

Reactions to the large-scale use of the Indian security forces in the Kashmir Valley have been varied. For one thing, the news about every attack or killing by the Government side got a lot of publicity and many friendly elements wonder how Nehru's India could permit such brutalities. The fact that the human rights activists in India have themselves been campaigning against excesses by the Indian security forces has had a sobering effect, but the question widely asked is: how does the Indian Government expect to end this veritable armed conflict?

One gets the impression that the present crisis in Kashmir evokes diverse response in different segments of Pakistani public opinion. For instance, some people look upon the present Indian predicament over Kashmir as a rebuff, if not revenge, for India's help to the Bangladeshis in 1971 which led to the slicing off of the eastern wing of Pakistan. This is natural in the case of the old Army hands who still seem to smart under the defeat in 1971. At the same time, it needs to be emphasised that in all circles that one met, the prospect of a full-scale war with India is ruled out. The continuation of the low-intensity proxy war is more or less taken for granted.

In this context, there is reticence to discuss the question whether at any stage Pakistan would accept independence of Kashmir instead of its annexation to Pakistan as the Azad Kashmir leader Qayyum elaborated quite openly. There was curiosity to know if New Delhi has been making any efforts to placate Shabir Shah and his supporters, to isolate the aggressive pro-Pak Hizbul elements.

The more intransigent elements do not seem to trust India. They say that it was India which on its own took the Kashmir case to the UN Security Council, and then when the Security Council diplomacy indicated the solution through plebiscite, India backed out of it. In Simla, it was a defeated Pakistan on which India imposed its terms that henceforth all outstanding problems with Pakistan would have to be solved on bilateral basis. Hence, today India's insistence on talks is taken by this angry old group as just stonewalling and not an earnest move for settlement. Incidentally, there was curiosity as to what Prof P.N. Dhar, who was Indira Gandhi's Secretary, had to say about what had transpired at Simla. Not unexpectedly, the old bureaucrats deny Bhutto had given any oral assurance to Indira Gandhi, while others are noncommittal. However, there is a lot of curiosity as to what Prof Dhar had written on the subject. One could detect an urge to discuss the subject—as a sort of joint post-mortem between the Indian and Pakistani participants at the Simla talks. An idea which is certainly worth exploring.

The need for talks with India is not denied but the initiative, they say, must come from India. Also, there is expectation that India could take some initiatives preparing the right ambience for talks between the two Governments. Withdrawal from Siachen is mentioned as one such item. It is interesting to note how different leaders view the question of breaking the ice with India. Nawaz Sharif, for instance, emphasised its need and took the credit for himself having held discussions with Chandra Shekhar and Narasimha Rao. As for Benazir Bhutto, she had met only Rajiv Gandhi about whom one can detect a special feeling in her circle.

Incidentally, all Pakistani leaders appear to have a soft corner for V.P. Singh about whose health they all enquired.

This is because they look upon V.P. Singh as one who risked his tenure as the Prime Minister but did not give in to the communal clamour over the Babri Masjid. In contrast Narasimha Rao, in the Pakistani perception, suffers from the handicap that the Babri Masjid was dismantled without his having taken any steps to save it. This is an aspect of Indian politics which baffles Pakistani observers. Quite a few of them have a good impression of Atal Behari Vajpayee as the Foreign Minister, but they are disturbed that the BJP could gang up with the Shiv Sena for the purpose of election politics.

A striking aspect of the present Pakistani scene is the widespread feeling against the USA today. There are many reasons for that. The denial of US arms and aid to Pakistan under the Pressler Amendment has offended the sentiments of the Pakistani public—a development that needs to be clearly understood. The Pakistani argument is that throughout the Cold War Islamabad had remained loyal to Washington, and after that threat was over, the USA has been ditching Pakistan. Secondly, the US pressure on Pakistan's nuclear weapons programme is resented, as the bomb has become a symbol of power in world affairs since Bhutto's days. Thirdly, it is mentioned that the US side had contracted to sell a number of F-16 aircraft for which payment was duly made by the Pakistan Government, but not yet delivered on the excuse of the Pressler Amendment ban. There is also a feeling of resentment that the US authorities had made use of Pakistan as their base of operation against the Russians in Afghanistan which has led to the notorious injection of Kalashnikovs and drug traffic into Pakistani life breeding anti-social elements on a monstrous scale. One hears such grudges even among those who are at home in the

American intellectual circles. There is also a feeling in Pakistan that the USA is now tilting towards India which, in their view, has been assiduously cultivating the USA, particularly the American business circles and the Fund-Bank high-ups, for large-scale investment in India—thereby the advantage that Pakistan had in the past vis-a-vis the US over India is now negated, and as the bigger supplicant India would get more from the US.

It is in this background that Prime Minister Benazir's recent elaborate visit to the USA is viewed by different sections of Pakistani society. Her own circle of admirers and supporters think that she is the one leader who has kept open the window to the world for Pakistan. They say that her campaign in the USA would help to soften the rigours of the Pressler Amendment and perhaps the F-16 aircraft which Pakistan had bought might be delivered. It is also generally conceded that Benazir has an active lobby in the Democratic Party, but the recent Congressional election has negated that advantage with the Republicans being now on top in the Hill. Benazir's supporters say that it was to rectify this position that her extensive public-relations campaign in the USA this time was necessary and has been useful. Generally it is known that the Pak military brass enjoys a special relationship with the Pentagon, and it was because of this that she, with her old ties in Washington, has been able to enlist friendly support from the military bosses in Pakistan, as could be seen from the days of the elections.

In this context, it is worth noting that Nawaz Sharif is more or less a *persona non grata* with the Generals. While he gets the support of all the anti-Benazir forces including the influential religious lobby, it would be a mistake to think that his influence is confined to Punjab alone. One has to look at the poll figures to note that Nawaz's Muslim League has made a sizeable dent even in the Sind politics.

Even a brief visit to Pakistan makes it abundantly clear that the old euphoria for Benazir Bhutto, which was evident at the time of the General Elections, has gone. Apart from other reasons, the crisis in Sind, particularly Karachi, accounts for it. The sustained Army operation against the Mohajirs has brought her no kudos, while in the interior of the province, the Sindhi landlord community is not infatuated with her. In fact her mother, Nusrat Bhutto, seems to have more possibilities in that constituency. To some extent, the taint of corruption associated with her husband has become a sort of liability for Benazir.

The impression that one carries back from Pakistan is that although Benazir Bhutto still commands the support of her father's followers, she has the rather difficult job of keeping in good humour the very Army junta which had killed her father. This is sometimes rationalised by the rather unconvincing distinction sought to be made between the image of the villain in General Zia-ul-Haq and the rest of the top brass who are presented as decent chaps. Benazir has supporters among the educated intelligentsia for standing up to the mullahs, particularly with regard to women's rights. On the other hand, she has hardly consolidated the huge mass support that her father had whipped up with his strident call for *roti, kapra our makan*—the euphoria that she had inherited but had not been able to sustain. Nor has she been able to reconcile the contending interests of the diverse regions that constitute Pakistan. The Pakhtoon area has been badly messed up with the aftermath of the Afghan civil war in which Hekmatyar has been playing a major role but totally negative. The Baluchis have never been admirers of the Bhuttos after the military operation that Benazir 's father had ordered against them in 1973-74—the fatal flaw that undermined his democratic standing and made him dependent on the Army which led ultimately to his imprisonment and execution at their hand.

Benazir's efforts at building a constituency abroad—on a number of occasions this reporter was reminded how many days she had spent in overseas trips in the last two years—did not fetch dividends within the country. Bouquets abroad can't stave off brickbats at home. Rather she has come to be known as being more anxious to cultivate her American connections. But in Pakistan today, the reputation of being a favourite of the Americans is hardly an asset for any political leader.

The Pakistan Government's forays into the Central Asian Republics have hardly scored any point. For one thing, the situation in the whole belt stretching from the Caspian to the Karakoram is fluid, and Pakistan possesses no special credentials for establishing a niche in the region. Rather its record, as providing the jumping-off ground for the Americans in their superpower rivalry with Moscow during the Cold War, has earned Pakistan no passport to Central Asia. However, Benazir has not abandoned the adventure as could be seen from her forthcoming visit to Tashkent. Pakistan's relations with Iran are at a low key, and it is understandable there is curiosity everywhere to assess the impact of President Rafsanjani's visit to India and the tripartite accord between Iran, Turkmenistan and India.

In the coming days with Washington's blatant provocations to bully Iran there is a danger of the country developing into an international crisis-point. The impact of such a crisis inside Pakistan may turn out to be imponderable. Benazir's position certainly would not be reinforced as a result, because to be marked out as an ally of the US does not make a leader popular in Pakistan today, while Iran standing up to the American bullying may get the applause of a large section of the Pakistani public, much beyond the Shia community. Nawaz Sharif's party is bound to make hay in the circumstances. Can any Government in Islamabad afford to side with Washington against Teheran?

Pakistan's economy, on the face of it, carries no signs of an impending crisis. The social polarisation is obvious, but it has not yet created any tension. At the same time, few will vouch for its durability in the event of a war. The opening up to the market forces has taken place slightly earlier than in India, and the widening of disparities as a result, is acknowledged on all hands.

Which way would Pakistan ultimately turn? Geographically it is certainly an important limb of South Asia. But after the collapse of East Pakistan and the emergence of Bangladesh, Bhutto's mandate for his countrymen was to go west—to the Gulf and the Middle East. This is a strategy which has certainly helped Pakistan through the Afghan misadventure but it has had a negative effect on the country. The Islamic attachment was more in the nature of a political ploy as could be seen in the persistent refusal to take back the thousands of hapless Urdu-speaking Biharis from Bangladesh. Even during her latest visit to Islamabad, Begum Khaleda Zia could not persuade Benazir to hold out any hope on this score. For Pakistan, these brothers-in-faith—the so-called Bihari Muslims stranded in Bangladesh—are as good as having been written off.

In this context, it is interesting to find among a section of intellectuals an effort to identify the ideological roots of Pakistan as a nation. They do not depend on Islam as the binding force for the nation, since today Pakistan has less number of Muslims than India or Bangladesh. They reject the view that Pakistan is just a split-away part of India. By this view, the homeland of the Pakistani nation stretches along the catchment and basin of one of the world's greatest rivers, the Indus. It is argued that although the British imperial administration put this region under the Raj in Delhi, it has throughout retained an identity of its own. From Mohenjodaro this ideological descent of Pakistan is stretched. Its protagonists are confined to some of the brightest intellectuals of the country—not just arm-chair scholars, but even such people who have been in the thick of politics, have suffered prison terms during the Martial Law regime, and became part of active politics under Zulfikar Ali Bhutto. One of them has just signed a contract with a well-known publisher of international reputation, and the bulky tome is expected to be published before the end of the year.

While a thesis like this needs to be discussed in detail—which its author is very keen to hold—one realises that through five decades of tension, prejudices and mis-information we have ourselves built a high wall of quarantine between ourselves. There is the almost total lack of media interaction, the absence of exchange of news, the virtual embargo on exchange of books and publications, while an intense Cold-War propaganda is conducted by those who have made a vested interest in spreading misunderstanding. Irrespective of the views held, the appalling lack of information about our next-door neighbour is something grotesquely absurd and a total misfit in civilised society. The Partition has not only divided the country between two territorial entities but has succeeded in instilling into us with amazing emphasis the fear and hatred of the image of a monster living across the frontier. Whatever the politicians may say or do, it is time that at the level of the common people, there must spread the fresh air of freedom. It's time indeed for people-to-people diplomacy between Pakistan and India.

(May 13, 1995)

45

Conscience and Charar-e-Sharief

One month to date after the destruction of the shrine and mosque at Charar-e-Sharief a team of journalists reached the township. As one looked round the ghastly devastation of rows of burnt houses with their walls standing as mute witnesses to the crime, spontaneously it came to one's lips: if you have tears, prepare to shed them now.

As one slowly climbed the stone slabs at the threshold of the complex, one could almost sense that on those stones have fallen for six hundred years thousands upon thousands of footsteps of devotees, Muslim, Hindu and Sikh, who came to pray at the shrine of Sheikh Nooruddin Noorani—Nund Rishi to Hindus and Sikhs. The saint was honoured as Alam-Dari Kashmir, and was called "Param Guru" in the hallowed days of harmony among communities that lived in the Kashmir Valley.

With the hapless crowd of those rendered homeless by the fire that destroyed the Kasba and finally the shrine itself, one could not help breaking down by the agony all round—the agony of the hundreds rendered destitute through no fault of their own, as also the agony that has engulfed the whole of this picturesque Valley. Throughout the one-hour drive back to Srinagar, one could not help pondering over the searing misfortune that has befallen upon the entire State of Jammu and Kashmir and for which the entire nation is responsible. That guilt can't be covered up by finding alibis in Pakistan or elsewhere.

From the beginning of the period of Ramzan, the Army had cordoned off the Charar-e-Sharief and held the cordon for sixtyfive long days from March 7. Nearly three quarters of the local population quit the township as it was brought within the firing line from both sides. On May 8, many of the houses were set on fire. Three days later, in the night of May 10-May 11, as the time for celebration on the morrow was about to begin, horror struck the people that the sacred shrine of six hundred years was put to flame.

That was the moment for tears such as angels weep. For with that act of vandalism, the very ethos of our Republic was violated, as the shrine of Sheikh Nooruddin Noorani, Nund Rishi symbolised what this great subcontinent had stood out for in History—the symbol of brotherhood and harmony.

Who was the culprit whose hand committed this act of unholy profanity? The official version given in special briefing was that Must Gul, the Afghan chief of the Harkat-ul-Ansar, and his gang were taking shelter at the shrine; that they set fire to the Kasba on May 8 and two days later, torched the shrine and escaped. An ideological gloss was sought to be put on it by adding that Must Gul had entered the shrine with his boots on and assaulted the head priest there, and thereby wanted to destroy the symbol of Kashmiriyat and assert the primacy of Islamic fundamentalism. The Army had put pickets round the township to keep a watch and could not move in when the houses were set on fire because of the firing by Must Gul's men, and so by the time it could make the breakthrough, the shrine had been turned to ashes and Must Gul and his men escaped.

This version is totally contradicted by the entire populace of the township and a large number of people outside, who all hold the Army responsible for it. According to the residents of Charar-e-Sharief, the Army laid siege to the township two months earlier, right at the onset of the fasting month of Ramzan. And they asked the people to move out. Fearing that there would be an armed clash between the Army and the militants, most of the residents moved out of the siege and took shelter in nearby places, some even coming to Srinagar. Then on May 8, the Army did a clean-up operation by setting the empty houses on fire, planning thereby to encircle the militants in and around the shrine and then force them to surrender. And when there was no response to the surrender call, on the night before the festive day of Id, a helicopter dropped incendiaries that burnt down the shrine. Must Gul and his men escaped.

The Army refutation of this version of the residents is that it has no night-landing helipad in the neighbourhood. What is intriguing is that during the critical days, there was no publicity by the Government about the alleged recording of Must Gul's speech. When the Army had laid siege to Charar-e-Sharief for 65 days—which was widely publicised—its objective as announced was to save the shrine and catch the militants. On both these counts, it failed. If after laying siege for two months, it could not catch Must Gul, that was by no means a very impressive record, though the Chief of the Army Staff in a subsequent statement pompously declared that there was nothing for the Army to be ashamed about.

It is also worth noting that after the first report of houses having been gutted at Charar reached Srinagar, one of the Opposition leaders, Yasin Malik, rushed there, but was arrested on the way and brought back. The same happened to Shabir Shah and Abdul Gani Lone of the Hurriyat Conference. Even the local leaders of the place like G.M. Hubi of the People's Conference, and Abdul Qayyum, the Janata Dal MLA of Charar whose house had been gutted, were kept away.

The local people showed us empty mortar shells and empty cases of other ammunitions with Indian markings picked up at the spot. Another journalist reported that a mortar shell and a khaki coloured small parachute with Indian Ordnance markings had been recovered from the spot. And General Rao, the Governor's remark was that "the Army could have fired flares and smoke bombs to cover its advance into the township". Could not some of them hit the mosques and the shrine which were of wooden structure and combustible? A strange blanket of silence has been maintained by the authorities on this score.

It is difficult to understand how the Government does not realise that there are hardly any takers for the official version of the destruction of the Charar. A leading figure in the Congress told this writer that he felt that the Army was responsible for the destruction of the shrine. As for Must Gul, he was known to have been in the Valley for the past four years, and the authorities are not unaware of it.

What was heart-rending was the total apathy and mismanagement in relief and rehabilitation work at Charar-e-Sharief. The journalists' team had gone there with

Government clearance and stayed at the spot for more than two hours. Hundreds thronged there to tell us of their woes, most of them had received little of relief and less of rehabilitation help, despite all the publicity about relief and rehabilitation from the Prime Minister downward. The Imam of the shrine himself was deprived of any such relief, though he is without a roof over his head. No tents could be seen, not even any temporary shades. People are living in the open: soon the scorching sun will be followed by rains and then the winter snows. The authorities at Srinagar denied the charge of paucity of relief and rehabilitation and insisted on having a relief officer there, though he was invisible to us during our stay there.

The tragedy of Charar-e-Sharief is a matter of national shame. This is no hyperbole but the measured utterance of a senior officer holding very important responsibilities. It is the height of folly and dishonesty on the part of the Government not to have initiated a highest-level investigation into the entire happening. One can understand why the Government should by fighting shy of such an enquiry as many other dirty skeletons might come tumbling out of its cupboard. For the affairs of Kashmir in the last few years, when revealed, may turn out to be the most horrendous scandal of our times. If the Government fails to wake up, it is the bounden duty for conscience-stricken citizens of the country—there are quite a large number of them—to come forward and set up a people's tribunal to go into the Charar-e-Sharief calamity. And with it must come from all sections of our people generous donations for the reconstruction of the sacred shrine which was the place of worship not of one community but of all three—Muslim, Hindu and Sikh—a *sangam* indeed.

Today, Charar-e-Sharief stands as the challenge to our conscience.

(June 17, 1995)

46

Freedom Day at Amritsar

Three landmarks to cover in a single day—that was how some of us spent our fiftieth Independence Day.

The first of the pilgrimage was to the Indo-Pak border post at Wagah to celebrate the anniversary of the freedom at midnight.

Reaching Amristar by the Shatabdi Express in the late evening of August 14, about a dozen of us led by the President of the Citizens for Democracy, Kuldip Nayar, we were received by a huge crowd at the Amritsar station itself which included many dignitaries including leaders from the SGPC. From there, the hour-and-a-half drive to the border itself was filled with memories of that great day fortynine years ago which Jawaharlal Nehru had christened as "our tryst with destiny".

In the pitch darkness of the night—there were those of us who are old enough to recall that day of freedom sweated with the bloody Partition which had been unleashed in the country. By this very road and many others, thousands upon thousands had trudged and been killed by the fiendish hatred that the Partition had brought about. The memory of freedom's arrival on that fateful midnight was soaked with the blood of our very kith and kin. All this and more were in our thoughts as we drove to reach in time to celebrate the anniversary of that historic midnight on the very border that marked the Partition of the country.

As our cavalcade reached the security zone of the border the BSF authorities, on prior information, let us in. This was a pleasant surprise because this entire border check-post is normally closed by late afternoon. By that time, the celebration participants, numbering over 200, were all let in. We stayed there for about two hours, candles and torches were lit and as we could go up to the very border-line, much beyond the electric fence, to the emigration and customs and the Indian flag-mast, it was a moment of joy interspersed with trepidation if those friends in Pakistan who had informed us of their enthusiastic support for this demonstration of amity would be able to make it to the border from their side. From the Pakistan Rangers who stood guard on the same side of the fence, it was gathered that nobody would be allowed to come to this point. Later we heard that a group of eight had come but were turned away by the Rangers.

No doubt this was a disappointment, that the Pakistan authorities should have debarred such a crystal expression of mutual cordiality at the popular level as distinct from the official demonstration of mutual acrimony. But there was nothing to be disheartened as a message had already come to the Citizens for Democracy from a distinguished group of eminent Pakistanis who identified friendship with neighbours as being in consonance with their citizenship. Their message appreciated the initiative of the Indian friends and called for an early and amicable end to all disputes between the two countries and strongly supported the efforts at the popular level for such a task. The signatories included Asma Jehangir, the President of the Pakistan Human Rights Commission, among other well-known public figures of that country.

At the Wagah border meeting, the Indian response was equally forthright. Read out in candle-light amidst deafening calls for Indo-Pakistan peoples' friendship, the Indian resolution, while acknowledging the ups and downs in the relationship between the two neighbours, pledged to work for the removal of barriers of suspicions and mistrust between the two countries: "We have no doubt that we shall overcome." As the heart-warming songs of friendship and brotherhood by the Nishant Natya Manch rent the silent midnight, the message was inscribed for our brothers and sisters in Pakistan to sense that there are hundreds and thousands in both our countries who are determined to build bridges across the frontier, breaking the barbed-wire fences that stand there. That was the way it was that some of us welcomed the advent of the fiftieth year of our Independence.

Next morning, the morning of auspicious August 15, we were at the Golden Temple, the sanctum sanctorum of our brothers and sisters of the Sikh faith. Some of us had made the pilgrimage to this sacred place—both before and after the tragedy of the Bluestar, June 1984—but this time I could not help feeling the incongruity between the messages that came from Wagah and the Golden Temple. If one stood as a memorial to our freedom from colonial rule, the other is marked by a sacrilege which those in authority to rule in this democracy of ours, indulged in. It was a vicious act which was the very antithesis of that democracy, namely, the desecration of the sacred place of worship with the use of the bayonets of our armed forces. Whatever might have been the circumstances, it was a black day for Indian democracy that this holy shrine of the Sikh community was attacked and damaged by the armed forces, just as the demolition of the Babri Masjid was perpetrated eight years later, in 1992, with the elected Governments of our democracy choosing to remain inactive making no effort whatsoever to prevent the vandalism. These are the black marks on our democracy which one can hardly forget as one visits the Golden Temple, exuding the pure air of humility and devotion of millions, many more than the Sikh community itself.

No trip to Amritsar could be complete without a visit to another pilgrimage—the martyrs' memorial at Jallianwala Bagh. The solemnity of the memory of the martyrs has been heightened by the serene atmosphere of the spot where General Dyer had butchered hundreds hoping to terrorise the Indian people into submission. As one looked at the well where hundreds jumped in desperation as British bullets were showered on them, one could not but feel that the sacred trust that freedom had imposed upon us has been largely betrayed by subsequent generations of our rulers. Those among them who are today charged with gross corruption and misconduct in public affairs, can they be brought to this sacred spot and made to confess to their sins? Perhaps the politician of today is too thick-skinned to move before that pristine legacy of the freedom struggle that Jallianwala Bagh symbolises.

Incidentally, a little incident at Jallianwala Bagh brought out how our freedom struggle had woven the texture of our national integration. The caretaker at the museum, a young Bengali, I found, is the grandson of a Congress worker who came here at the behest of Gandhiji at the time of the Amritsar Conference, and stayed on to look after this sacred monument of sacrifice.

Later in the day, when participating at a symposium at

the Guru Nanak University on national consciousness, I could not help thinking how rich was this national consciousness left behind by the freedom struggle. General Dyer and his masters could not subjugate the unarmed Indian people by their terror and repression. The consciousness of freedom that was instilled into them by Gandhiji could not be muzzled by terror, and it rose to full heights when Independence came. But in these five decades since Independence, we have sullied our democracy through terrible lapses. The Bluestar on the Golden Temple represented one such act of apostasy of secularism. And the other, the one for which each one of us is responsible—the prolongation of hunger and deprivation for the millions of our countrymen who had pinned their hopes for a better living in this democratic Republic of ours.

As we proceed to celebrate the first half century of our Independence, let us remember the messages from those three centres of pilgrimage—the barrier of acrimony that divides us from our great neighbours that the Wagah electropost stands for; the desecration of the Golden Temple by the Bluestar operation; and the monstrous betrayal of the trust reposed on their countrymen by the martyrs at Jallianwala Bagh. It was indeed a thought-provoking Fifteenth August spent at the great city of Amritsar as the nation reaches out to half a century of its Independence.

(August 24, 1996)

47

South Asia: Come Closer, Know Better*

The declared policy of the present Government that its prior task in foreign affairs is to strengthen this country's relations with the neighbours has been widely approved by all political parties. Even in the difficult terrain of Indo-Pak relations, there is wide support in the country for our Foreign Minister Gujral's reiteration of the commitment to open dialogue with Islamabad the moment the Government over there is ready to reciprocate it.

This emphasis on improving relations with neighbours is born out of the realisation that in the new international environment after the end of the Cold War, there could be no effective pursuit of foreign policy for India without building a durable structure of peace and understanding in South Asia, and only on that basis can India really hope to strike out for an independent policy in the wider world context. Although the SAARC as a regional body has yet to grow into a vital organ of foreign policy for the countries of the region, there is little doubt that in today's world, there is little chance of our country making a mark if it is beset with an adversarial, or even a negative, relationship with its neighbours. This is true as much for India as for any or all the neighbours of ours.

During the Cold War, such regional unity was difficult to achieve as superpower rivalries disrupted the natural tendency towards regional understanding because the Cold War concentration tended towards military alliances cutting across natural regional interactions.

In this background, it is perfectly logical and wholesome that India as the country with its preponderating presence in South Asia should take up as its priority foreign policy concern the building of peaceful enduring relationship with all its neighbours. If belligerent relationship has to be abjured and mutual goodwill has to replace mutual animosity, it is most urgent that there has to be maximum effort at establishing enduring relationship. This to a large measure will depend on the policy of the Governments of the region and India, as the largest country of the region and more advanced in certain aspects of development, needs to take the initiative in this respect.

Difficulties galore will come in the way, and our Government has to move with the determination to overcome all the obstacles and pitfalls in progressing towards the goal. It is worth reminding ourselves that of all the seven countries constituting the South Asian region, our country is the one and only one which has frontiers with all these neighbours. In an adversarial relationship, this naturally generates the maximum of problems: every border breeds infiltration and smuggling, every transnational river raises the baffling problem of water sharing. At the same time, contiguity has its advantages. Cross-border trade and joint ventures thrive among neighbours. The harnessing of international rivers and inland shipping are time-honoured enterprises. Many of the state boundaries divide people belonging to the same cultural and ethnic matrix and when the border-fences are lowered, it very often helps to solder the breach and foster cultural solidarity of an abiding character. In other words, the dividing boundaries can be turned into points of unifying fraternisation.

There is, however, a tendency to wait for Governments to create the necessary climate for good neighbourliness. Certainly there are difficult barriers to surmount. For instance, between India and Pakistan there has grown up such absurdities as the special Indo-Pak visa system that more often than not innocent self-respecting citizens on both sides get put off by such humiliating restrictions. Even when the authorities on both sides of the frontier concede that such passport and visa restrictions cannot and do not prevent thousands upon thousands every year to cross the border illegally, the Governments of both the countries pathetically hold on to such restrictions and thoughtlessly flaunt these as the badges for upholding the sovereignty of their respective states. No doubt the lifting of such crazy restrictions on freedom of travel for the common people of the two countries would go a long way towards Indo-Pak amity and peace.

But there is a lot that can be done at the level of the public at large, even if the Governments of the two countries prefer to retain such primitive shackles. One can campaign for more and more access on the part of specific professional groups whether it is the case of the scientists and teachers, businessmen and industrialists, economists and mediapersons, cultural workers or sports groups. The more we meet our neighbours in our specific fields of activities the more shall we be realising how grotesque it is to paint as monster the people on the other side of the barbed wire fence. In recent years, there have been fruitful initiatives to overcome such barriers. The moves for regular conventions of India-Pakistan peoples' cooperation have borne fruit. Two sessions of such conventions at the initiative of concerned citizens and human rights activists have taken place in the last two years in Lahore and Delhi attended by a growing number from across the frontiers. The third session of this initiative is due to be held in Calcutta in the last days of this year.

At the media level, non-official initiatives have borne fruit in the last few years, and every time the more perceptive among journalists have realised how little we know about what's happening next door while news channels, print and electronic, tell us all about Princess Di's secret life or President Yeltsin's failing heart. The Governments of the two countries step in only when unpleasant or unfortunate incidents like the expulsion of diplomatic personnel takes place.

It is amazing that while we mark out our biggest neighbour Pakistan as our principal target for defence on the plea that we had three wars with it in the last fifty years, many among the elite care to know so little about the important happenings in that country. A participant in a recent media conference of South Asia held in New Delhi was the editor of a widely-known independent newsmagazine of Pakistan, *Newsline.* A quick glance at the latest issue of this journal presents one with a lavish fare on the recent happenings in that country. This issue of *Newsline* has devoted most of its pages to these developments with fearless professional excellence—from Asif Zardari becoming "The Billion Dollar Man" to Benazir's "Fall from Grace" and the "Undemocratic Article" that obstructs the democratic process. No Indian paper has published anything like this. If we have to regard the developments in Pakistan as of some concern for our country, is it wise at all that our people should be kept in the dark about them, or fed with measly fare by only a few Indian correspondents working from Pakistan? How much more rewarding would it be for every concerned Indian citizen to have the advantage of understanding how much well-equipped can we be about the happenings in our neighbourhood by getting their journals. We don't have to depend on the BBC version or a commentary in the *International Herald Tribune* to tell us the real meaning of what has been happening across the barbed fences beyond Wagah.

Lifting of the existing impediments to the free flow of newspapers has become a matter of utmost concern for us. The demand for the right to information need not be confined to matters of public concern within the country. Every thinking democrat in this country has to take up this demand as a matter of urgent priority if he or she has to play a right role in deciding on India's foreign policy perspective. And for the wider public of our Republic, the knowledge and understanding of the policies and actions of our brothers and sisters immediately beyond the frontier are of utmost urgency for the powerful building of our foreign policy priorities.

(December 14, 1996)

48

Pakistan: Wide-angle View

It is but natural for us to view the recent General Elections in Pakistan by our time-worn standards and to assess whether it could be regarded as free and fair. There were certainly inadequacies, some of them serious—particularly the prelude to it which involved peremptory dismissal of a duly elected Government followed by appointment of a caretaker Government chosen by the President and a snap election in the midst of the Muslim month of Ramzan fasting. But any major event in a country has to be judged in the context of its historical development. Otherwise the reality of the given situation is likely to be missed.

Over four decades now, the stereotype that we have formed of Pakistan politics is that it is heavily decided by the domination of a military junta, fed lavishly by a super-power for its own global strategic reasons. This has taken different forms according to the prevailing political vagaries. Quite often the politics of the country is dominated by unalloyed military dictatorship without any frills or cover. At other times, political personalities came on the stage because of the debacle suffered by the military bosses at home or abroad, or because of the unrest of the people which the top brass did not know how to control. The ignominious loss of Bangladesh led to the Bhutto interlude in Pakistan politics, while the seething popular unrest in some parts of the country or the other either led to the reinforcement of the bosses of the armed forces in the politics of the country as it happened in Bhutto's handling of Baluchistan or the discredit of the elected Government as it happened in the case of Benazir in the fiasco over Sind.

However, the umbilical cord that binds Pakistan's military junta to the superpower in Washington, particularly to the Pentagon, has had to face a totally different situation with the end of the Cold War. The rules of the game of world politics are yet to be set in the context of the new world in which the military rivalry between two superpowers has given way to a scenario in which trade rivalry and economic domination are sought to be enforced by the developed few over the rest of the world. The military elite spawned by the superpowers in different countries have to face a new situation, almost a crisis situation, and Pakistan's armed forces bosses are no better off.

The changed situation could be discerned by 1990 about the same time that the superpower Cold War had formally ended in the old form. However, the readjustment in Pakistan took time because of the situation in Afghanistan where the Pak Army, particularly the ISI, acted as the surrogate for Washington.

If the military dictatorship of General Zia was brought to an end by his physical extermination, the transition to civilian regime has not been easy. In fact, the latest election brings that out. When Benazir Bhutto won the election in 1993, it was taken, by and large, as a democratic victory. However, certain background developments of the time would be worth noting. Soon after President Clinton's victory in 1992, Benazir had gone to Washington, as she has had a strong lobby in the Democratic Party. About this time, she made a statement that she would agree to a General Election provided it was under Army supervision. Rather a strange statement from the leader of a party whose founder was hanged by the military dictatorship at that time. But this understanding with the military bosses was the price she had to pay for having an election to make her the Prime Minister. In the three years of her tenure as the Prime Minister, she never stood up to the military junta. Her quarrel with the President—even the present one who was her nominee—was over the question: who would deal directly with the Army brass? It needs to be emphasised that her major political setback was in Sind in dealing with the MQM, and her discredit came because of the indiscriminate use of the armed forces in trying to put down the unrest in Sind, particularly Karachi, with the help of the Army.

Even this time during the General Elections, Benazir thought she could rely on the Army brass. On the day before the General Elections on February 3, Benazir wrote a letter to the Chief of Army Staff, General Karamat, asking him to intervene as she feared there would be "electoral fraud" in 65 seats as she felt the Army could play a pivotal role in dealing with "ballot tampering and post-election fraud". The appeal was not to the Chief Election Commissioner but to the Army Chief. While throughout her election campaign, she attacked the President, she never suggested that the Army should be curbed.

One of the serious inroads into democratic Government in Pakistan has been the setting up by the President of the Council for Defence and National Security (CDNS) which has come under severe scrutiny by the media. This Council would consist of the three Service Chiefs and others as advisers and would oversee all measures in the interest of national security and economic development. It has not been made clear what its relation should be with the elected Cabinet. It is significant to note that Nawaz Sharif has already mentioned that the newly elected National Assembly would decide about the CDNS. No such demand has come from the Pakistan People's Party under Benazir.

The elections were conducted under the supervision of the Army as observers found Army personnel in election booths. In the last election in 1993, this was of course much more conspicuous. The poor turnout of the voters was, however, not due to the presence of the Army as such, but a perceived degree of apathy at the over-powering corruption and strong-arm rule under Benazir, particularly the notoriety earned by the misdeeds of her husband, Asif Zardari. The poor score of the PPP is mainly due to the slump in Benazir's personal popularity while she has not permitted any new leadership to come up inside the PPP.

Where then does the Army junta stand in Pakistan politics today? Nawaz Sharif's convincing victory is going to be a sore point for the Army and it poses a difficult challenge for the Army leadership. For one thing, Nawaz Sharif would not forget that he was displaced from power in the past because of the intrigue of the military bosses in league with Benazir. It would be interesting to see how the new Prime Minister would be dealing with the military bosses. In this context, one has to take into account the significance of Nawaz's convincing victory. He and his party represent what may be called the emerging commercial and industrial corporate sector of Pakistan. One finds them quite responsive to having normalcy in commerce and economic cooperation with India and other South Asian countries. It is worth noting that throughout the election campaign Nawaz, more than once, emphasised his readiness to open dialogue with India—which is in total contrast to Benazir's hectorings against India.

It would be difficult for the military junta to displace Nawaz Sharif, as it would be in India's interest to respond to his positive approach towards better understanding with India. If economic cooperation is the buzz word of the present global market, then Nawaz Sharif's rule has the promise of ushering in a new phase of India-Pakistan understanding, away from the sabre-rattling of the Cold War days. It is for New Delhi to discern the signs of a new era after the nightmare of the Cold War.

(February 15, 1997)

49

Breaking New Path after Fifty Years

Those who have had the unique fortune of being the witness to the birth of a free country and passing through five long decades of historic events with the morale of the country going up and down can vouch for the momentous character of the present day. We who have been witness to this cavalcade of history have to judge the importance of this day in this age. The break-up of one-party rule that the Congress represented; and the emergence of coalition politics which combined the Congress and anti-Congress parties as well, what exactly is the chief feature of this particular moment in the chequered history of India?

To answer this question one has to look outward and not inward because the answer is shining in full sunlight and not in the dark, dingy corridor of musty politics. If one looks with care and dispassion, one would realise where precisely the significance lies of this day in the annals of independent India. What has been the major achievement for the country to be taken note of in this year of the golden jubilee of the country's Independence? It is not in the achievement of enduring stability at home, where security forces are called to keep internal peace over vast stretches of the country. Despite all claims to growth, the economic pundits and policy-makers have to concede the existence of stark poverty over more than one-third of the vast population of the country, which by cold calculations will have more by the turn of the century than any other country of the world. Many of our economists today measure the advance registered by the country in terms of the growth achieved, not in terms of development of the human personality of this land of over 900 million men, women and children. And if we take politics in its conventional definition, one has to take note of the growing anti-social criminal elements, the mafia and their masters, in practically every part of this country of Gandhi.

Where then have we made a significant headway? It is in the painstaking efforts that have gone on the part of our Government in trying to build a structure of durable peace, particularly with our neighbours. In the past there were certainly moments of warmth and understanding but these have hardly come down from the close circle of protocols and official formalities. What has marked out in the last two years has been a steady improvement in our country's relationship with our neighbours. There were moments in the past when the country celebrated by extending the helping hand to our brothers and sisters in a neighbouring country trying to throw out the jackboot that had captured power in the state to which the struggling people at one time belonged and then extracting Independence with blood and toil. And to that sacred battle for freedom, our people and our jawans, our Government and our common people on the roadside, in distant hamlets and cramped bustees extended their wholehearted support. That was the birth of Bangladesh; in celebrating its emergence, we justly shared with all our hearts.

However, in the circumstances with its twists and turns, the people in Pakistan for some time took it as a defeat, the humiliating setback suffered by the military junta that ruled over them. This complex situation stood in the way of normalcy and good neighbourliness. Ironically therefore our joining in the celebration at the Independence of Bangladesh was dogged by the worsening relationship with Pakistan. Though there were official exchanges and meetings between the Governments of India and Pakistan, these have taken a stereotyped form as between two antagonists still licking their wounds of the Partition day and accentuated by the compulsions of Cold War animosities.

More than five years have passed since the end of the Cold War and inevitably the military junta today has had to yield place, step by step, to the authority of the elected Government in Pakistan. Years of mistrust could not evaporate in one day, and that is why in the last crucial years, there was the backlog of misgivings and distress which delayed the recognition of a new outlook in both the countries, India and Pakistan. While India, particularly under Inder Gujral as the Foreign Minister, made the forthright declaration for trade ties instead of military animosities, it has so far been a path that calls for patience and faith in neighbourly goodwill.

Perhaps the biggest testimony of India's persistent anxiety for good neighbourliness—which has come to be popularly known as the Gujral Doctrine—was provided by the frank and open discussion which marked the remarkable end of the squabble over water-sharing of the Ganga that had been held back for decades because of the stiff position taken by both sides. The breakthrough on the Ganga water has turned out to be a landmark in Indo-Bangla relations, which today perhaps rest on more solid foundations than at the time of Indira Gandhi and Sheikh Mujibur Rahman.

It is the striking success in India's relations with Bangladesh that has acted as a spur for renewed efforts at improving India-Pakistan relations. Apart from the fact that the military grip in Pakistan politics has definitely weakened with the installation of the Nawaz Sharif Government with a firm majority in the National Assembly. Equally conspicuous has been the firm urge of the new Pakistan Government to go in for open trade with India and other members of the SAARC which can make the concept of the SAFTA free trade zone a reality. Those who pessimistically hold on to the line that there could be no durable peace with Pakistan, obviously ignore the new climate of good neighbourly relations that prevails over many parts of Pakistan, particularly at the popular level. The visits by writers, poets, performing artistes and journalists from both sides have strengthened the faith of those who seriously believe in the impending breakthrough between the two countries.

No doubt Kashmir is a difficult issue that bedevils the relationship between the two countries. Surely, however, there is sufficient goodwill and statesmanship in both the countries which can find a way out of this particular impasse. If the talks between the two Governments take a fruitful turn—as the prospects seem to be—it may certainly be possible to discuss the problems relating to Kashmir between the leaders of India and Pakistan. And this need not be confined to the political leaders and Government officials. It is an area in which the common people—the non-official elite down to the youth and working people—can certainly contribute in a really wholesome manner. Gujral as the Foreign Minister had unilaterally relaxed many of the antiquated visa and travel restrictions and the results show that this had a salutary impact on the people in Pakistan. Of course, there are critics who will flare up at the very mention of Kashmir as one of the items of discord between India and Pakistan. The fact that Gujral has agreed to include it in the agenda for future bilateral talks between India and Pakistan would enrage this circle. What is forgotten is that Kashmir has always figured in Indo-Pak talks. It was India which had taken the question of Pakistan-backed armed gangs' intrusion into Kashmir to the United Nations, and put it not as a complaint against Pak aggression but as a plea for settlement with Pakistan. The results were, to say the least, unfortunate. When Sheikh Abdullah was released from detention and was Nehru's personal guest before his demise, he set out to Pakistan for an amicable settlement of the Kashmir issue with the Pakistan Government—Sheikh Sahib had in his mind the concept of a confederation between India and Pakistan with Kashmir as its third member. As he opened his talks with General Ayub, the death of Nehru put an end to that peace mission. In 1972, when Bhutto came to Simla for finalising the peace accord after the Bangladesh war, even then in the overall review of bilateral India-Pak relations, Kashmir did figure and there is a mention of that in the text of the accord itself. All this makes it abundantly clear that the inclusion of Kashmir in the agenda of any future talk between India and Pakistan can by no means be regarded as a concession but only the reiteration of reality buttressed up by antecedents.

The point to note is that we in India have to win over the goodwill and trust of the people of Pakistan. And once this gets going, there shall be nothing on earth that can hold back the settlement of the more difficult problems. If the barriers sedulously built for five decades are perceptively giving way, why should the Kashmir issue defy all solutions based on mutual confidence and goodwill? The opening function at the SAARC Summit at Male on May 12, 1997 has to act as an eye-opener for many of us. The Prime Minister of India got the warmest encomium from the Prime Minister of Pakistan. Has it ever happened before at any international gathering? We must not miss the signs of the times.

(May 17, 1997)

50

Scanning a Landmark

Important events are graduated into landmarks in History as they are invested with hindsight. Perhaps it would be premature to call an event a landmark on the very morrow of its happening. By this criterion, the meeting of the Foreign Secretaries of India and Pakistan at Islamabad on June 19-23, 1997 has a significance which needs to be taken into account.

For years at a stretch, there was no formal meeting at the official level to decide on the agenda for a business-like discussion of problems bedevilling the relations of the two countries. Although a number of brief summit-level encounters between the heads of Government of both Pakistan and India have taken place in the last few years, there have been no serious appraisal of the problems until last week's meetings at Islamabad with a short session at Murree. The importance of this round of meetings has been that all the issues that have cropped up between the two countries—ranging from trade and economic cooperation to Siachen and Kashmir—have been noted down as part of the agenda of official level meetings which would start in September. For fixing a regular agenda, the Islamabad meeting of the two Foreign Secretaries has been extremely important.

In fact, it can be safely stated that since the Simla talks in July 1972, there has been no such serious talks between India and Pakistan for the last 25 years. There are, of course, many differences between the Simla and Islamabad talks. For one thing, the Simla talks were held at the summit level, and therefore had the authority to take decisions binding on both the countries. The Islamabad talks were at the official level—that is between the Foreign Secretaries of the two countries—and therefore they were in the nature of fixing the agenda by the officials of the two countries and to that measure, it marks an improvement over the vague generalities about amity and goodwill that political leaders are accustomed to use as part of their protocol formalities. The agenda that has been set by the joint statement at the Foreign Secretaries level is not only detailed: the problems that beset the two countries on which fixed positions have been publicly taken by the two sides, but about which a lot of ground has to be covered. In a sense it is a very bold document but at the same time signifies the seriousness with which both the Governments have undertaken to go in for a settlement of the major issues that have become the bone of contention between not only the two Governments but even stirred up acrimony between the public of the two countries.

The most serious of these challenges has been the question of Kashmir. On the side of Pakistan, the argument raised boiled down to the point that for seven long years, there has been armed militancy, particularly in the Valley, which the Indian security forces have not been able to put down. Besides, this phenomenon has attracted wide international attention not merely on the sore of human rights violations but as part of the urge for self-determination. The Indian argument that the militants who have been active mainly in the Kashmir Valley were trained and armed by Pakistani outfits could carry little weight since it became more and more known that the Indian authorities have been unable to run normal administration in the Valley. Although this argument was particularly confronted by the fact that even under security protection a full-fledged State Assembly election could take place and an elected Government has now been installed in the State of Jammu and Kashmir, the fact is that the urge for autonomy is still very strong in Kashmir—in fact on both sides of the military Line of Control, a situation which can hardly be wished away.

Orthodox Indian opinion has long held that the State of Jammu and Kashmir, having acceded to the Union of India as early as 1947, there could be no reason why New Delhi should permit Kashmir to become the subject of discussion with other states, particularly with Pakistan. This standpoint was held at times by the Government of India, as also by the more orthodox political standpoint represented by the BJP, among others. In fact, a section of those who generally support the Congress have sometimes taken the same view. It was, therefore, a Herculean task on the part of the present Gujral Government to have agreed to the Pakistani demand for the inclusion of Kashmir as part of the agenda of Indo-Pak talks. No doubt, it was Prime Minister Gujral's personal initiative which has enabled Foreign Secretary Salman Haider to include Kashmir in the future official-level Indo-Pak talks. For, it is known that in the list of priorities for Prime Minister Gujral's foreign policy the improvement of Indo-Pak relations comes at the very top of the agenda, and as a realist, he has understood that there has to be an understanding between India and Pakistan over the issue of Kashmir.

The argument which has often been trotted out by the hard-core Indian circles has been that Pakistan has no business to be invited or consulted with regard to any decision on Kashmir that New Delhi may arrive at with Srinagar. But if one looks back at the record of the last five decades, it needs to be emphasised that New Delhi has never kept Pakistan out of any discussion on Kashmir. This could be seen from the fact that in 1948, when India took the Kashmir issue to the UN, it was not as a complaint against aggression by the armed tribals coming over from Pakistan, but for a settlement of the dispute between India and Pakistan. In 1964, when Sheikh Abdullah was released after a harassing trial spread over years, he was invited to the Prime Minister's House in Delhi as the guest of Jawaharlal Nehru and from there he set out with his known views for bringing about a confederation of India, Pakistan and Kashmir. Whether such a confederation was feasible is a different question, but there is no doubt that, in Nehru's view, there could be no final solution to the Kashmir issue without involving Pakistan into it. Again at Simla in 1972, Indira Gandhi met Zulfikar Ali Bhutto mainly to discuss the sequel of the Independence of Bangladesh, but the issue of Kashmir came into the parleys and found its place in the accord that was signed there.

In recent times, the issue of Kashmir figured prominently in Pakistan politics and in the last General Election Benazir Bhutto took a hectoring posture over it. In contrast, Nawaz Sharif, who won the poll with an overwhelming majority, only expressed his hope to come to an amicable understanding between India and Pakistan. It is known that the present Government of Nawaz Sharif generally reflects the viewpoint of the corporate sector in Pakistan which is keen on better economic relations on the part of the present Pakistan establishment for an enduring Indo-Pak relationship.

The military establishment in Pakistan is known to be largely dominated by the line of the Pentagon, and it is quite possible that the present Clinton Administration might like to play host to a Camp-David model settlement between India and Pakistan. It is on this point the two sovereign countries of South Asia have to display their strength, wisdom and sense of independence to work out their own agenda for a settlement of outstanding issues. If the Kashmir issue has to be settled in the ambience of amity and understanding, the settlement has to come through understanding between India and Pakistan alone.

One has also to take into account the temper of the common humanity in the two countries. After five decades of acrimony, there are distinct signs about the turn of the tide, and that is precisely what is reflected in the clear drafting of the agenda as embodied in the Islamabad accord between the Foreign Secretaries of India and Pakistan. It is the hope of millions in this country as also in Pakistan that this round of highest official level deliberations will pave the way for laying the foundations of a structure of durable peace. It is symbolic that these talks holding out hopes of amicable understanding should take place exactly twentyfive years after Simla and in the middle of the celebrations of fifty years of Independence in the two countries.

(June 28, 1997)